RACING

Faith, Love & Triumph Over Loss

FORWARD

bright sky press
HOUSTON, TEXAS

2365 Rice Blvd., Suite 202
Houston, Texas 77005

ISBN: 978-1-939055-91-0

10   9   8   7   6   5   4   3   2   1

Library of Congress Cataloging-in-Publication Data on file with publisher.

Editorial Direction: Lucy Herring Chambers
Editor: Cristina Adams
Managing Editor: Lauren Adams
Designer: Marla Y. Garcia

Printed in Canada through Friesens

TO MY SON DONALD CAMERON DUNCAN III
AND HIS WIFE, BO:

THANK YOU FOR PUTTING UP WITH ME.
YOUR LOVE AND UNDERSTANDING SUSTAINED ME
DURING THE WORST TIME OF MY LIFE.
YOU ARE MY HEART,
AND DONNIE, THE GRANDCHILD YOU GAVE ME,
IS A SOURCE OF INFINITE JOY.
I LOVE YOU.
MOM/MIMI

RACING

Faith, Love & Triumph Over Loss

FORWARD

MICA MOSBACHER

bright sky press

HOUSTON, TEXAS

PROLOGUE

Just a few months ago, I was driving my grandson, Donnie, to pre-school when he asked a question that really took me by surprise.

"Mimi," he said in his sweet five-year-old voice. "Does everyone die?"

"Yes, darling," I replied. "Everyone dies sometime."

"Mimi," he said again. "Am I going to die?" You could have knocked me over with a goose-down feather. I couldn't believe he was asking such a question, but I had to give him an answer. So I did.

"Yes, Donnie," I said, choking up. "But not for a long time." (*Please, Lord, protect him,* I silently prayed.) He then explained that his beloved turtle, Yertle, had died the week before, and he was sad about losing him.

See, Donnie is packed full of love; he lives big and loves large. He is in a constant state of wonderment for everything the world has to offer: a pink sunset, a gray rock, a seashell, his mother's cooking. Suddenly, in his shiny, new corner of the planet where he sees an unbroken landscape of endless possibilities, he has experienced loss. It took him by surprise and disturbed him. If God is good and His love protects us, how can such a thing happen?

Loss. How I hate that four-letter word. When loss is a death, it feels very final. I do not feel that it permanently separates us, though. We certainly will meet our loved ones again. But death temporarily isolates us from our loved ones and wreaks havoc on our lives. My late husband, Bob, and I were a May-December couple. With a twenty-six-year age difference between us, it was always a foregone conclusion that he would precede me in death. Bob had lost his first wife, Jane, to leukemia, and her passing left an indelible mark. He never got over losing her.

"Mica, please, please don't leave me," he once said to me when I found myself in the emergency room suffering from an acute allergic reaction. "I can't bear it another time."

Lightning struck when I met Bob Mosbacher. He was my best friend and is my eternal soul mate—a grand passion. I was the luckiest woman on the planet! He understood me. We shared common political goals; we wanted to make the world a better place. Service was our main focus—we felt blessed and lucky and wanted to give back. Bob often said that I was in love for the first time, and he was in love for the last time. Sadly, I lost him in January 2010 to pancreatic cancer. It was then that I finally understood how he felt and how he had suffered when he lost Jane. Until you have survived the death of a loved one—in fact, until you have become the lone survivor—it's impossible to understand the gut-wrenching grief that pulls you down and renders you senseless.

Loss comes in many forms, with death topping the list. We all experience loss; it's part of life. It includes break-ups, divorce, injury, disabilities, illness, friendships and careers, even a loss of innocence. These are all disappointments of different stripes, and nobody escapes them entirely. Loss catapults us out of the warm, safe nests we feather for ourselves and our families, and brings the road we were on to an end.

It takes grit and resilience to transition from survivor to thriver; a certain mindset is key to making that journey. Change has to be your best friend. You have to acknowledge it. Embrace it. Kiss it good night. And then move on. Change can bring wonderful rewards and blessings. Don't look back. Be there to welcome it. Race forward to meet it. You'll be amazed at the new gifts that come your way.

TABLE OF CONTENTS

This portrait was taken when Cameron was
six-months-old. I decided to let "sleeping babes lie."
His birth was one of my miracles.

CHAPTER ONE

STUCK IN THE MUD

IT WAS FALL IN HOUSTON, a dark gloomy Friday, and I was packing up to leave the office after a long day. I was working as a sales assistant for the managing partner at Oppenheimer and Co. The markets were closed; the relentless, grating sound of the thirty-plus phone lines on the PBX system at my desk had, at last, gone quiet. But the silence seemed ominous.

As I was getting ready to walk out the door, I saw a letter on my desk. The return address read Oppenheimer.

"Perhaps it's a bonus check," I thought. I opened it and read that, along with several others in the firm, I was being laid off with two weeks' severance. My heart sank.

It was 1992, and I was a thirty-nine-year-old single mother with a six-year-old son. Rent was due; bills were due. The timing of this pink slip couldn't have been worse. Times were a little tough back then. I was divorced and felt like a two-time loser after yet another failed relationship. Back in 1990, I had landed in this business because I needed a job. I had no background in finance, but I had been desperate for work. I was on the rebound from the failure of my marriage to Donald Duncan, my son Cameron's father, when I met a charming, charismatic man at church. Willem (not his real name) was from South Africa. He seemed caring and focused on my needs. We went to church, took dance classes, and cooked dinners together. I found him easy to talk to. He also made me laugh.

Willem presented himself as a stand-up guy: an Oxford-educated attorney, entrepreneur, big game hunter and amateur racecar driver. We became inseparable, and he was very good to Cameron, which made him even more attractive to me. He pushed me to get married. Even though I thought things were moving too fast, we were soon engaged and moving in together. He even convinced me to quit working and hand over control of my money to help him establish his own business. Naively, I thought he was older, wiser and more mature. I trusted him. What's more, my brother, John McCutchen, and my friends were crazy about him.

Initially, I failed to spot how controlling he was. When my mother called, Willem would tell me not to take the call. Looking back, he was obviously trying to separate me from my family and friends. He was needy and insisted I go everywhere with him. It was suffocating. My instincts kicked in, and I started to feel ambivalent toward him. I began to notice that some of his background didn't add up; there were holes in his story. He said he had a former wife and children in South Africa, but he wasn't in touch with them.

Early on, there were several red flags that I conveniently rationalized. In fact, the holes in his background kept getting bigger. He used no credit cards and at times he even used an alias. Finally, I quit making excuses for him and decided to end our relationship. We were out to dinner in a Katy-area restaurant when I told him that things were moving too fast, and I wanted to take a break. He pleaded with me, but I was firm.

When I got up from the table to call a taxi, he turned angry, grabbed my arm hard and virtually dragged me out of the restaurant. I tried to get someone's attention, but nobody noticed. Not wanting to make a scene, I didn't scream. He overpowered me and slammed me into the car. I was terrified. Shaking, I tried to keep control as he sped away. It was déjà vu—a flashback to a terrifying time I had experienced in childhood.

He then tried to sweet-talk me. "I love you so much; you are my angel," he told me, his eyes even tearing up. Once home, I raced inside and locked the door. He had not technically assaulted me, so I couldn't call the police. I had nothing to report. The guy was merely possessive and in love. He followed me, but I locked the doors and ignored the pounding.

Scared, I called my brother. John liked Willem and said he was just jealous and obsessed with me. He reassured me that Willem was a good guy. I have to admit that I did like feeling protected, and I enjoyed having a man around the house. Before I knew it, I had rationalized things away again, while ignoring all the classic symptoms of abuse—controlling me, separating me from my family, taking control of my finances and making me feel dependent. My mother remained skeptical; she was the one hold-out who smelled a rat.

I refused to hear her concerns, and Willem and I were quietly married a few weeks later. She was not happy. It turned out she was the wisest of us all. One night some weeks later, the doorbell rang at about two o'clock in the morning. I opened the door to find a sheriff flashing his badge at me. Shocked, I asked what he wanted. He had come to arrest Willem for failure to stop and render aid in a car accident. Two people had been badly injured. I had no knowledge of any accident and no clue what he was talking about; I was completely blindsided. Fortunately, he knew an honest reaction when he saw one and was very kind to me.

He and his deputy arrested Willem and took him away, and I called my mother in tears. She lived in our neighborhood and came over a few minutes later to comfort me, even though deep down she had never liked or trusted Willem. The next day, she called the South African consulate to ask if they had any background information on him. She was told that he was considered "a person of interest" and was on an international watch list. He had fabricated his credentials. Willem had never attended Oxford University—much less graduated from law school. My mother also learned that he was in the country with an expired visa. It became clear to all of us that he was pushing me to marry him so that he could have legal status in the U.S.

The consular official wanted to speak to me directly and gave my mother a number to call after business hours. Nervous but determined to hear the truth, I called her back that night. She warned me that Willem might be abusive and to distance myself from him. While she was not willing to provide any specific details, she was concerned for my welfare. Based on this unpleasant information, we contacted an attorney. Needless to say, we did not post bail.

I sought an annulment. I also wanted my day in court to expose him and his deceitful ways—it seemed that he targeted widows and divorcees and preyed on them. But he didn't show up in court. I will never forget the reaction of the female judge when she heard my case. She became emotional when I told her my story, but said that the laws had "no teeth" in them. We could not have him locked up and have the key thrown away. Sadly, Willem moved in with another woman and assaulted her. I had been so lucky.

In an odd coincidence, years later when I met Bob, one of his close friends confided in me that his sister had also been involved with Willem. This friend put me in touch with his sister and we discussed how foolish we felt after learning his true identity. She said that there had been several victims. He was so charming and totally sociopathic, and our experiences with him would have been great material for Lifetime television.

Now, in the wake of humiliation and heartache, I was also unemployed. Willem had gone through my savings. Cameron and I temporarily moved in with my mother, intending to stay only until I got back on my feet. Of course, my former husband was not happy about the situation, and who could blame him? Unfortunately, things heated up between the two of us, and Cameron was caught in the middle between two people he loved.

We eventually worked things out but had to hire a lawyer, and lawyers are expensive too. I needed to find a job posthaste. My mother loaned me some money, but I needed to make my own living and support Cameron. My self-worth was on the line, and I needed to feel good about myself. I did not want my parent supporting me. I began networking and spent hours calling everyone I knew. One call led to another referral and another. Finally, I learned that there was an opening at Oppenheimer and Co. in downtown Houston.

I made a phone call to human resources and was told to come in the next day for an interview. I was wearing a pink dress and probably looked like a wilted Southern belle. The partner was a bright guy and quite personable. He alluded to Oppenheimer's dog-eat-dog environment. Not only was he in charge of all the brokers, but he was also responsible for the Syndicate Desk. He said he was willing to hire me, but it would be a steep learning curve. He questioned if I could survive the heated, frantic and demanding pace of an investment banking firm.

I didn't budge. He seemed eager to fill the position, and I started immediately. I had found a job in one week. Soon after that, Cameron and I moved into The River Oaks High Rise, and he continued preschool at St. Francis Episcopal Day School. He saw his father on a regular basis, and I started counseling. I determined never again to be taken in by a dishonest person with no integrity. I wanted to heal from my divorce and to create an emotionally safe environment for my son.

My days were long. They started at six o'clock in the morning, when I would get up, feed Cameron and leave the house by six-thirty. The school was in the opposite direction of my work. I was due at my desk by seven o'clock for research calls from New York and broker's meetings. I was expected to attend, and there was no wiggle room from being late. I was an owl and Cameron often stayed up late too. I finally gave him an alarm clock and he got himself up each day. He also decided to sleep in his school uniform to save time in the morning. He was resourceful.

My career as a writer and editor for two prominent energy companies had not prepared me for the chaotic world of my new job. It was culture shock—sheer insanity at times. The hours were long, the business rough around the edges. It was a boisterous, tense and hardscrabble environment. The brokers were on straight commission and under a lot of pressure. The F-bomb was hurled frequently. It was like a high stakes game of Texas Hold'em. Compared to the civilized corporate world I knew, working at Oppenheimer felt like working on the docks in Brooklyn.

Under any other circumstances, I might have looked for a job more suited to my skill set. I was learning a lot, however, and I was pleased that after a year, I had survived. I was seasoned by then, but the job was a dead end for me and offered no viable career path. I had the option of studying on my own time for the Series 7 exam to become licensed to trade, but my days were full, and I did not want to neglect Cameron. He needed me. And I asked myself if it was a career I really wanted to pursue. After some soul searching, I felt it was not a good fit. I trusted my gut and felt that if I bided my time, something more suitable would come along.

Truth is, I probably would never have left that job if God and fate hadn't seen fit to give me the boot, so to speak. Even so, when it happened, I panicked. It was another mixed blessing of course. Despite all my hard work, I was still living practically paycheck-to-paycheck. I had come through my divorce with debt, and the child support I did receive barely covered the cost of the childcare I needed while I was working. What's more, I had no safety net. My father, John McCutchen, a prominent lawyer and neurologist, had died just before Cameron was born, his life cut short by a brain tumor. My mother, a divorcée, worked as an administrator at the Art Institute of Houston, but she had to plan for retirement. There was no one to help Cameron and me but me!

However, my parents were both great examples of people with a strong work ethic. While attending medical school at Case Western Reserve University, Dad had sold shoes at Halle Brothers Co. department store in Cleveland, Ohio, and my mom had worked at a bank. And they had two children under the age of three. A pity party was not in my DNA. The rent was due soon, and my livelihood depended on that job. I had started out to prove that I could support my son and me without receiving handouts. It hadn't mattered that I hated my job; I had grown up being told to play the hand I was dealt. So I'd stuck it out—for the money and out of fear of the unknown job market. Now I was going to have to face that job market again, despite my misgivings.

Leaving the downtown offices of Oppenheimer offices that night for the last time, I knew I would just have to play the bad hand I'd been dealt. It wasn't the first time I'd have to rely on an inner strength. Never mind Willem or losing my job or the divorce. I had experienced other, more important, times when all seemed lost, such as when I was pregnant with Cameron in 1986.

I met Donald Duncan at a wedding at River Oaks Country Club in Houston in 1984. He was a successful attorney working for Pennzoil; he was good-looking and kind, and I immediately liked his down-to-earth attitude about life. His father was dying of cancer. My own father had just died, so we had some things in common and plenty to talk about. Neither of us were in a celebratory mood. I was missing my dad and we both felt sad.

Donald's family ranch was near Burnet, and I was working for Southern Political Consulting and assigned to the Ed Walsh for Attorney General campaign in nearby Round Rock. He frequently visited his parents in Burnet, so we started seeing each other and got married that December. It was a quick courtship, and I don't feel that we really knew each other well. We settled in Houston, where I continued to work for Southern Political. I found out early on that I was pregnant. While commuting to Round Rock, I was exiting Interstate 35 in Austin and totaled my car in a horrific accident. It was a miracle that the baby and I survived. Donald bought me a new car and I slowed down.

Then, one Saturday morning in mid-February 1986, I woke up in a pool of blood. Donald and I had been planning to attend the Wildcatter's Convention in San Antonio, and instead wound up in the emergency room at the Women's Hospital of Texas. On arriving, I was poked, prodded and tested, and then admitted.

The diagnosis was complete placenta previa, a rare condition in which the placenta plants itself across the cervix rather than at the top. Ironically, I had always been called "wrong-way Mica" because of my bad sense of direction. It seemed my placenta was also good at getting lost; it was in a precarious position. I would be lucky to carry the baby full-term.

I was discharged with strict orders to stay in bed. Bed rest. What did that mean? I had been jogging, I had been taking care of myself, and I had been eating well. How could this happen? My doctor, Leon "Bubba" Daily laid it out for me: no cooking, cleaning, exercising or any other activity that could jostle the placenta. I would have to work from home. I called the partners at Southern Political. They agreed I could work at home. God bless them!

The condition was serious. After I was released, I began acquainting myself with the concept of bed rest. I worked the phones. A few weeks went by and once again, I started bleeding heavily. We went back to the hospital, except this time there was no brief visit and discharge. Dr. Daily admitted me to Women's Hospital to stay. We spoke to a battery of neonatologists and other specialists to prepare us for a premature baby. I also consulted a few specialists on ways to keep my body from going into labor. I thought I could will myself to not have contractions. I was very naïve. Or was it wishful thinking?

All these efforts didn't do any good. On Easter weekend, my body did what it wanted to and went into labor. A former Army nurse named Mary rushed me to intensive care as the contractions started coming hard and fast. Dr. Daily came, as did my mother; Donald was at the ranch in Burnet keeping his newly widowed mother company. I was terrified, but determined not to lose this baby. I was convinced I was having a boy, despite what the ultrasound had showed, and I believed I would not survive losing him. I couldn't explain it, but it was as if I knew he would be my only child.

Dr. Daily told me he was preparing to give me a Caesarean, but I refused. I knew instinctively that my baby would not survive. My mother pushed me to listen to my doctor.

"No," I said.

"We might lose them both," the doctor whispered to my mother. I heard him loud and clear.

I was bleeding heavily by then. Fine, I thought to myself. You can bury us both. I asked to be left alone. "Clear the room," I said. I wanted to scream. It was Good Friday. Ironically, my father had died the year before on Good Friday (as had his mother), and I still felt his loss keenly. I would not lose this baby, too. I had never felt so scared or desperate. I began praying. Soon, a sense of peace and reassurance flooded my being. Dr. Daily came back into the room.

"Mica, time is of the essence," he said.

"No. Absolutely not," I said. "No."

I told him that I had prayed and believed that everything would be okay, despite appearances to the contrary. Worried, Dr. Daily shook his head and left the room. Thirty minutes later, the contractions stopped. When he came back to check on me and saw what had happened, Dr. Daily shook his head again, this time in wonder.

A devout man of Jewish faith, he said, "Mica, I believe you made a Christian out of me!"

After that weekend, I wasn't afraid anymore. My days weren't different; I still watched reruns of *Perry Mason*, *Dragnet* and *Bewitched*, along with the news. I had no DVD player. On a good day, I was allowed to take a shower. I wasn't permitted to go outside—even in a wheelchair, even just down the hall. I was very large then and could hardly eat because the indigestion was so bad. I craved grilled-cheese sandwiches, and the nurses indulged my every craving. My situation continued to be precarious.

One day, Donald brought my mail, and in it was an invitation from Nancy Reagan to attend a tea for the Republican National Committee at the White House. Having been involved in politics, both with Young Republicans while in school and later as a professional, I was elated. Unfortunately the timing wasn't quite right because it was two weeks away. I had always dreamed of going to the White House. So, this was a loss.

Meanwhile, I had a baby to bring safely into the world. I still went in and out of labor several times a week and found myself on the Labor and Delivery floor on a regular basis. My life seemed to take place in a revolving door between my ward and intensive care. I was given corticosteroid injections to boost development of the baby's lungs. By then I knew he was a boy, and boys had a slightly lower chance of survival as preemies than girls. I debated pumping drugs into an unborn fetus, but developing his lungs was the highest priority. I lived in fear and in prayer.

By the time Dr. Daily scheduled a C-section for June 10, I had been in the hospital for almost five months. I had blown up like a piñata from the steroids, but Cameron had enough lung capacity to survive. The amniocentesis indicated that I would give birth to a healthy son. Donald attended the birth—as attentive a father as ever existed. It was a joyous day, one I would never forget. We had survived. Our son was a special gift.

Not every woman is as lucky as I was—and am. Another woman who was on my hospital ward during my bed rest lost her baby. I still remember her screams. I was grateful then as I am now. I was lucky, and I knew it. In my darkest moments, I remember the arrival of this baby—now a grown man with a child of his own—as a blessing and a joy. He had made it through a car accident and a precarious pregnancy.

Following my release from the hospital, I gradually felt like my old self. Not one to sit around, I started a public relations consulting business and worked from home. My life had been put on hold, and I needed to get back in touch with me. In addition to going to baby Gymboree, I took singing lessons. It was something I'd always wanted to do. I also began volunteering for then-Vice President George Bush, first at his downtown office and later at his "Advance Office" at the Houstonian Hotel.

The night he announced his run for the presidency, I was downtown at the Hyatt Regency ballroom helping with the news media. While I was standing in the audience listening to the Vice President's speech, a member of the Secret Service tapped me on the shoulder to say that they had received a phone call from Donald. He had taken Cameron to the emergency room. "Don't worry," the agent said. "Your son was given Percodan." Why was he given a painkiller? I thought to myself. I remained anxious until I could get in touch with Donald. It turned out he had an infection and was given Pedialyte™ for dehydration. What a relief!

I attended the Convention in New Orleans and was later invited once again to the White House, This was a thrill. Nancy Reagan was so gracious, and I was honored to be there as a guest. It was an exhilarating moment. Sadly, I couldn't say the same about my marriage.

I was just going through the motions. Donald and I had very few interests in common, and we were not pulling the same yoke. We were making each other miserable. We tried marriage counseling, but it only served to further define our differences. It was hard on all of us, but we decided to divorce. He needed someone who loved him and was not trying to change him—and frankly, so did I. He was a marvelous, loving father, and I know it hurt him to be separated from his son. Divorce is a loss, and in our case, we were two well-meaning people who just were not right for each other.

The adversity I faced during my pregnancy and subsequent divorce had toughened me up. The situation with Willem had shaped me into a strong woman. My mother was an example of someone who bounced back from adversity. She had learned to fly a plane; she was determined and independent. A hard worker, she was also positive and self-sufficient. I had inherited some of her Viking DNA and used my new-found resiliency to face my current obstacles.

I had learned a bitter lesson from my involvement with Willem. Now I was wary of men—especially those who were not part of my crowd. Going forward, I would be less needy and choose wisely. Meanwhile, I had to find a job.

Being pink-slipped from Oppenheimer would prove to be a gift. At the time, it did not seem that way. I needed a job; just not this one.

I could wallow in the sludge of self-pity, or I could dust myself off and set a new course for my life. Cameron was my priority. I wanted to create a stable home for him, a place where he felt safe and provide him with an education in a Christian school environment. I wanted to prove I was a worthy mom.

My divorce from Donald had already rocked my son's world; I was prepared to do almost anything to take care of him. If that meant going without breakfast or lunch to give him extras like T-ball at the local YMCA, then I would just go without. I had, in fact, skipped more than a few meals over the past several months, and I'd do it again today. It's what mothers do.

Reflecting back on the Easter weekend when I almost lost him reminded me of what was important. Jesus was crucified and suffered horribly, but his suffering resulted in transformation and the resurrection. That day in the hospital had been the "darkest before dawn" for me. But God heard my prayers and answered them. I knew he would answer them again. As my grandmother, Dorothy Jolley, always said, "It's best to never look back. Look at the road ahead!"

So when I packed my bags at Oppenheimer and left, I focused on the future.

Meeting famous balloonists Maxie Anderson
and Ben Abruzzo during the International Bennett
Race in Los Angeles. This was one of my first
assignments while writing for *Houston
Natural Gas Magazine.*

CHAPTER TWO

GOD CAN'T STEER A PARKED CAR

I FIRST HEARD THE EXPRESSION, "God can't steer a parked car," in 1972 during my sophomore year at The University of Texas. I was participating in a Campus Crusade Bible Study and trying to find my way. I had transferred from Hollins University in Roanoke, Virginia. The Bible lesson was referring to prayer—while prayer did not always involve action, God didn't expect us to sit around and act helpless. The first move was ours. We needed to contemplate the Holy Spirit and the word in the Bible, but we also needed to take action. With ourselves in motion, God could then steer us in the right directions.

Unsure of my major during my freshman year, I had prayed for guidance. During the short mid-term at Hollins, we were required to intern in the career of our choice. My choice had been KPRC-TV, the

NBC affiliate in Houston. I had written the legendary news director, Ray Miller, about a possible internship. "I will sweep the floors if I have to," I told him. The station accepted me on a volunteer basis.

Joanne King (later Herring), who would become so well known for her actions recounted in *Charlie Wilson's War,* was the only female broadcaster at the station. She had her own show. Ray told me during my first week there that Joanne was talented and would make a good role model. I was given routine duties and sent out on a regular basis with one reporter or another, many who were happy to help and encourage me. One even let me do a voice-over for the radio show.

In 1970, there were virtually no female reporters nationally. In Houston, Jessica Savitch at Channel 11, the ABC affiliate, was a rising star. On a reporting assignment, Kay Bailey Hutchison, who was then planning to run for the Texas House of Representatives (and would go on to become a U.S. senator), introduced herself to me and told me that she had been the legal correspondent at KPRC-TV and one of its first on-screen reporters. In Joanne and her, I had two amazing role models.

I soon learned that my voice wasn't authoritative enough, so I worked on my delivery. The feedback I got from the producer was only helpful, not negative, and I flourished in that environment. I gradually began doing regular on-camera interviews. It was exhilarating to sign off a reporting segment on air with my name.

One day, I was sent to the Harris County courthouse downtown to be a place-holder at a jury trial. Following the longest murder trial in Texas history at that time, the jury had begun deliberating. Richard "Racehorse" Haynes was the defense attorney, a celebrity lawyer who had been involved in a number of high-profile cases, including the murder trial of Dr. John Hill. Haynes was a larger-than-life character. Silver-tongued and theatrical, he was formidable as a defense attorney for his client, a Hispanic painter.

I had been in the courtroom for five minutes, when the jury marched back in. Everyone, including Jessica, was on a coffee break. The jury, it seemed, was hung. After the judge's announcement, it was bedlam. Jack Cato, the station's police beat reporter, was there with me, and together we went over to speak with Richard Haynes. Much to our surprise, he granted us an on-camera interview.

"What would you do differently?" I inquired.

Unfortunately, I don't recall his answer, but I had the exclusive. And for a little bit, I was a minor hero in the newsroom. I received regular on-camera assignments after that and got a kick out of saying, "This is Michele McCutchen, Big 2 News On the Scene."

Later that month, my parents met Ray Miller at an event. He wrote me not long afterwards to tell me he had met them and told them he thought I had real talent. It meant the world to me. I was so surprised and pleased that he'd taken time to reach out to a young woman and offer her encouragement. KPRC-TV sponsored me for an on-camera training course and invited me back the following summer. His vote of confidence in my abilities would sustain me during what would prove to be an exceptionally hard year.

That experience whet my appetite for journalism. As Hollins had no formal program in journalism, I had transferred to the University of Texas. I met with the dean of the School of Communications, who wasn't all that impressed with my credentials. He even had the gall to tell me that I might be overreaching with my ambitions. It was a typical attitude toward women in the business in the early 1970s; it was also the first time I truly understood what was meant by "the gender gap."

Instead of listening to him and letting him discourage me, I went to work at the *Daily Texan*. At Christmas, my parents announced they were divorcing. My brother and I were devastated. My mother didn't take the news well, either. There was upheaval on the home front, and I was trying to keep things on an even keel. It was a tough time for all of us. My mother weathered the aftermath and went back to work. I continued to worry about her, but she proved her mettle. John and I returned to UT for our spring semester feeling defeated and heavy-hearted. Our home was no longer a safe haven.

Following my sophomore year, I went abroad with a group of friends on a chaperoned trip to Europe. We sailed from New York to the UK on the *S.S. France* and had a wonderful time. One night in London, we went to a popular restaurant known then as the Elizabethan Room. The wine was flowing freely; our glasses were refilled after every sip. During the meal, a well-dressed strange man approached our table and started flirting with me. I tried to ignore him. In my mind, he was too old for me.

The evening progressed, and he returned to our table several times. I became firmer and less friendly. Finally, he seemed to give up. I was relieved. But that relief was short-lived. As we got up to leave, he approached me, draped his arm around my shoulder, and roughly pushed me out the door. Then took my hand with a firm grasp and tugged at it. I called to my friends to come back, but they were already moving on, laughing. I tried to pull away, and this time he latched onto me harder. I was scared. My girlfriend hung back and called out to me but he propelled me into his car before she could get back to me.

He took me to another local bar. When we got there, I was feeling confused. I asked for water and he handed me a drink. I took one sip, then another. Suddenly the room was spinning. Where were my friends? Where was I? I was losing focus.

"Take me to my hotel," I said.

Looking back, I am certain that I was drugged. He guided me to his car and drove to the hotel where I was staying. I was fighting the sensation. My head was reeling, and I was unsteady; but I jumped out of the car and walked away from him as fast as I could. He tried to follow me to my room, but a security guard stopped him. I got upstairs and fell into bed with my clothes on. I was safe.

Minutes later, there was a knock on the door. Not thinking, I opened it. There he was. All I remember is that he overpowered me. Then he left. I woke up the next morning with the sheets and my dress stained with blood. I still remember that knit dress. It was white.

My reaction was classic: throw away the dress and tell no one. I didn't want to make waves. Ashamed and in shock, I got dressed and joined our group at St. Paul's Cathedral. I walked around, thinking of Christ and what he had endured, and I managed to hold myself together. I was so angry with myself. What had I done to cause this? How did I lose control of the situation? It was not like me to go anywhere with a perfect stranger. I had not gone willingly, but I was surely at fault for not fighting hard enough to extricate myself. Surely there was something I could have done.

I was also in a foreign country and ignorant of their laws. In the U.S., I knew the victim was often blamed for bringing the assault on herself. I just knew I would be accused of having too much to drink or being too flirty or having somehow invited the attack. The culture had not evolved in general, and women were often viewed as "flirts."

Surely "no" translated into consensual sex. No one will believe my story, I thought. I couldn't handle any further humiliation; I saw no way out except silence.

I was scheduled to join my father and some family friends for a tour of Bordeaux's wine country the following week, but I couldn't face him or the trip. Instead, I called him and asked to come home. He didn't understand why I was backing out, so I made up the excuse that I needed to take Spanish at summer school. It was a lie, but he let it go. I was speeding away from the scene of a crime—while I might have been in the driver's seat, I did not feel in control.

Shell-shocked, I began my junior year. When my grades began suffering, I took a semester off and went to work at the State Capital for the Senate Education Committee. I retreated into a kind of cocoon and almost made a game out of being friendly. In truth, I had shut down emotionally. I was frozen inside. Disillusioned and distrustful, I kept my secret bottled up, ticking away like a time bomb.

That summer, I traveled to New York. With the encouragement of a friend, Lindsay Wells, I made an appointment at the Ford Modeling agency. When I met the legendary Eileen Ford, she told me to lose weight. At five-feet, six-and-a-half inches, I weighed 125 pounds. She felt I had potential, and I returned to Texas and modeled on a part-time basis. But my father adamantly disapproved, so eventually, I went back to school on the "five-year plan."

Eager to go to work full-time and leave Austin and my bad memories behind, I began freelancing as a writer. My heart was no longer in my studies. I wanted to go to work. After several query letters, an editor in Houston assigned me two articles for *Houston Town and Country Magazine*. The day I got my first check for those articles was a happy one, indeed. Encouraged, I asked for more work—and got it.

I continued to knock on the doors of local television and radio stations, but there was a hiring freeze. So I went to work as a writer, first for a local non-profit organization and then for *Houston Natural Gas* as editor of in-house publications. There, I had a mentor: Alex Chesser, the senior vice president in charge of the communications department.

CEO Robert Herring wanted to expand the department. The full-color, in-house magazines were meant to showcase the company's profitability and diversity. Soon I found myself traveling to cities where Houston Natural Gas had operations, accompanied by a freelance photographer. In 1977, we covered the Gordon Bennett Balloon Race in Long Beach and met famed balloonists Maxie Anderson and Ben Abruzzo (who died years later in a tragic balloon accident). The following year, I went down into the Zeigler coal mines (despite it being bad luck to have a woman in the mines), spent a week on a towboat on the Mississippi, visited factories in Montreal and was sent on many fascinating international assignments.

My work was interesting and varied. I traveled non-stop with a generous budget and finally hit my stride. By the end of the second year, our publication and my stories had been nominated for several awards. I proudly accepted these accolades and enjoyed being part of an amazing team.

As one of the few female executives in the company, I was mindful to stay professional and to avoid any whiff of impropriety. There were no incidents on any of the business trips, and the men I worked with were consummate professionals. I remember wearing Brooks Brothers business suits and carrying a briefcase. The experiences and training I received were invaluable; my self-confidence returned. I had landed on my feet and the qualities of overcoming a traumatic experience while in school had steeled me. I was no longer a tortured soul.

I had gotten my car out of park, and God had steered me into an exciting career.

———————————

Time raced ahead. Before I knew it, it was 1992. Change often brings introspection, and looking back I saw how time had flown by, fast and furious. It was almost twenty years since I had left the University of Texas. Looking back on my earlier career and the ways roadblocks had led to exciting new avenues, my new status as an unemployed person did not undercut my self-esteem. I knew that problems had solutions, so I went to work calling friends in my Rolodex. I was confident that I would land on my feet.

I reached out to my friend, Maria, who worked at Saks Fifth Avenue. We had met when my dad and his wife Pam opened Courreges at the new Pavilion, the upscale mall where Saks was located. Maria was older, widowed and more experienced in the ways of job-hunting, so I asked for her help in finding a job at one of the stores in The Pavilion. She had worked in retail for years and, luckily for me, had all the right connections. By Christmas, I had a part-time job that would pay the rent. There is dignity in work, and I enjoyed sales, so I didn't feel that being a sales associate in retail was necessarily a demotion.

My temporary job turned into a permanent one, and I spent many pleasant days selling designer clothes. A steady stream of friends stopped by regularly to visit and shop; I was sent to New York for training. It was a reprieve from the grind at Oppenheimer, and I was enjoying it. More importantly, I had time to resume my writing career. I had the energy to be creative, as I wasn't going home drained and exhausted every night. I also did some modeling for print publications and fashion shows.

After Cameron went to bed, I would write. I queried local magazines and was eventually assigned features and human-interest stories. The work was a great outlet for me and slowly helped me build a portfolio. I was beginning to feel whole again.

In terms of my social life, I was dating, but much more selectively. I was understandably wary. I became friends with a wonderful neighbor, Jay Moore, who bonded with my young son. We weren't lovers, just friends, and he was helpful in advising me about finances and other matters. I was grateful to him and other friends who lent me support during those hard times. As for dating, well, you kiss a lot of toads before finding a prince. There were a couple of bad guys who were double dealing—one was dating me while at the same time trying to reconcile with his ex-wife.

Dating isn't for the faint of heart. My mother kept reminding me that I did not need to waste time and energy on Mr. Wrong. If it wasn't working for some reason, I needed to move on. The right guy would come along, and in the meantime I had my son. I had experienced enough drama and certainly didn't need another guy with no scruples to break my heart yet again. I learned not to excuse bad behavior. "Next" became my mantra. I defined very clear boundaries and set my standards much higher.

Cameron remained an exuberant, happy kid, despite a few bumps in the road. I will never forget one day when the police showed up at our door. We were still living in The River Oaks, and I had left him alone in the condo to go downstairs and get the mail in the lobby. Apparently, I took too long because when I got back upstairs, the police were there. Cameron had called 911 because he was worried about where I was. The police laughed at Cameron's resourcefulness and told me not to feel defensive. I realized that I had to learn to relax and not worry so much about trying to be the perfect mother.

During that time, I began to feel less tentative and more secure in my judgment. The counseling I had forced on myself was helping me to build a better future. I really didn't want to keep repeating past mistakes. I needed to learn from them and move forward—for myself and for Cameron. It was a time of growth and rebirth. It takes courage to face one's true self in the mirror, and that's exactly what I was doing. I was going through self-analysis and learning to be discriminating in all choices—trust but verify.

I realized that love was more than just romance. Making it through hard times took maturity and character traits like trust and integrity. I had been easily wooed by Willem and his hard sales tactics. He was a master at his game, but I was never going to be a victim again.

To that end, I enrolled in self-defense classes and took lessons at a skeet shooting range. I had learned to hunt with my dad and brother; now I worked on honing my skills. Meanwhile, Donald found true love and married a lovely girl named Ellen. Cameron took to her right away. My mother continued to help with Cameron, and I was grateful as a single mom to have her assistance. Perhaps someday I too would find my perfect match.

Women were considered bad luck in coal mines, but I was welcomed into the Ziegler mines during a reporting assignment.

CHAPTER THREE

YELLOW FLAGS & ROAD HAZARDS

ON A RACE TRACK, the solid yellow caution flag universally requires race car drivers to slow down. The flag marshal warns drivers of a hazard or obstacle in their path, signaling drivers to exercise extreme caution as the roadway is potentially dangerous. Wouldn't it be amazing if we could be forewarned of hazardous conditions or roadblocks in our emotional lives?

Bad relationships, like losses, don't often come with warning radar; more often than not, they come in the form of unexpected—and unwelcome—surprises. The aftershocks can be life-changing. Sometimes we can discern red flags in our relationships, as I should have with Willem. The signs were there. However, I didn't heed the warning. Once we learn to trust our instincts, we can halt, detour or disengage, and save ourselves from heartache and angst. Nobody can totally control or change a negative circumstance. We just have to motor past it. What is, *is*. All we can do is accept it and move on. Loss does not have to define us and regrets only hold us back.

I often want to analyze what went wrong, but that's really just a delay tactic. Taking no action causes us to stall in a crisis, when action is needed. Action is the solution. The way we choose to react is what tests our reactions and strengthens our character and resilience. Though wounds can be deep, we can find a new GPS setting and recover enough to lead a fulfilling but different life.

Any and every unexpected change feels like a loss. Whether it's a garden-variety loss that we all inevitably must face—the loss of a parent or a pet—an unexpected loss—of a job, a marriage, or our self-esteem—or a more catastrophic loss—the death of a spouse or a devastating illness or injury—the aftermath is always disruption and chaos, and it drains our tank of emotional energy.

For those who face extraordinary loss, the end result is permanent disruption. No matter what caused the loss, life as we knew it ceases to exist. Loss pulls the rug out from under us. It threatens our sense of security and tests our faith.

I am inspired by the stories of heroines and heroes who have shown exceptional resilience and courage. The families affected by wars and catastrophic accidents and still go on are remarkable. Thor and Margret, an Icelandic couple who live in Austin, are raising a non-verbal autistic son named Kelli, and he has learned to compose music. Together with actress Kate Winslet, Margret produced an HBO movie titled *A Mother's Courage*. This family is actively inspiring and helping others.

We can learn from that brand of superhero resilience—whether it's a blind runner, someone with a prosthesis participating in the Special Olympics, or a parent caring for a special-needs child. A change in our day-to-day world can also present an opportunity. Whenever my path has changed and I've been forced to take a detour, wonderful gifts have come my way. My unplanned departure from Oppenheimer ultimately led me to meet Robert Mosbacher, oilman and twenty-eighth U.S. Secretary of Commerce, who would become my husband.

In 1993, I was still selling designer clothes by day and writing feature stories at night.

After Cameron went to bed, I stayed up and wrote into the early morning hours. Fortunately I am an owl and managed to get by on very little sleep. I didn't own a computer, so I wrote in longhand and then went to a Kinko's store on Sundays to tap out the copy onto a rented laptop.

If I was on deadline, I would drop Cameron of at school and head to Kinko's before reporting for work at Saks. I was writing steadily for three magazines, including *River Oaks Monthly*, keeping my fingers crossed that a full-time position would open up at one of these publications.

Meanwhile, the weekend and evening hours of retail were taking away time I could spend with Cameron. Once again, I felt I was heading toward a dead-end and needed to make a U-turn. The job at Saks had provided an opportunity to take some time out from a high stress career. It had allowed me enough room emotionally to be creative again. It was a rest stop, but I needed to look at the future.

By mid-1994, I had enough published articles to apply for a full-time job in journalism. I was an admirer of Lynn Ashby, then editor of the *Houston Post,* one of the city's two daily newspapers. That's where I wanted to work. Creative by nature, I was anxious to restart the writing career that had begun with the newsletter I distributed in the neighborhood as a girl and was furthered by my experience writing for energy companies.

But I had taken a hiatus from writing in my thirties, and I discovered my starter was stuck. That's when a mentor is so valuable. Finding a good mentor isn't hard. Alumni associations, professional associations, or a local chamber of commerce are all good places to start networking. Getting involved in your place of worship, volunteering for a non-profit organization and applying for an internship in your field of choice also present opportunities to meet established professionals who are doing interesting things.

Email wasn't common in those days; a phone call or letter from a mentor was necessary to reach key figures in a company. I am always reminded that there are no substitutes for face-to-face meetings. Email is impersonal and can never take the place of a real conversation. It's much harder to cold call a stranger on the phone or meet in person, but it's also much more effective. Networking in person is one of the keys to success.

We all need mentors. Even if an introduction helps us get onto the first rung of the career ladder, after that we must learn to sell ourselves. A mentor can provide encouragement and candid advice, in addition to warning you about any pitfalls. The advice I received from those who were successful was to get out on the road and meet as many people as I could. During my time at Houston Natural Gas, a senior editor of *National Geographic Magazine* had become a friend. He taught me that it was important to form genuine friendships; people don't like to feel they're being used.

I had been active in professional writing organizations and networked as much as I could. I also volunteered in political campaigns. Through my activities with the presidential campaign of George H.W. Bush I met veteran sports reporter Mickey Herskowitz. He had been a ghost writer for President Bush, and he became my mentor, helping me to get a foot in the door at the *Houston Post*.

Gail Borden Johnson started the *Post* in 1880. I liked the fact that Gail had been ahead of her time. For many years, the *Post* was owned by the Hobby Family; Oveta Culp Hobby, the first Secretary of the U.S. Department of Health, Education and Welfare and first commanding officer of the Women's Army Corps, was the newspaper's president and editor. An extraordinary woman, she was encouraged by Eisenhower to run for president in 1960. She served on multiple boards and cared for her ailing husband. She was a formidable role model.

The hiring process took awhile, but after a second interview I was hired. It was late March 1995. I was over the moon with a sense of accomplishment. I had set a goal and achieved it. I couldn't wait to learn from the talented people at the *Post*. Like many women who take a hiatus and return to the job market, re-entry was tough. Following my divorce, I had interrupted my career. I had taken jobs that provided stability in the form of health insurance and steady work, but this unilateral progress left me restless and dissatisfied. I knew it was never too late until it was too late. While a job at the *Post* wasn't going to make me rich, it was the creative outlet I wanted and needed.

My dad had gone to law school at South Texas College of Law in the 1990s at the age of forty-nine and was among the few with MD/JD after his name. He had encouraged me to pursue a law degree while I was the University of Texas. He often pointed out that I loved to argue and seemed to thrive on opposition. I had encouraged him to pursue his doctor of jurisprudence degree instead. If Chaucer wrote the *Canterbury Tales* at age eighty, my dad could pursue his dream in his late forties. Former Judge Mary Bacon, another mentor of mine, told me "you can do everything you want in life, but not necessarily at the same time." She had raised a family and returned to school in mid-life and accomplished great things on the Bench.

While I had the aptitude to pursue law school, I didn't have the fortitude. I was not a linear thinker. Besides, I felt that the world had enough lawyers already. My father was concerned about my career in a low-paying job like journalism. He wanted me to be financially secure, and journalism didn't provide a clear path to a robust salary. But in the end, we have to live our own lives. I stuck to my chosen field.

Despite these concerns, it was my writing career that ended up supporting me. "If you choose work you love, then it won't feel like work," one of my mentors reminded me. "Stress in life often comes from doing things we don't have a passion for." I was passionate about writing. I loved interviewing people, getting a glimpse into their lives and developing a story. Everyone has an interesting story to tell, and I liked recording bits of people's lives.

In April 1995, the Hearst Corporation bought the *Houston Post* and shut it down, dashing my dreams. Journalism was changing in the late 1990s, and news reporting was much more colorful. Almost gone were the days when the news was reported "who, what, when and where." Just the facts ma'am. When I had interned at KPRC-TV, language was free from gender and group stereotypes. The news mostly reported straight facts without bias. I remembered that Ray Miller, one of my mentors, did not always subscribe to the "if it bleeds, it leads" school of thought. KPRC-TV had strict standards for reporting the news, and they didn't always include showing corpses on the nightly news. News then was not entertainment as there were no cable stations and all-day programming slots.

The *Post* was a legendary newspaper in Houston. How could it shut down? Newspapers were struggling, and the culture needed to keep up with trends. It was getting harder to sustain a daily newspaper. At the *Post,* circulation had been dropping, and revenue had been shrinking. It was emblematic of the changing times. Digital forms had not cropped up yet but would soon enough.

Few people at the paper had any warning that they would lose their jobs. Most of them had to get out and pound the pavement. The *Houston Chronicle* absorbed many of the *Post's* most talented reporters, but not new kids like me.

I had to find a way to regroup and get motivated. "God can't steer a parked car," I would tell myself. "Put yourself in gear. Move it or lose it." I began to feel like Job in the Bible. I had attended several bible study classes in the past, and I now found strength in re-reading passages from the Book of Job at night. In faith, I believed that God would return "twice as before."

One evening not long after the news of the *Post's* demise, I left Cameron with my mother and walked through the Houston Galleria to window shop and clear my head. I walked around the ice skating rink, watching the skaters. They seemed carefree and light-hearted. I felt heavy in my heart and spirit. One step forward, two steps back seemed to be the dance in my life. I walked around the mall feeling sorry for myself; I felt beaten down. Then I saw it. A sign—literally and figuratively. In the window of the Louis Vuitton boutique was a small sign advertising the 1995 Louis Vuitton Cup Race in San Diego.

The LV Cup Races are a selection series of sailboat races. The winner goes on to race in the America's Cup, one of the world's premiere sailing events. Held every three to four years, the races are a test of boat design and sailing skills, and they attract the top sailors. The 1992 winner, *Il Moro di Venezia*, spent more than $200 million on the construction of four boats. To me, it's one of the most exciting races in the world.

My interest in sailing wasn't random. As a girl, I was a competitive Sunfish racer at Casa Mare, a Girl Scout camp on Galveston Bay. My father was a boating enthusiast; my brother, John, and I owned a catamaran and took it out on weekends. We thought of ourselves as true Galveston "Bay Rats." Back then, there was nothing I loved more than the smell of the ocean and the sea spray on my skin. As Isaak Dinesen once said: "The cure for anything is salt water: sweat, tears and the sea."

I spotted a 'help wanted' sign by the LV Cup poster. Without missing a beat, I went in. The sailboat race might just be the thing to drag me out of my doldrums. After meeting with the manager, Patricia, I was hired. She needed help in sales, but more importantly, she also needed help planning a large debut party for the new store. Next to sailing, I absolutely love entertaining. Party planning on a big scale appealed to me. Walking out of the store with a creative task and a job with more 'mom-friendly' hours, I felt buoyant and light-hearted.

While I was destined, it seemed, to continue selling, I was also charged with the task of planning a grand-scale event. Louis Vuitton Moet Hennessy Corp. (LVMH) had deep pockets, and we had a generous budget.

John connected me to. Scott Ziegler, a friend of his. A respected commercial architect and sailor, Scott raced at Texas Corinthian Yacht Club (TCYC) near Kemah on weekends. TCYC is a serious racing club, so I thought it would be a natural audience for the LV event. Scott agreed to help host and brought in a terrific friend, Martha Farish Oti, who offered to sponsor the group for a party at the Bayou Club on Memorial Drive.

Martha's husband, José, was a serious sailor who knew members of other yacht clubs. Meanwhile Scott, a Wisconsin native, knew previous America's Cup winner and former Olympian Buddy Melges. He invited Buddy to come down and speak at the event, and Buddy agreed. Witty and charming—as well as an internationally known sailor—Buddy would bring tremendous cachet to the party. I knew it would be a big success.

Over several conversations and a lot of laughs, Buddy and I became telephone friends. In the process, he asked me to invite his good friend, Bob Mosbacher. He told me that he had beat Bob at a previous Olympic trial in San Francisco. It sounded like a friendly rivalry, so I agreed to call. I rang up his office and gave the evening's details to Bob's personable assistant, Syd Dudley.

Meanwhile, I was hard at work on the all the details as the RSVPs came rolling in. LVMH, the parent company of Louis Vuitton, wanted everything to be first class. The company adhered to high standards, and so did I. I focused on the food, the décor and the ambiance; this party had to be perfect. Architect Mies van der Rohe said that God is in the details.

The night of the event, I was busy juggling logistics, caterers, guests and our guest speaker. It was my job and I needed to excel. Bob Mosbacher introduced himself to me. He was handsome and charming, but immediately surrounded by old friends. I might have mumbled something like, "Nice to meet you" before dashing off to attend to another task. Buddy hit it out of the ballpark with his talk. The evening was a rousing success. I went home and collapsed in a heap on my bed.

As a thank you, Scott, his wife Yvonne and I were flown out to San Diego to watch the training that was underway for *Mighty Mary,* the 1995 America's Cup team—a women's team organized by billionaire Bill Koch. He had won the previous America's Cup with Buddy at the helm of *America 3. Mighty Mary* was named for Bill's mother, and Buddy was one of the coaches. The ladies' team didn't win, but I had a rare opportunity to sail on the boat during practice. I became friends with some of the women crew members who later came to Houston at my invitation to speak at the Houston Yacht Club.

Several months went by. I wasn't dating anyone special, but I wasn't concerned. My brother had gone to work for Fisk Electric, and Joanne Herring Davis was now married to its CEO. We became reacquainted, and she fixed me up. Our paths kept crossing, I believe there are no coincidences. After my past experiences, I was gun-shy and very cautious. It seemed inappropriate to introduce my son to a steady stream of acquaintances, so I would meet dates in the lobby of our high-rise. Usually I went out on Wednesdays or on weekends when Cameron was staying with his dad.

I wanted to insulate my son from strangers. I had not given up on love. I figured if it was meant to be, it would find me. In the meantime, I wasn't in a hurry to get married again. Of course, I dreamed of true love. What girl doesn't buy into the fairy tale of Prince Charming and the glass slipper? However, I was much more realistic now. Cameron and I were a package deal. He had an attentive father and didn't need a male role model. I was fiercely independent and still smarting from the imposter who scammed me. Cameron and I needed stability and trustworthy people in our lives.

Scott Ziegler had offered me a marketing and public relations job at Ziegler Cooper Architects in the fall of 1995. My hours would be school hours, so I could be there for Cameron. Scott's commercial architectural business had taken off, and he needed someone to help tout the company's reputation. I would also have time to pursue freelance writing on a broader scale. I happily accepted his job offer and went to work. It was a talented and creative group, and I learned a lot about city planning and historic preservation during my time there. My passion for fine architecture, cityscapes and planning ignited.

My writing started to bear fruit. Former *Houston Post* editor Lynn Ashby was now editor-in-chief of *Inside Houston* magazine, a topnotch, glossy publication. I submitted several story ideas to him and his editor and got a bite. They liked the idea of a story on Suite 8F of the former Lamar Hotel in downtown Houston. Leased by George Brown of Brown and Root Construction, Suite 8F was a meeting place for the state's top business leaders in the 1940s and 1950s.

Known as the unofficial capital of Texas, it was a place where power brokers like Jesse Jones, Herman and George Brown, James Abercrombie, Gus Wortham, Sr., and James Elkins, Sr., came together to talk shop and politics. Governor William P. Hobby, who owned the *Houston Post* and KPRC-TV during that period, was also a frequent guest. Of course it was an all-male club.

The group played a little poker, helped to support elected officials and laid out the economic growth of Texas from their special haunt. Lyndon B. Johnson, John Connally and a few other larger-than-life figures came and went, participating in conversations here and there. Few people know for sure what was discussed in Suite 8F, but the group's influence extended to Washington, D.C. Together, they put Houston on the map.

The article I wrote was well received; it even won a *Houston Press* Award. A jury of fellow journalists selects the winners, so I was especially honored by the recognition. After that, Lynn Ashby assigned me several more interesting stories, and I ended up learning a great deal about Houston history in the process. I was assigned more cover stories and won yet another writing award for an article on Westheimer Road, the longest street in Texas. My work was fulfilling, and I was happy.

As for my personal life, I continued going on dates, but there was still no one really special.

Then, one day in 1997, my phone rang. It was Bob Mosbacher. I was absolutely speechless. He was the last person I'd expected to hear from. He asked how I was and what I'd been doing for the past few months, and then he invited me to dinner.

"Sure," I said. "When?"

"How about now?" he asked.

I had just gotten back from a run at the Houstonian Fitness Club; I was wearing stretchy black jogging pants and a lumpy, brown cotton hoodie jacket. My hair was pulled back in a ponytail. I had no make-up on, and I was hot and sweaty.

It was a Wednesday night, and Cameron was with his dad. Okay, I thought, I can be spontaneous. So I agreed to meet him. When I arrived, Bob looked me up and down. A dandy, he was immaculately dressed. He was so handsome and had a dazzling smile. I, on the other hand, had left the house without changing. I was a mess!

"Well, most women would have made some sort of effort," he frowned. "That's an ugly jacket."

"Ouch," I said and started laughing. So did he. He had an infectious laugh. As Eleanor Roosevelt once said, "No one can make you feel inferior without your consent."

"Take me as I am," I challenged him. "This is me—a soccer mom."

Bob fixed me a "see thru" (vodka and soda water) and, over a spaghetti dinner that he had cooked himself, we talked for hours. Cooking isn't one of my strengths. My son grew up to become an excellent chef, and he often tells people that he learned to cook in order to survive. I couldn't believe that I'd met a man who actually liked to cook. Bob was athletic and self-deprecating, kind and very old-school—and absolutely charming. He wore his tie the entire evening!

He told me that he was having trouble adjusting to life after serving as U.S. Secretary of Commerce. He had gone from having a huge staff of handlers and aides and rides on Air Force One, to having one assistant and flying in coach on Continental Airlines.

"Do you know how to pump gas?" I teased him.

An energy man and wildcatter through and through, he was working nonstop to take command of his company again. He had to distance himself from Mosbacher Energy while in office. He was traveling a great deal and seemed spread a little thin. I sensed that he'd temporarily lost his footing. I told him that we had moved to Houston in 1969 so that my father could join Dr. Michael DeBakey's heart transplant team. The conversation got serious as he asked me some philosophical and existential questions. What did I want to accomplish in life? How did I feel about women working and the pay gap? Was I anti-Semitic? His own parents had been Jewish, and he remembered being left out of Cotillion parties as a student at Choate; the boarding school he had attended in Connecticut.

I told him that I was keenly interested in gender equality and in human rights. I wanted to build bridges among different religions, cultures and nationalities, and I was bothered by prejudice and hatred of those who were different. I hoped one day to work on a significant project on tolerance and diversity. I also said that I wanted pro-choice/pro-life and gay issues off the table and the Republican Party platform. He shared with me that his daughter, Dee, was gay and that he had worked hard to make her feel loved and accepted.

Here's the thing, I said. While I didn't always agree with other people's lifestyle choices, it wasn't my place to judge. Our children needed role models, not misbehaving celebrities. I told him that Yvonne Ziegler and I had been part of a team that implemented Elayne Bennett and Alma Powell's Best Friends Foundation character education project in schools in the Houston Independent School District. Launched in 1987, the program was showcased as a solution to teenage pregnancy.

Earlier that year, I told him, I had been introduced to the Raoul Wallenberg Committee's "A Study of Heroes," a school program dedicated to teaching children about heroes and character traits. Named for the Swedish diplomat who ferried thousands of Jews out of Nazi-occupied Hungary during World War II, this program depicts real heroes and gives real examples. Children are encouraged to take "the hard right, not the easy left," and the curriculum teaches students to stand up for those who are being bullied or how to help a new kid fit in.

Together with the members of the Wallenberg Committee, a group of concerned Houstonians and I had pitched the program to the Board of the Houston Independent School District, and it had passed. I wanted to make a difference in some small way and did what I could as a busy single mother. I talked about my goals, my dreams and my failures. We connected.

Bob and I began seeing each other off and on. He was separated from his wife and gun shy. At times, he decided we couldn't date anymore. Having been married three times, he was understandably ambivalent and conflicted. Another year would go by before I introduced Cameron to Bob; it was a period of uncertainty for all of us.

Meanwhile, I was finally able to be self-supporting as a writer and went out on my own. It was a joy to be able to spend more time with Cameron after school. He was thriving. I was so proud when I could finally afford the tuition at St. Michael's School. He had been on a scholarship for the past year. Now we were independent.

One night, Cameron came racing into my room and said that Bob Mosbacher had been mentioned on an episode of The *Simpsons*. I was speechless; I had never spoken to Cameron about Bob. It turned out, as Cameron told me, that he'd seen Bob's name come up on caller ID. Out of the mouths of babes, right? Bob became my son's new hero. Anyone who starred in or was mentioned in *The Simpsons* was okay in his book. (*The Simpsons* was—and still is—Cameron's favorite show.)

After Bob and I had been seeing each other for several months, things started to get more serious. I got an inkling of that change when Mossy (as I called him) invited me to take a trip with him to the Bahamas. He had arranged to borrow a sailboat, known as *Babe,* from Tommy Dickey, a friend from Houston. Tommy kept the boat at Man-of-War Cay in the Abaco region of the Bahamas. We decided to stay nearby in Green Turtle Cay at the Green Turtle Resort and Marina. Founded in the eighteenth century, Green Turtle Cay was one of the first settled islands in the Bahamas; the island's residents can trace their ancestry back to the British Loyalists.

We arrived and rented a runabout boat called an Albury. That night, the resort's power went out, but we didn't care. The starry sky was breathtaking. Bahamian sunsets and star-filled night skies were always a thing of joy for Bob. The next day, we started out in the Albury to find *Babe* and get sailing. We stopped for gas at Black Watch Sound. I noticed right away that the gas gauge on the Albury didn't seem to be working. I asked the attendant how far a tank of gas would take us.

"Ma'am, you can go all the way to Florida and back," he said.

Comfortable with those odds, Bob bought a Cuban cigar and we headed out. Twenty minutes later, we were climbing aboard *Babe* for a sailing adventure.

After a full day of fun in the sun, we headed back to port. We hopped into the Albury and sped off; just as the sun was beginning to set, the engine sputtered. We were running out of gas. I upended the gas tank. Sputter, sputter. Up ahead was an unoccupied cay; we sputtered in and anchored there. "No Name Cay" was overgrown with vegetation, and I was nervous about setting foot on it in the dark. We opted to stay in the boat.

In the Bahamas, few boats move around at night, as the channels and hazards aren't well marked. We decided it was best to just stay put. The boat had no canopy, and no radio nor cell phone, and it was just fifteen-and-a-half feet long. You had to slide under the seats to lie down. The only provisions were wine, a cigar and some matches. Not long after we anchored, it started raining. The "no-see-ems," the Bahamas version of mosquitoes, were biting. This was definitely not my warm bed at the Green Turtle Resort.

The next morning, Bob spotted a man in a boat nearby taking his wife to work. He took off his shirt, draped it on our only paddle and began waving it around. The man motored over, looked at Bob, then at me.

"Man, have you been out all night?" he asked.

"Yes," I mumbled, sleepy and itchy.

"I will be right back," he said. And he was. He came back and gave us a tow back to harbor.

Bob told Tommy what had happened. Soon the story was making the rounds at cocktail parties. Folks were dining out on it. Bob would later tell Tommy that he thought he'd told him the story in confidence, but Tommy just laughed.

"No way!" he said. "A world-champion sailor running out of gas. It's too juicy. I told everyone!" That Christmas, Bob's family gave him a ship-to-shore radio. We would laugh about No Name Cay for years to come.

I continued to see Bob off and on, and the more I got to know him, the more I loved him. He was true blue. If he said he would call, he called. He traveled extensively on business and was heavily involved in the Houston community. Yet somehow despite his juggling, he proved he was reliable and trustworthy—a rare breed indeed, and a true gentleman.

In August 1997, we went to Paris. There, while driving through the Pont de l'Alma tunnel, I had a strange experience. Out of nowhere, chills ran down my spine, so much so that I had to buckle my seat belt. We were heading to Cannes, where we planned to cruise on Bob's and Max Fisher's boat, *Hallelujah,* to the Costa Smeralda in Sardinia. Bob had invited close friends director Peter Masterson and his actress wife, Carlin Glynn, to join us. I had never been to Sardinia and was looking forward to it.

We spent several days cruising, swimming, eating and laughing. On August 29th, we dropped anchor at the Hotel Calve di Volpe in Porto Cervo, Sardinia, a classic, refined and exclusive watering spot. We arrived for lunch and had just been seated when we spotted Dodi Fayed, then Diana Princess of Wales' boyfriend, in the restaurant. I felt those chills run down my spine again. Princess Diana wasn't with him, but later, when we were leaving our tender to *Hallelujah,* we passed her on a nearby tender to another yacht. She ducked her head as we passed by, but there was no mistaking that elegant, exquisite beauty.

On August 31st, I woke up feeling queasy. I'd had a nightmare and as a result hadn't slept well. Once up, the crew told us that Princess Diana had been killed in a car accident and that the crash had occurred in the Pont de l'Alma tunnel. My family has joked that I am "spooky", that I have uncanny intuitive powers because sometimes I just know things. The premonitions I often experience are jolting; the flashes of insight come out of the blue. In Sunday school, I was taught that we are surrounded by angels who are our spirit guides. I like to think that these psychic flashes are really my guardian angels guiding me.

Our trip had been surreal, and we left for Paris sharing the world's collective sadness. The princess had been a bright light; her life was an example of service. Once again, I was reminded of how fragile and precious our lives are. They are a gift from God and should not be wasted. *Carpe diem,* I told myself. Seize the day.

The happiest day of my life was when I married Bob on July 20, 2000. Here we are at home with Dave Peterson, Pastor of Memorial Drive Presbyterian Church.

CHAPTER FOUR

ON A FAST TRACK

BOB ASKED ME TO MARRY HIM IN 2000,
two years after we started dating, on the eve of the in-
augural ballgame at what was then called Enron Field
(now Minute Maid Park). We were sharing a "see-th-
ru", and I was teasing him, telling him that I thought
he was a confirmed, irrepressible bachelor.

"Yes, I am," he teased back.

The next thing I knew, he was down on one knee, proposing. From confirmed bachelor to gallant suitor in a matter of seconds—I pinched myself, not entirely sure that what I thought was happening was actually happening. But it was, and I said, "Yes."

I didn't have much time to feel euphoric, however, because in his next breath Bob told me he was too old to be engaged. He asked not to tell anyone. Seriously? I couldn't believe it. Can you imagine joining a group of close friends at a ballgame and not being able to share this secret? But it was his request, and I honored it. Reluctantly.

Bob planned the wedding; he wanted to marry on July 20th, my birthday. In his previous marriage, he had eloped, and now he wanted something more real and intimate: a wedding at home with all his family.

"Let's just tell friends to come to a formal birthday dinner," he said. "We can surprise them with our marriage announcement."

He selected the wines, planned the menu, chose the flowers and the cake. It was touching to see his careful attention to detail, and it made me love him all the more. I had a simple, strapless satin gown made for me in New York City. My brother, John, gave me away, and my sister-in-law, Karen Garrett, was my maid of honor. Dave Peterson of Memorial Drive Baptist Church officiated, along with Charlie Shedd, a former pastor and author who baptized Bob when he was married to his first wife, Jane. She had brought him into the Presbyterian Church. Many close friends joined us for the celebration, including Max and Marjorie Fisher of Detroit, Kelly and Robert Day of Los Angeles, Denton and Louise Cooley, Jimmy and Susan Baker, Berdon Lawrence and Bob and Janice McNair. Bob's son, Rob, was his father's best man.

We honeymooned at the Lyford Cay Club in Nassau, The Bahamas. This time, we were definitely not going on a boat; I wasn't taking any chances. Located on the western side of the island, the Lyford Cay Club is rich in old-world tradition. It was built in the 1950s and has hosted many notable residents, including actor Sean Connery. Several of the James Bond films he starred in—*Thunderball,* among them—were filmed in and around Lyford Cay. President John F. Kennedy stayed there at the home of Canadian businessman E.P. Taylor during talks with British Prime Minister Harold MacMillan. And, an episode in season two of the television series *Mad Men* was filmed at Lyford Cay. The area has also figured in a number of high-profile murders, some of which remain unsolved to this day. Colorful legends about brigands and pirates add to the lore of this magical place.

We leased one of the club cottages—No. 91—on the beach. Ocean front, its an idyllic setting with shimmering blue water and a pristine white beach. The fact that Bahamians are some of the friendliest and most welcoming people in the world was a bonus. I had been going there for twenty years, so I already knew how much I loved it; nowadays, it's still one of my favorite places on earth.

After a couple of relaxing, magical days, we flew to the Republican National Convention in Philadelphia. It was my third convention. At the 1988 gathering in New Orleans, my role had been to help out in the press office. Now, my role was that of political spouse. I joked that my honeymoon was shared with delegates, elected officials, protesters and the Bush family.

Bob had told me that he was done with fundraising, even though he was one of the Republican Party's most successful fundraisers ever. Fortunately, I never believed him. I knew he couldn't stifle his passion or his talent for persuading others to open their wallets. Sure enough, once we were at the Philadelphia convention, he went into what former Commerce Department staffers called his "high energy mode."

He went from one television interview to another, schmoozing with fellow contributors and head-huddling with old friends about current policy issues. This was a very different man from the one who had cooked dinner for me and proposed on bended knee.

———————————

Bob Mosbacher was a bona fide political animal, and he loved every aspect of the process. I heard story after story about him. One of my favorites was told to me by California developer Don Bren. Bob had flown out to see him and to ask for a large contribution to the party.

"I will dance on the coffee table if you give me money," Bob had said to him. According to legend, Don and others wrote checks, and Bob did exactly that. *Danced.* It was his way. He was charismatic, fun and irresistible, a presence whenever he entered a room. Few people could say no to Bob. He was hard to resist.

John "Jack" Hennessy, former chairman and CEO of Credit Suisse First Boston and part-time Lyford Cay resident, told me at the convention that Bob had the "Midas touch". I got scared. For some reason, it made me think of the Cole Porter lyrics "Get out of town before it's too late...why not retire to a farm and be contented to charm the birds from the trees." In this case, the birds were political contributions from a forest of friends.

He was certainly charming, but there was no way he would ever retire to a farm. Once I'd fallen in love with Bob, there was nowhere for me to run. I knew that I would need tennis shoes to keep up with him. We weren't destined to lead a serene life in the country.

I never dreamed that soon we would be on a presidential campaign trail. We were on our feet all day long at the Convention. Several wives and veteran campaigners gave me tips on how to survive the long, gritty days. Gayle Wilson, former first lady of California, advised me to have rubber soles put on my shoes because it would make standing on hard surfaces for long periods of time much easier. Another political wife told me to always have a stash of antiseptic wipes handy to cut down on the risk of infection from shaking so many hands.

I appreciated the advice and insider knowledge, especially the part about the rubber soles. Those saved me and my feet! Bob and I would go on to entertain and host fundraisers for statewide and federal candidates throughout most of our marriage and I often stood for hours.

Interestingly, only a small percentage of wives get involved in the fundraising side; many leave it to their husbands to handle. But Bob taught me how to raise money and encouraged me to do it on my own as well. The first phone call was always the hardest. And even if the answer was no, I didn't take it personally. Learning how to ask for money also taught me how to handle rejection gracefully. It was a great education.

Bob used to say that money was the mother's milk of politics. He wanted to see more women involved in the process, and so did I. I still do. Women are a significant economic force in this country, and the number of women-owned businesses continues to grow every year. There may be a gender gap in what was once the "good 'ole boys club," but that's changing. Maybe, just maybe, the pendulum will swing more forcefully when we have a female U.S. president.

I will say this: Once Bob and I joined forces for fundraising, we became expensive friends to have around. Our hearts and souls were committed to helping qualified candidates, so we weren't shy about asking others to assist, financially or otherwise. No one, it seemed, could resist Bob's enticement. Sharing his political interests, I enjoyed fundraising. Working in sales for so long, I realized it took some finesse. You had to learn how to read people. I also knew when it was time to back off. No one likes hard-sale tactics. Some needed to have time to contemplate and size up a candidate, too.

The first years of our marriage were a constant juggling act for me. Cameron needed a mother, and I wanted to be involved in his life. I experienced the push-pull that all mothers feel; sometimes it was country first and family second. Bob and I had decided early on that our projects for the most part would be joint projects. We discussed it and agreed on how we would spend our time. We were a team. Yet balancing on the high wire act of our lives took planning and commitment.

Wanting to be engaged in the community, I joined several boards independent of Bob, and I agreed to chair some galas. I was anxious to make my mark. It was important to me to give back, so I got enthusiastically involved and wound up spreading myself too thin. Soon I was overcommitted and stressed. I hadn't learned yet to pick and choose my priorities outside of the obvious one, which was my family.

The first time we went over our family calendar, we found ourselves discussing our commitments six months to a year out. I wasn't even sure of Cameron's school schedule then. It was overwhelming; I also felt like Bob didn't know how to say no. I often commented that if he was a woman, he would be pregnant all the time. If he had been an old-fashioned girl, his dance card would have been full every night of the week. He liked to be helpful, and he never wanted to let anyone down.

Accommodating and gracious, he was respectful and kind to people from all walks of life. It took some major negotiations on my part to get him to slow down and catch his breath.

I was always wrangling for "date nights" with just the two of us. We needed some down time and hardly ever got it. I also felt pressure to look my best wherever I went, and grooming took time. I was not used to this—in fact, I had trouble being "on" all the time.

I felt that I was expected to be perfect, look perfect and be the perfect wife and mother. Early on, it became clear that Bob was velcroed to his phone. He was on it when we were together in the car and at breakfast. He was obsessed. It was why he was so successful. Feeling neglected, I decided we needed to establish "no-phone zones" when we were together. There was no "Cell Phones Anonymous" twelve-step program, but staying connected every waking moment with everyone was becoming an issue; it was intruding on our private time. The iPhone didn't exist yet, so emailing and texting weren't yet the norm—thank goodness!

So soon, if I wasn't with Bob, he was serial-calling me. I loved staying connected, but sometimes I was in the middle of something else. Bob's favorite daily call was from Max Fisher of Detroit, one of his mentors. The oldest man on the *Forbes* 400 list, Max was a very wise man who gave Bob—and on occasion me, too,—very good advice. I have often said that I hope God gives us phones in heaven. Bob would certainly be miserable without one.

Bob and I were so much alike in our personalities, but I was more easygoing. Here's a typical example. We were driving new cars and had met over at his barber shop. At Bob's insistence, I had come to meet his lady barber to give my input on a haircut. As we were leaving, I noticed that Bob and I were parked opposite each other. I assumed he would let me back up first. Ladies first, right? As it turned out, we backed up at the same time and collided. We both got out, and it looked like it would be unpleasant as sparks began to fly. Then I started to laugh, and soon we were both laughing.

Election Day in November 2000 came, and we went over to the Tanglewood home of former President George H.W. and Barbara Bush to watch the election returns. Mrs. Bush was focused on the news. While I sat there with this strong, vibrant woman, I was aware that she was watching, not as former First Lady, but as a mother. She was in control, but concerned—as any mother would be.

During the historic post-election vote recount, James A. "Jimmy" Baker, III, former Secretary of State and family friend of the Bushes, was dispatched to Florida to oversee the situation. Meanwhile, Bob and I joined former President Bush at the opening of the M.D. Anderson Cancer Center facility in Madrid, Spain. Bob was a two-time former chair of the board of M.D. Anderson Cancer Center and former President Bush was the incoming chair-elect of the Board of Visitors. Standing in the group photo with the directors and the president of M.D. Anderson, John Mendelsohn, and his wife, Anne; was Juan Carlos, King of Spain. The King let out a shout when he saw Bob, and they began kidding with each other. He then turned and introduced himself to me; his eyes were dancing. I could see there was a very special friendship and rivalry, as they were both irreverent with each other. H.M. King Juan Carlos told me that we would be hearing from him soon with an invitation to very special event.

From Spain, we traveled to London to shoot pheasant at Glympton Park with the Bushes. Owned by Prince Bandar, the Saudi Arabian Ambassador to the U.S., Glympton is a glorious former deer park set on 2,000 acres; the residence, Glympton House, dates back to the eighteenth century. That was my first shoot, and the days were filled with fun and activities. I enjoyed watching the beaters and loaders do their jobs. The former President was his usual jovial self until he came in from shooting; the election recount was still going on and he was either glued to CNN or talking to Jimmy Baker. He was clearly worried. In this case, he was a father first, a former President second.

In the end, the U.S. Supreme Court declared George W. Bush the winner. We attended his inauguration, but it was so cold that we watched the ceremony from our hotel room. We did, however, manage to make it through the freezing rain to attend the Texas Inaugural Ball.

About this time, we began receiving phone calls and troubling letters from a woman named Nancy Crawford. She had approached Rudolph Guiliani, then mayor of New York City, at a political event and told him that she was Bob's lover. *Houston Chronicle* columnist Maxine Mesinger had also received a call from her stating that she was going to marry Bob.

Nancy had bothered Bob for years and had been arrested on several occasions. We contacted a Houston Police detective, who expressed concern about my safety. He said that Nancy might perceive me as "being a rival" and could possibly harm me.

Letters from her came in almost daily. As she had stalked Bob at his former home in New York City, we hired a night guard. It was another rude awakening to life in the public spotlight.

One of our first official overseas trips as a married couple was to Kuwait in 2001. It was the tenth anniversary of the first Gulf War, "Operation Desert Storm," and we were flying on a Kuwaiti airliner with former President and Mrs. Bush, former U.S. National Security Adviser Brent Scowcroft and General "Stormin'" Norman Schwarzkopf and his wife, Brenda. On landing in Kuwait City, I asked General Schwarzkopf if he thought we would be safe traveling there. Without hesitating, he said that we were safe anywhere that the former President wasn't. Saddam Hussein was still in power, so his comment wasn't all in jest.

The General earned the nickname "Stormin'" because his troops noted that he had a temper. He had commanded the build-up of 700,000 international coalition troops after Iraq invaded Kuwait in 1990. The war was waged by thirty-four nations and led by the U.S. in response to that invasion. Passionate and effective, "Stormin'" led a successful hundred-hour ground offensive and an extended air campaign—and got the job done. I have enormous respect for him and for General Scowcroft. Before joining the administration of George H.W. Bush, General Scowcroft spent years as National Security Adviser under President Gerald Ford and as assistant to Henry Kissinger when he was National Security Adviser.

Soft-spoken and candid, General Scowcroft is known as someone who always strikes the right tone and looks for balance in diplomatic relations. He had written extensively on policy and the war. A brilliant tactician, he seemed more inclined to find a diplomatic solution, if possible. He was obviously close to former President Bush, and the two were on the same page in their handling of that first Gulf War. He shared many observations with me.

I had to pinch myself at times because of the rare insight I was getting into that military campaign. Here I was, a footnote to history, witnessing how the Kuwaitis treated this group of men, which also included former Chairman of the U.S. Joint Chiefs of Staff General Colin Powell, with deference and as heroes. On the second day of our visit, General Powell spoke at a reception held in the courtyard of the U.S. Embassy.

"We renew our determination that evil will not prosper...that freedom will live and breathe in this part of the world and that honored heroes so they did not die in vain," he said.

His words resonated with me. I looked around at the audience standing in the hot desert sun and watched their reaction. Our fine leaders in the military were heroes, loved and revered by the people they helped liberate. General Powell was presented with a medal by the Emir of Kuwait, Sheik Jabbar al Ahmed al Sabah; former President Bush received a welcome and reception worthy of a superhero.

At a luncheon hosted by the women honoring former First Lady Barbara Bush, I was struck by the gratitude and respect they all had for the Bushes. The ladies had each prepared a favorite national dish; some wore the latest Chanel suits, and others covered up with traditional *abayas*. My tablemates shared horrible stories of their husbands, sons and brothers being rounded up and marched off by the Iraqi invaders. I felt we had more in common than not—we all loved our families and our countries, and we all wanted to keep our children safe. As Americans, we are fortunate to live in a very free and open society. Yet we take those freedoms for granted too often.

At the closing ceremonies, the names of those who lost their lives in Operation Desert Storm were listed on the screen. I became very emotional. Somewhere there were broken hearts—mother and fathers who had lost sons or daughters. The stories were profoundly sad, but I sensed hope in the room. I felt that that, if given a choice, every soldier would go again, without hesitation, to fight for those essential freedoms we hold so dear. Those soldiers put everything on the line to fight for us, and they deserve our respect and support.

None of us who have not experienced the loss of a child can comprehend the pain of the military families who lost their son or daughter. But even if we have not experienced loss on this scale, we are all broken somewhere along the journey we call life. For me, practicing optimism and gratitude is an important way to deal with pain. Sometimes, it's simply a matter of making a mental list of what you do have. To begin my list, I thank God I have my sight and my limbs. A gratitude list is especially helpful on those bleak days when you either feel like screaming or crawling into bed and pulling the covers over your head. My faith sustains me on those days; God can always talk me off the ledge.

Our trip continued when the Bushes invited us to join them in Saudi Arabia. I had brought along a modest black pantsuit, just in case. And after reading that women were obligated to cover their hair, I stopped at a market and bought a thick, black veil. When the plane landed in Riyadh, I pulled it out and placed it over my very blond hair.

"No, you don't have to wear that," Mrs. Bush said to me. "You are with my husband."

"But my hair is so blond!" I protested. But Mrs. Bush just shook her head.

Walking down the red carpet that had been laid out for former President Bush was a surreal experience. Bob, following the tradition of Saudi men, asked me to walk behind him. I refused and remained at his side as we walked down the carpet. If I was going to liberate my hair, then I certainly wasn't going to walk five steps behind my husband!

We were greeted by Amabassador/Prince Bandar, a member of the Saudi royal family. Riyadh, which means "the gardens," is home to about six million people and the urban center of the region. There were very few high-rise buildings, but there were some incredible architectural wonders, including the $2 billion Kingdom Center and Al Musmak Castle. The Prince escorted us to the Palace, where we received a warm and royal welcome.

At the Palace, we met then-King Fahd bin Abdulaziz Al Saud, who had suffered a serious stroke in 1995 (and passed away in 2005). While former President Bush had a private meeting with the King, Mrs. Bush and I attended a fabulous lunch at the gorgeous and very ornate Palace. Surprisingly, we were invited to dine with men—women and men rarely dine together in those kinds of public situations in that country. The fact that we were not only included, but also entertained, was clearly due to their great respect for Barbara Bush.

Before we left, Bob and I were each given a Bulgari watch—a gift I cherish. There wasn't time to visit the marketplace, but if there had been I would definitely have covered my hair. I enjoyed my time in the birthplace of Islam, and I left wanting to know more about the Kingdom and its traditions. Again, I felt we had more common interests and concerns than we had differences.

As citizens of the world, we can't let misunderstanding and fear poison our relationships with other countries. We have so much to learn from each other. Let's be honest: we are, all of us, living in less-than-perfect societies but we are fortunate to live in America. Our country isn't perfect but as Bob used to say, "No one is perfect but you and me."

From the left, the Duke of Arion Spain, H.M. King Juan Carlos, Bob, myself and the Duchess of Arion wait curbside in the Isle of Wight for a ride during the America's Cup Jubilee.

CHAPTER FIVE

SUMMER RACING

THE SUMMER OF 2001 brought lots of sailing adventures. Over several months, we sailed our seventy-five-foot "Little Harbor" sloop, Rhapsody, to many ports in the Northeast, including Newport, Nantucket and Martha's Vineyard. I caught up on my reading along the way, occasionally subbing for Bob; our Captain, Bill White, and our Admiral—Bob—took turns at the wheel. I wasn't a bad sailor and enjoyed learning more from Bob. He was a perfectionist and was always teaching me how to maximize the wind.

We stopped in different port towns to visit friends, among them Robert and Kelly Day in Martha's Vineyard. It was there, in Edgartown, that I met Walter Cronkite. Best known as the voice of CBS News, his career spanned decades of world-changing events—from the assassinations of President John F. Kennedy and Martin Luther King, Jr. to the Space Program.

Walter invited us to sail on his boat, *Wyntje*, and we immediately accepted. His charming wife, Betsy, joined us. I couldn't believe I was sailing with one of the most distinctive and respected broadcasters in the history of TV news, but I decided to take advantage of having him as a captive audience by asking questions like, "Why is there more bias now in the news than in the past?" and "What happened to just reporting straight facts?"

He told me that cable television had changed everything, including the news format, and there was more pressure on stations to compete in the ratings wars. News had evolved into a form of entertainment. I shared with him my experiences in the University of Texas School of Communication. He laughed when I told him I'd said that I was eager to get to work—and then promptly dropped out of school. He admitted to also being a college dropout. But that's where the similarities ended.

He was a legend in the news media; I was a freelance writer. The fact that there's a Walter Cronkite Plaza outside The University of Texas' Moody College of Communication, not a Mica Mosbacher Plaza, speaks volumes. We laughed a lot that afternoon, and he patiently posed with Bob at the wheel of his boat. It was a memorable day.

The following March, I hosted a Senior Prom-themed party for Bob's seventy-fifth birthday. As we were gearing up for the celebration, a box was delivered from a local florist. Inside was a gorgeous traditional senior prom corsage from Walter and Betsy signed with love. I pinned it to my gown that night. It was a lovely gift, one I have cherished over the years. I keep it framed in a shadow box in my office to remind me of the wonderful afternoon we spent with this iconic man whose legacy I so admire.

In July 2001, we celebrated my birthday and our anniversary aboard *Rhapsody*. We grilled fresh fish, opened a perfect bottle of Chassagne Montrachet, and toasted one another and our good fortune to have found each other. We were in our favorite place in the world; romanced by the moon and the stars, we were content and very much in love.

In August 2001, we joined King Juan Carlos of Spain for the ultimate sailing adventure: racing in the America's Cup Jubilee at Cowes on the Isle of Wight in England. I had been reading up on the history of the race. It began in 1851 with a challenge by John Stevens, commodore of the newly formed New York Yacht Club. He formed a syndicate with the goal of building a boat that would be a worthy rival to its British counterparts. The new schooner, *America,* was built and designed by George Steers. Following some correspondence, the Earl of Wilton, then commodore of the Royal Yacht Squadron Yacht Club, invited *America* over for a visit.

Headquartered in an imposing castle, the Royal Yacht Squadron is rich in tradition. No ladies, except the Queen of England, are allowed to enter its hallowed halls. It was then—and remains today—one of the most prestigious yacht clubs in the world.

Not long after arriving for a visit, *America* was entered in the Royal Yacht regatta. On August 22, 1851, she beat the opposing fleet and proclaimed victory. Despite protests and controversy over the route she had taken, the results stood. She had won. Ever since that historic race, the competition has been known as the America's Cup. The actual trophy was held at the New York Yacht Club from 1857 until 1983, when the Cup was won by Perth,Australia.

To celebrate this special anniversary, the New York Yacht Club and the Royal Squadron agreed to stage an elaborate joint celebration. Planning was meticulous and took several years. A week of races, balls and exhibitions were planned; the guest lists included royalty, such as Princess Anne of England, Prince Henrik of Denmark, the Aga Khan and King Juan Carlos de Borbón of Spain, as well as sailing luminaries Buddy Melges, French Olympic sailor Thierry Pepponet, Dennis Connor and New Zealand winner Russell Coutts. Other notables in attendance included CNN founder Ted Turner, Bill Gates and duty king billionaire Bob Miller.

In addition, 200 of the world's most beautiful yachts that had competed in previous America's Cup races were invited. An exact replica of the original ship, *America,* was racing, as were vintage classics like *Shamrock V* and *Endeavor.* These yachts were iconic, and many of them were more than 130 feet long. Also featured were the modern twelve-meter (thirty-nine-foot) boats.,including two-time winner, *Intrepid,* skippered by Bob's brother, Emile "Bus" Mosbacher Jr. The J class boats and the high-tech boats—the more recent winners—were there, along with super yachts. For anyone who was even a little interested in sailing, it was a fascinating floating museum.

Bob was competing in the IMS Modern Division aboard the boat *Bribon.* There was an august crew scheduled to sail on *Bribon,* including the Spanish America's Cup winner Pedro Campos, Duke of Arión, and, of course, Bob, a two-time world champion and Olympic finalist himself.

We flew to Mallorca on August 14th to join King Juan Carlos and Queen Sofia at their summer retreat. We left the airport, stopped at their gracious home (really more of a palace), threw on some boat shoes and grabbed bathing suits, and we were off to *Bribon,* the King's boat. Once we sailed out and found a tranquil spot to anchor, we enjoyed a lovely picnic lunch and an afternoon swim. Far removed from paparazzi, everyone onboard seemed relaxed and happy. It occurred to me then that it must be very hard for people in their position—high-profile, very public lives—to find private time where they could let down their guard.

Queen Sofia, also an Olympian, introduced us to her family at dinner. It was there that I met then-Crown Prince Felipe—now King Felipe. He was single at the time, devastatingly handsome and personable. I was sure that hearts would break all across Europe when he eventually decided to get married. The family welcomed me with open arms and a down-to-earth attitude. I felt instantly comfortable, especially when the King said he wanted Bob and me to feel like we were part of his family. We might not be royal, but we certainly got the royal treatment!

The King and Bob both spent lots of time laughing, kidding, and trading stories. My favorite was a story about when then-Prince Juan Carlos visited Texas for a regatta. Bob and his late wife Jane and the Prince and Princess (now King and Queen) were staying at the same hotel. Then-Princess Sofia called out to Bob from her balcony, which was above his. He innocently walked out onto his balcony to answer and was doused with a cold glass of water. Apparently, he looked up and she burst out laughing.

Another time, Bob presented a puppy as a birthday present to the Queen. The puppy was brought to the dinner in a silver-plated covered dish. When the lid was removed, the puppy let out an adorable puppy bark, and the delighted Queen rewarded him with a dazzling smile.

That evening, I learned that Bob had won the Gold Medal in the World Championship Dragon Boat Regatta in Palma de Mallorca and that the King had presented him with the trophy. It occurred to me then that he had been so modest that I knew very little about his accomplishments in racing. From that night onward, their chance meeting at a competition evolved over the years into a deep and rare friendship.

Regrettably, we received word that night that the boom on the King's racing boat had broken during practice. She needed a new one, so arrangements were made for us to fly over to Cowes the next day in a cargo plane. We were all crowded around the boom in the passenger part of the plane. The King was a good sport and didn't seem to care at all that he wasn't flying in first-class comfort.

We arrived in Cowes a happy group. The Louis Vuitton Media Center was headquarters for the race, reminding me of how Bob and I first met. My life had come full circle. It was a splendid day with an almost carnival-like atmosphere in the town. It reminded me somewhat of Nantucket. So many of the grand ageing beauties from past America's Cups floated elegantly in the water. On High Street, people were dancing and banners were flying. There was a general feeling of celebration.

As Bob ran into many old friends—fellow icons in the sailing world—it seemed like a Who's Who of Olympic sailors and sports reporters. We retreated to a private home on the outskirts of town that had been rented for the week for the King and his crew. Ever gallant, King Juan Carlos traded his larger bedroom for our smaller one.

"I was in the Army," he explained. "I got used to barracks."

It was a very generous—and not at all unusual for him—gesture. At dinner that evening, I was seated on the King's right. He regaled me with many sailing stories. Later, we met the crew. They seemed determined to win. Losing, it seemed, was not an option in their world of competitive sailing.

The next day at dawn, the actual America's Cup trophy returned to England in a style befitting a queen. Escorted by commodores from the New York and Cowes Yacht Clubs as well as flag officers of the Royal New Zealand Yacht Squadron and Maori Warriors, the Cup received a hero's welcome, complete with a fearsome war dance performed by the Maori warriors. The crowd loved it!

On Saturday, the Jubilee was officially opened by Prince Philip, Duke of Edinburgh. Charming and eloquent, he brought a certain *savoir faire* to the occasion. The opening ceremonies were followed the next day by practice races. Several of the team wives and I hopped onto a spectator boat to watch the matches. It was thrilling to see the King, his crew and my husband race together.

The seas proved rough that day, and when I went to disembark later, I landed hard on the dock. My foot twisted just the wrong way, and I heard a crunch. Ouch! At first, I acted like nothing had happened. But soon I was limping. By the time we went to dinner that night, my foot was swollen and throbbing. The next day, while hobbling around town shopping for souvenirs, I was stopped by a journalist wearing a soft cast on his foot. He had broken it the day before and urged me to go to a clinic and have it looked at.

I didn't want to miss anything, so I ignored his advice. By the time I'd limped through a reception, a dinner party and a fireworks show, I was in agony. I went to bed that night convinced that it would be better in the morning. The following day, it didn't hurt quite as much—probably because I'd slept for eight hours and so had stayed off the foot. At lunch, King Juan Carlos introduced me to His Highness the Aga Khan, who was also a friend of Bob's. He had contributed to so many important causes through his charitable foundation, and yet he never publicized it. I admired how he kept a low profile while doing good works behind the scenes.

The re-enactment of the actual America's Cup race around the Isle of Wight was the highlight of the day. Because of tidal conditions, it couldn't take place on the actual anniversary; but, when it was finally held, it was an amazing event. Seeing so many yachts from different eras, including the boats on which Bus Mosbacher had sailed to America's Cup victory, was thrilling—like a glorious pageant, an Easter parade.

On the sixth day of racing, King Juan Carlos and his crew won their race. At a small press conference earlier in the day, he had expressed optimism about their chances and delight in the opportunity to compete.

"The feeling I have sailing here is of great happiness and excitement," he said. A keen competitor, he once again proved his prowess on the water that day.

At a ball that night, we were all in a celebratory mood. Despite the men mistakenly wearing navy blazers when the dress code called for black tie, the group was in top form. It was a magical evening, and I forgot my aching foot. When we arrived in Houston a couple of days later, however, I went straight to an orthopedic specialist and ended up with my foot in a boot. He couldn't believe I had been wearing high-heeled sandals all week, because it turned out it was broken.

Boot and all, I got back to my routine. Cameron had to be driven to football practice, and the two King Charles Cavaliers taken to the vet. Fairytale trips aside, life goes on. I went from hanging out with kings and queens back to being the family chauffeur. Someone had to go to the supermarket and make sure dinner was ready. We had no nighttime help.

Re-entry was a little rough. Bob had a backlog of work—a mountain of paper, really, piled on his desk, and I had my own enormous stack of mail to sort through. It was life back to normal. Everyone has a unique brand of stress. Ours was a very fortunate situation, but with that good fortune came what we saw—and I continue to see—as a responsibility to give back and to be generous in helping others. We received many requests, so it was hard work, too.

One morning I woke up and felt like something had bitten me. Allergic to wheat, nuts and bees, I have a tendency to go into anaphylactic shock. I felt like I had sustained a shock to my system, but I wasn't short of breath. Still, I called my allergist, Dr. Inteliano, as a precaution. He said to go to the ER if things got worse. We had an event that night so I went to the hairdresser instead. While I was getting my hair done, Syd from Bob's office called. She sounded concerned.

Apparently, Milagro, our housekeeper, had spotted some brown spiders in the bedroom. The bite of brown recluse spiders can cause serious problems. Syd had called Dr. John Wolf at Baylor, and he wanted me to meet him at the hospital.

Reluctantly, I went home to pick up spiders. I absolutely have a phobia of these eight-legged creatures. Milagro handed me an Evian bottle full of spiders. She also showed me the back of the upholstered headboard. It was a spider convention. Something had hatched. Repulsed, I threw the bottle in the trunk.

I drove to the hospital with wet hair and handed the bottle to Dr. Wolf. He took it away and came back, nodding, "Yes, it's a brown recluse." There were several species in the bottle, but the offending spider was there as well. He examined the bite on my thigh, froze the spider and whisked me away to grand rounds so the interns and residents could see a "documented poisonous spider bite."

I stripped all linen and upholstered furniture and the rug out of the master suite and hired Mike, an exterminator, who came almost daily for a while. Bob had been bitten too, as had Cameron. The spiders were everywhere. Friends who heard the story teased me and called me the Spider Woman. This brand of super heroine did not appeal to me.

Before I knew it, September had arrived, and we were on our way to visit former President George H.W. and Barbara Bush at Walker's Point, their summer home in Kennebunkport, Maine. It was a gracious home with a breath-taking view, and we were honored to be their guests. After enjoying their hospitality for a few days, we headed to Portland, Maine on September 9th, where we were catching a US Airways flight to New York.

My injured foot was still wrapped up in a boot, so Bob dropped me off at the check-in counter and left to return the rental car. A friendly attendant brought me a wheelchair, got my boarding pass, and wheeled me to a somewhat deserted gate area to wait for Bob. The only other person there was a striking, dark-haired man sitting by himself; for some reason, the attendant parked me next to him. I smiled at the man, who just glared back at me. I froze in my seat.

Something felt wrong. I tried to read my magazine, but I felt antsy. I kept glancing sideways at this man, who was clearly unfriendly—even hostile. I was anxious for Bob to show up. When he did, I whispered something about everyone being so helpful and nice, except this guy.

Once on board, I was on edge. During the flight, I kept telling Bob that I wanted off the plane. Something wasn't right. A dark haired man behind me was acting strange. His female companion talked the whole time. Bob was used to my "psychic moments" and knew I wasn't a white-knuckle flyer. He held my hand and tried to reassure me. When we landed, I stood behind a young man and commented to him that the terminal bus was taking a long time. He seemed hostile. Naively, I thought that maybe he didn't speak English. I was relieved when the bus finally pulled up to take us to the terminal. I studied the two men who were at odds with the environment; I knew it was rude to stare, but I did so anyway. There was something about their mannerisms that just wasn't right; I knew it in my bones.

On Sunday, September 10th, we flew from NYC to Houston. The next morning, on September 11, 2001, we drove to the campus of Strake Jesuit College Preparatory School where Cameron was starting high school. During the new parents' orientation session with school

President Father Daniel Lahart, we were interrupted by the horrifying news that two planes had crashed into the World Trade Center. Words like "terrorists" and "al-Qaeda" made their way around the room. Before we knew what was really happening, four planes had crashed and more than 3,000 people—mothers, fathers, sons, daughters, all someone's loved ones—were dead. The unthinkable had happened.

Needless to say, the orientation session was cut short. Like most stunned Americans, Bob and I went home and tuned into the news. The following morning, there were photographs of the terrorists—suicidal fanatics, as it turned out—in the *New York Times,* I looked at the photos one face at a time, and that's when I recognized not one, but three of the faces of evil. Mohammed Atta had been sitting next to me at the Portland Airport gate; the other two terrorists had been aboard the plane in first class and I had spoken to the two of them.

Bob saw the horrified expression on my face, and I told him I recognized Atta. He didn't doubt me and immediately called the Secret Service and the FBI. I spoke to an agent almost daily. It turned out that two of the seats on the airplane were unassigned. It was my fate to have been on that plane I guess and were the last to see Atta alive. Bob and I outed the cell in Portland.

—————————————

As the year wore on and America slowly regrouped from the devastating shock of that day, Bob complained increasingly about a constant pain in his hip. His joint was wearing down, and it seemed he would need a hip replacement. We scheduled the surgery, everything went smoothly, and after about a week, he came home. That should have been the end of it, but it wasn't.

One evening, I came into our bathroom to find Bob coughing up blood. Alarmed, I asked him how much he had coughed up. He brushed it off.

"Oh, this is nothing," he said. "I coughed some up earlier, too."

The obvious concern was that there was a blood clot, a not-infrequent side effect of joint-replacement surgery. Bob's internist was out of town, so I insisted that he go to the emergency room at St. Luke's Hospital. We went, they gave him a complete work-up, and he was discharged.

That night, he coughed up blood again, and I became frantic. After speaking to a nurse at the doctor's office, I decided it was time to go back to the hospital. He refused, but I insisted. "They missed something," I told him. Again, he said no.

I don't view stubbornness as a sign of strength; I view it as plain stubbornness. Bob had dug his heels in, so unless I could drag him, he wasn't going to go. I played my trump card and called his wonderful cardiologist, Dr. Ali Massumi. He told me to give him extra blood pressure pills and then wait. Eventually, Dr. Massumi predicted he would have trouble breathing and would not resist my overture to drive him to the hospital.

It was a long night. Keeping vigil, I called my mother, crying, terrified that Bob was going to die. She told me to call an ambulance and get two burly attendants to take him to the emergency room.

"That won't work," I said. "He will not go back."

Fortunately, Dr. Massumi called me early in the morning—about 4 o'clock and told me to meet him at the emergency room around 6 o'clock. I had had no sleep. When I checked on Bob, he was gasping for breath. I prayed mightily, knowing that Bob's life was in God's hands. I had to trust that everything would turn out well. Finally all the fight went out of Bob. He could barely stand up.

I drove the car around to the front door, grabbed his crutches, and asked the male nurse to help me load him into the car. Then I drove like the wind; I felt like I was running out of time. We arrived at the hospital, but there was nobody there to help me. Running on sheer nerves and adrenaline, I muscled him into a wheelchair and ran all the way down the corridor.

Dr. Massumi met us there and wheeled Bob away. An hour later, he came out and told me that it was, in fact, a blood clot, and it had passed through Bob's heart. Another physician was going to thread a filter into a vein in his leg to prevent anymore clots from traveling through his heart.

After what seemed like hours, Dr. Massumi emerged to tell me that when the other doctor was threading the filter, she literally "caught" a large clot moving through his vein. It was such an unlikely thing to happen and a miracle that she had intercepted it. The procedure saved his life, and not a minute too soon. Bob was admitted and would stay there for several weeks.

"I cheated death," Bob declared. With Bob in the hospital, my days were now spent driving to and from the house and St. Luke's. I tried to be home every day by the time Cameron got back from school. I had the route between the hospital and home memorized; I knew how to time the lights on Kirby Drive, and I could recognize virtually every tree on Sunset Boulevard. In the meantime, Bob seemed to be suffering from one setback after another. Every time he called, he would tell me in shaky voice that he had another medical problem, and I would dash back to the hospital. I felt like I was literally driving around a racetrack, with home as a mere pit stop.

As frazzled as I was, I prayed often, scared that each day might be Bob's last. Finally, the strain began taking a toll on me. On evenings when I came home late, I had more than my share of wine. I wasn't coping well with the schedule, and life at home was being neglected. I was on the verge of giving up, when my mother offered to stay over and help with Cameron so I could move into the hospital suite. It wasn't the ideal solution, but it was better than doing nothing at all.

Sure, there were sacrifices. I missed an important event that Cameron hosted at our house; I wasn't there when he came home from school or from sports practice. Once again, I was reminded that motherhood is a lot like a circus act. We balance and juggle family, children, spouses and careers like acrobats. Keeping all the balls in the air without falling off the high-wire takes great skill—and lots of practice. None of us gets it entirely right. It's a series of compromises and cutting corners at times. Women multitask and often fail to take care of themselves.

I had conflicting priorities, but Bob was in crisis and Cameron wasn't. They both needed me, but fortunately my son was very fond of my mother, his Nana. He was in good hands, and I could be there for my husband. While it was touch-and-go for a while, Bob's condition improved. It was soon time to pack up and go home. I was elated.

––––––––––––

Before Bob's health scare brought everything to a screeching halt, we had made an offer on an architectural gem in the lovely River Oaks neighborhood. Built in the 1950s by prominent architect Hugo V. Neuhaus for his family, the house had won many awards for its mid-century modern design. It was set back on Lazy Lane on two acres of stately oak trees.

One of the things I loved most about the house were the floor-to-ceiling glass windows.

They were literally walls of glass; when the sun shone through them, the light sparkled throughout the house. At night, it danced off the pink terrazzo floors. It was marketed as a tear down, but I knew it was a keeper the minute I walked in. Our realtor and close friend, Laura Sakowitz Sweeney, had taken me to see the property in September 2001, and it was love at first sight. With its spacious lawns and wooded areas, the house was a perfect place for the three of us. I knew Cameron would also enjoy spending time with his friends there.

Another plus: the kitchen had recently been updated. Both of the men in my life were passionate about cooking. The kitchen in Bob's bachelor pad, as I referred to it, was tiny; we were always colliding at dinnertime. Envisioning many happy times in that kitchen, I called Bob. He came over immediately to take a look.

We tended to think very much alike, and his impression mirrored mine. In fact, he surprised me by making an offer on the spot. I was over the moon. The walls were purple and there were deep holes in the ceiling—it was obvious the house needed a lot of tender loving care. It looked like Miss Havisham from *Great Expectations* might have once lived there. But it would be my first home.

Given Bob's health problems, we had postponed closing on the house until he was out of the woods. Once he turned the corner, we signed the closing documents from his hospital bed. The new home represented an important new chapter in our marriage. Like many women, my surroundings are very important to me. I couldn't wait to restore the house to its full glory. I envisioned that happy day of taking our time to plan the renovations. We needed to find an architect, a contractor and a designer. Fortunately, we already had a place to live, so there was no rush to move. My office was at home, so by staying put, we could avoid the construction noise. I could take my own sweet time to plan the move, which was exactly how I wanted it. I like organization.

It was late October by the time Bob was ready to leave the hospital. That's when he made a surprise announcement.

"When I go home on Friday, I would like to go home to the new house," he said.

"Uh, what?" I asked. "It needs a lot of work, sweetheart."

"I know," he smiled, the dazzling smile he was known for that melted my heart every time.

I started to protest, but decided to roll with it. He clearly needed and wanted a fresh start. Nursing Bob back to health had been my project for a while, and now I had a new one. I tried not to panic. On the way home, I called Max Movers. They weren't available until the very Friday he was scheduled to be released. I raced around our house attaching yellow Post-Its™ on essential furniture. I also ordered a home hospital-style bed for Bob. Before I knew it, Friday was here and it was show time. I let the movers in and drove to the hospital. Armed with a to-do list, my mother took over. As always, she was a godsend.

I picked up Bob at St. Luke's and drove him to Lazy Lane. Laura was there to meet us with the keys. As we pulled into the driveway, the moving van drove in right behind us. Laura got out of her car and looked at me in disbelief.

"You're moving in today? Now?" Her face was white.

"I'm an impatient person," Bob grinned. "I don't buy green bananas. They take too long to ripen." She was flabbergasted but I knew how Bob thought. He could be impulsive and I was adaptable.

It was a scene of controlled chaos. I got Bob settled into his new portable bed in what would become his library. With no clear floor plan, the movers set the furniture down in key rooms and left. Over the next few weeks, Bob's bed became a kind of command station. With the assistance of Dickens, our King Charles spaniel, he happily supervised the contractor, George Gazis, and his crew. As for me, I went with the flow. The house was a fishbowl; I had to be careful in the mornings not to walk by the windows in my nightgown because I never knew who was going to be on the property. With workers everywhere, my home was yet another ring in the circus that was my life.

Bob wanted an instant house and was clearly not willing to wait on a proper design scheme. I decided that I needed some help and sent up a flare; David Lewis and Ernest Maese of Lewis and Maese Antiques and Auction came to the rescue. They helped me place the furniture and also found a few extra pieces to fill in some "decorative holes." Sofas and rugs showed up from Meredith O'Donnell, and well-known local designer Patty Hubbard, also a family friend, lent a hand. Social icon Lynn Wyatt came over to help advise me. She pushed my living room sofas around and gave me advice. She was so amazing. It took a village of friends and experts to help me pull the house together, but we managed. And it was worth it.

I named our home *Reflections* because of the splendid way the light bounced off the windows. At night, the reflection in the windows made by a fifty-year-old live oak in the backyard made it seem like there were a dozen trees, not just one. It was a magical place, morning, noon and night. "I like your home, Mrs. Mosbacher," Bob said to me over and over. He clearly loved it, too, and was tickled to have bought it for me. I was blessed.

Cameron's friends started coming over, and the house became party central. I don't recall many specifics about that period, except that there was lots of laughing and joy. We were thrilled to have Bob home and alive. At some point in there, I realized that life with Bob was always going to be exciting and unpredictable, like driving a race car in the rain.

As the house came together, I began to notice just how much in tune Bob and I were with each other. Of course I loved him and of course I found him charming and challenging at the same time, but I didn't quite realize how much, over time, we'd begun to find our rhythm as a couple.

One day, for instance, I went to the Mattress Firm to buy a new bed. I chose it in just under an hour and went home, pleased with myself for having crossed one more thing off the list. When I told Bob, he looked upset. He insisted that we go back to the store and pick it out together. So back we went, and he proceeded to lie down on a few store models. Finally, he announced that he'd found the bed that was just right. The manager walked over and pointed to the one Bob had selected.

"Are you sure you want this one?" he asked.

"Yes sir," Bob answered.

"Well, good, because that's the bed Mrs. Mosbacher picked out earlier today."

Bob and I had a good laugh over that experience. It was increasingly typical of us. I could finish Bob's sentences, he could finish mine, and our tastes were very much in sync. Occasionally, we would butt heads, but the make-up sessions made the battle well worth it.

A few weeks later, I came home to find Bob sitting in his car listening to music. His doctor had just cleared him to drive. I asked him if everything was okay, and he nodded, hands on the steering wheel.

"How long have you been sitting here?" I said.

"Oh, a good hour," he looked at me. "It means so much to me to have my freedom back." It was then that we both understood just how much we took for granted.

One thing we never took for granted, however, was the amazing skill and care our doctors gave us. We later presented Dr. Massumi with a statue of a bronze angel. At the dedication in the Ansary Atrium at St. Luke's Hospital, we saluted his compassion as a doctor and the great care he gave Bob. As far as we were concerned, he was one of Bob's guardian angels and had helped save his life.

When Bob went back to work, I found my own way back into my routine. There was much catching up to do. Thanksgiving came and went; by Christmas, our home was pulled together enough to host a family gathering. Over a delicious Christmas dinner, Bob's children, grandchildren and extended family members toasted us. We went to bed that night feeling grateful to God for all His many blessings—especially good health.

Going through the Straits on Bonifacio, Corsica on *M/Y Hallelujah*.

CHAPTER SIX

NEW ROAD CONDITIONS

ON CHRISTMAS DAY, we left on what would become our annual trip to Lyford Cay, Bahamas. Arriving in the evening, we settled into Rhapsody. *At the time, we co-owned the boat with Bob and Janice McNair. We took in the breathtaking sunset and finally began to exhale. Bob had two speeds—start and stop—and the only time he ever truly relaxed was when he was on his beloved boat.*

Captain Bill was a good friend and a wonderful companion; he made sure everything ran smoothly on *Rhapsody*. We ventured out the next day, and the wind was on our nose. Bob didn't care. He was used to sailing windward; the greater the challenge, the happier he was. There was another upside to being aboard *Rhapsody*: it was one of few places where Bob would finally ignore his perpetually ringing cell phone.

After a wonderful trip to the Abacos Islands and romantic walks on the beach, we returned home relaxed and happy. At that time, all was right with the world. Bob jumped back into wildcatting and fundraising, and I divided my days between Cameron and Bob, pursuing my own interests in between. I met with Anna Mod, a noted historic preservationist and author. She helped us obtain city, state and national historic designations for our house. Like Anna, I felt terrible every time an architectural jewel was torn down. Neither of us thought of buildings as bricks and mortar; we saw them more as keepers of social memories and history.

One of our first receptions at *Reflections* was held in the spring for Anna's group, Houston Mod. A non-profit group, it was founded to promote appreciation of mid-century modern architecture in Texas. Among the guest lecturers at our home was Stephen Fox, the well-known Houston architectural historian and Rice University lecturer. He explained that the twentieth century had brought tremendous and enormous wealth to Houston as well as a dramatic expansion of its population and urban territory.

That period also saw the construction of unique houses, including the home of John and Dominique de Menil, designed by Philip Johnson, and ours, designed by Hugo V. Neuhaus, who was then Johnson's co-architect. Dr. Fox went on to explain that mid-century modern, or "mod," houses were built to showcase wealth in the 1950s and 1960s.

"These striking examples are an integral part of our landscape," he had written in a paper.

"There was a gentility and civility in this era."

He explained to the group that in 1915 the city of Houston had hired renowned architect George F. Kessler to lay out Main Boulevard and Herman Park. Those spacious green spaces would become integral parts of the city. He also noted that Will C. Hogg and his sister, known as Miss Ima, had built their own lovely residence, Bayou Bend, on fourteen acres on Buffalo Bayou near Memorial Park and close to our home.

The Hogg siblings left Bayou Bend and its incredible collection of historic American furniture and paintings to the Museum of Fine Arts, Houston. Interestingly, a house known as Rienzi, which was next door and also now belongs to the Museum, was a wedding present from Miss Ima to Carroll and Harris Masterson III. My mother remembered meeting Miss Ima, and said she was the grandest of ladies. Kind and also imposing, she greeted my mother with such elegance and grace that my mother never forgot her.

Bob and I truly felt that we were mere caretakers of our home and that we were trusted to preserve it for future generations. I had always been interested in historic preservation and architecture, as my uncle, Harold Seckinger, was a noted Florida architect. During my time at Ziegler Cooper Architects, I had learned about the city and about master planning. I became active in historical preservation. In an attempt to choose projects that also coincided with my interests, I joined the boards of the Houston Ballet, the American Hospital of Paris and Strake Jesuit. My plate was full, but my heart was happy.

Life kept moving in fast-forward. I was constantly going, racing to meetings, school activities, dinners and galas. I was always running behind. My easygoing, Type B personality was quickly becoming an extreme Type A.

Every day had a new set of demands, and I was having trouble getting used to the fast-track pace. The first two years of marriage had brought adjustments and crises. We were also blending families, which is a tricky thing to maneuver. Cameron got along well with Bob's extended family and fit right in with the six grandchildren. Bob's daughters—Dee, Kathi and Lisa—were polite to me, but I felt they were having trouble adjusting to yet one more wife. After all, I was Wife Number Four. In a heart-breaking turn of events, the Mosbacher kids had lost their mother when they were at tender ages. I could relate, as I had lost my father when I was a young woman. But they didn't need a mother at their ages, and I still felt like an interloper. To everyone's credit, we all tried for Bob's sake. My stepmother, Nancy Hall, had made my father very happy at the end of his life. I wanted to please Bob, I loved being part of a big family.

On top of the strain of adjusting to my new crazy schedule, I was feeling tired all the time. On several occasions, I got dizzy and fainted. It seemed I was pushing myself too hard. As I had when Bob was first in the hospital, I was reaching for an extra glass of wine to give me enough energy to get through the evening. Memories of a childhood kidnapping began to surface. I couldn't sleep; I had nightmares and flashbacks. A few times I experienced emotional flooding. I was on hyper alert. Bob and Cameron became concerned enough to stage an intervention of sorts and convince me to get help.

That help came in the form of Dr. Alice Gates. She diagnosed me with post-traumatic stress disorder resulting from a combination of the traumatic childhood event, the sexual assault when I was in college, Bob's health scare and the September 11th experience. Years before, I had quit smoking cold-turkey, and now I stopped drinking while I processed what was happening to me. I learned to cope in healthier ways. After many sessions and much hard work, I started sleeping through the night. I continued to have flashbacks from childhood but the healing had begun as I finally felt safe.

I would continue to suffer from PTSD and disassociated from time to time. Even at rest, I was constantly running a marathon with my mind racing. My adrenaline was going full tilt, and the wine had been acting as a kind of sedative—self-medication. Once I went on proper medication, things returned to a more normal rate, I didn't need the wine to unwind.

Through counseling, Bob realized he was pushing me too hard as well. Our schedule would have been challenging for even the most experienced social hostess! We needed more of our own time and more family time; I couldn't be "on" every night. We began to put family first, and he let me talk about my feelings without feeling as if he had to fix everything.

For my part, I needed to get used to being in the spotlight as a couple, and Bob understood that. We had our fair share of press, which brought with it a lot of social pressure. I felt like I had to look perfect every time I left the house. Raised by a father whose parents were Main Line Philadelphians, I had been taught never to show my emotions in public. So I had tucked my emotions away and soldiered on.

Adding to the social pressure were the occasional nasty stories in the press. One article, in particular, appeared in the *New York Post* on the famous Page Six and compared Bob and me to oilman Howard Marshall and Anna Nicole Smith. It was a weak comparison, as Bob wasn't in a wheelchair, and I was not a stripper. Additionally, I was missing certain anatomical assets. Even Cameron was included in the story. He was an innocent child, and I was outraged at this mean-spirited attack. We were not even married at the time of its publication.

At the time, I was also mortified. I had been mentioned before in society columns, but never in nasty ways. Maxine Mesinger, the legendary society columnist who worked at the *Houston Chronicle* for decades, was a friend of my father's; she was always kind in her mentions of me. As for Bob, he had extensive experience with the press, especially as Commerce Secretary. He was accessible and receptive and not used to slash-and-burn pieces.

Not long after the article appeared in the *New York Post,* the rumor mill began grinding away that another venomous article was going to be published, this time in *Vanity Fair* magazine. It was too much for me. Fortunately, the article never appeared. I don't know who spoke with whom—I think Bob's old friend, Barbara Walters, may have bent the right ear—but I was grateful.

Over the months of therapy, I came to terms with many things, including the notion that I had to be perfect to be loved. We are all scared and fragile when we make ourselves vulnerable, and it takes supreme trust in another to do that. So we have to be accountable for our actions, and we have to be trustworthy. We literally hold another's life in our hands.

Bob was as needy and fragile as I was. We could both be tough cookies, but really we were more like Oreos™: hard on the outside, soft on the inside. He seemed like a tough guy—and he was in a business environment, but not at home. He needed bolstering, too. We learned to treat each other more gently and to not take out our fears and frustrations on one another. We shared tender moments, we helped build each other up, and we let past mistakes stay in the past. No one likes to have their faults pointed out to them. Marriage isn't easy, but it's worth the hard work. We were not going to let ours fail.

At the suggestion of Susan Baker, I joined a Bible class at St. John the Divine Episcopal Church. "Seek out like-minded people," she advised. "Please God, not people." What a wise lady! Former President and Mrs. Bush were also supportive of me at this time and reminded me that newspapers are used to line birdcages and to house-break puppies. My mother chimed in, too, reinforcing what our friends were telling us.

"If they don't like you, they don't appreciate you," she would say to me.

So I listened. To all of them. I stopped trying so hard to win approval, and I started to relax. If my roots showed because I hadn't been to the hairdresser recently, so be it. If I wasn't liked, so be it. Seeking approval was exhausting, and I was tired of being tired.

About this time, we began mending fences with the past. Bob needed to devote some attention to his family and to regroup with his sister, Barbara. His daughters needed him—so did his son, Rob. For my part, I continued working on being less self-critical. We all had lost time to make up for.

Like so many women, I put my needs last. We are, after all, the hub of the family. We are the caretakers, the peacemakers and, increasingly, the breadwinners. I was lucky enough to have household help; many mothers don't, but they're still expected to be Wonder Woman.

Part of the problem is that we don't have adequate, affordable childcare for working mothers. In Iceland, for example, there isn't much of a gender gap at all. Women and men can take paid maternity leave, and both have government support for equal pay. No wonder so many American women resort to comfort food and alcohol!

During this time. I learned to be even more flexible and to react to a change in the road conditions of my life. One of my favorite themes in the Bible is found in *1 Corinthians 9:24*: "Know ye not that they which run in a race run all, but one receiveth the prize? So run, that ye may obtain." Life tests our perseverance and endurance while we run our spiritual races. I needed to run my race and so did Bob.

CHAPTER SEVEN

ONE SMALL STEP FOR WOMANKIND

LIFE CONTINUED TO MOVE on a fast track. I was fully engaged as an active member of the Strake Jesuit College Preparatory School board and also involved with several charitable organizations that were honoring Bob. As I got more or less used to the frenetic pace of our lives, I figured I should run flat out now because I could always rest in my grave.

Cameron and his friends were in and out after school and, of course, always hungry. I became a pretty good short-order cook, as I often found myself feeding what felt like the entire football team. Sometimes it seemed like our kitchen was the most popular restaurant in town!

In June 2003, I was honored by the American Hospital of Paris Foundation board at a luncheon in the City of Lights. The event was held at the ambassador's residence in the U.S. embassy compound on the northwest corner of Place de la Concorde. It is our country's oldest diplomatic mission, the very one where Benjamin Franklin and Thomas Jefferson served as ambassadors.

When we arrived in Paris, Bob left his bag at the airport curbside. The driver was sent to retrieve it. He later called and said in a heavily French-accented English, "It blew up." Bob, slightly hard of hearing said, "I know you blew it." "No, no, it was blown up." The suitcase was returned a short while later. Bob's gorgeous new suits had holes in them. We were due at the Embassy in about an hour so he rushed out to buy a new suit.

I had never been to the Ambassador's residence before. With its jaw-dropping décor—gilded paneling on the walls and dazzling chandeliers—the residence was a beautiful example of French style. The reception hall was impressive, replete with priceless works of art, and the elegant dining room rivals any woman's beauty. It was humbling for me to be recognized in such an iconic setting. Ambassador Leach laughed when Bob produced a jacket full of holes. "I hope this doesn't spark an international incident," the ambassador said.

Cameron and my mother attended the luncheon the next day in my honor. Our friends Beatrice and Julio Mario Santo Domingo of New York and Paris, Becca Cason Thrash and Donna Josey Chapman of Houston, and various members of the Foundation and Hospital boards came to support me. Afterwards, we co-hosted a symposium for women at the American Hospital featuring a well know surgeon.

A word about the American Hospital of Paris: Located in Neuilly-sur-Seine, a lovely suburb of Paris, the hospital was built in 1906 to treat the ever-growing influx of American expatriates with U.S.-trained physicians. In 1913, Congress granted federal status to the hospital. It was twice designated a military hospital; from 1939 to 1945, it treated soldiers and civilians under the banner of the Red Cross.

This was Cameron's first trip to Paris, so we took in all the sights, including the Louvre, Napoleon's Tomb and the Eiffel Tower. I was in a cast yet again—this time, I'd sustained a stress fracture on the golf course. There was so much to see, and seeing it through my son's eyes was one of the greatest pleasures of all. After a day of touring, he and my mother would sit in the hotel's lobby bar and people-watch. My favorite part of the trip was visiting all the museums, especially the Musée Rodin.

Of course, there was the food. Bob and I loved to eat, particularly in Paris, where it's almost impossible to get a bad meal. Le Grand Vefour, next to the Palais Royal gardens, was a favorite spot of ours. This 200-year-old *grande dame* of restaurants is truly a trip back in time. The sumptuous cheese trolley, the tableside service and the sinful desserts—it was all irresistible. But we weren't limited to *haute cuisine*. We also loved popping into corner bistros and outdoor cafés. An adventurous eater, Bob especially enjoyed a hot dog he bought from a street vendor.

We celebrated Cameron's birthday, belatedly, at Le Jules Verne, the gastronomic jewel that sits in the Eiffel Tower. With its futuristic décor and sweeping views of Paris, this restaurant was a truly special dining experience. There was simply no place quite like it. Bob and Cameron sampled caviar, pâté, fish and beef dishes and several desserts. As I watched them make their way through plate after plate, I thought they were eating as if it were their last meal. With Cameron along, Bob had a partner in mealtime crime.

After a heavenly week, Mom and Cameron returned to Houston; Bob and I continued our vacation, losing ourselves in Paris. We enjoyed walking (I kept up as best I could) and absorbing all the sights, sounds and smells that are uniquely Paris. It remains my favorite city in the world; if I had only three days left on earth, Paris would be where I would spend them.

In July 2003, we celebrated my fiftieth birthday in the south of France on *Hallelujah* with close friends and family. Typical of Bob, he had arranged a birthday dinner party at the Hôtel du Cap-Eden Roc in Antibes.

Built as a private mansion by the founder of *Le Figaro* newspaper, the hotel was originally a popular refuge for writers. In 1889, it opened as the Grand Hôtel de Cap; the Eden Roc pavilion was built later. As a hotel, it quickly became a destination for a variety of actors, politicians and aristocracy, including Elizabeth Taylor and Richard Burton, Marlene Dietrich, Orson Welles, the Duke and Duchess of Windsor, John F. Kennedy, Winston Churchill and Ernest Hemingway.

Bob had meticulously arranged the dinner menu to include all my favorites: caviar, Dover sole and a splendid birthday cake. Friends and family who were vacationing in France that summer—Lynn Wyatt, Barbara Taylor Bradford, Joanne Herring, my brother John and his wife, Karen, Kathi Mosbacher, Pete and Carlin Masterson, and others—were invited to join the celebration. It was a magical birthday full of touching gestures from my always-romantic husband. I felt very fortunate to have a life partner who made every occasion extra special.

The dinner was proceeding beautifully until the bill arrived. For many years, the hotel didn't accept credit cards; that was still the case in 2003. Bob knew it and had wired the hotel enough money to pay the bill. However, there was mathematical glitch somewhere, and he owed more than he had originally thought. I remember a very heated conversation in French and English. Bob offered to pay the balance by check, and the hotel's maître d' kept insisting on cash. Finally, Bob pointed to our boat, the *Hallelujah*.

"There's my boat, and we are leaving tonight," he said. "Take the check or leave it."

He saw reason and took the check.

Once back on the boat, I sat on the stern feeling very nostalgic. I thought back to another milestone in my life—my sixteenth birthday on July 20, 1969, when a man first landed on the moon. My parents had planned a small dinner party for me at Brennan's in Houston.

Knowing that the lunar landing was imminent, Dad had brought a portable television set. Mom had decorated the table with green cymbidium orchids (among my favorite flowers) and had put corsages at each place setting.

Earlier that day, my parents had given me my first horse. Named for a famous trainer, J. Miller was a gelding American Saddlebred. Not expecting such a lavish gift, I was truly surprised. At dinner, sometime between the Turtle Soup and the filet mignon, Neil Armstrong took his historic first steps on the moon. I remember going to bed that night feeling like the luckiest girl in the world.

Thirty-four years later, here I was, celebrating another milestone and overwhelmed with happiness. During my toughest times, I had read and re-read the Book of Job and had felt that I, too, was going through a kind of "stripping" process. My outlook had been bleak; everything appeared to be in shades and gray, white and black. The years of feeling like Job seemed far behind me.

Looking back on that period in my life, I remembered the emotional pain of the past and realized that, like Job, I was being tested at the time. I had to trust the Lord and accept whatever came my way. During those grim days, I didn't see a light at the end of my tunnel, but I did believe there was one. I knew that those old wounds and experiences had created more room for compassion and understanding for others. While I had better clothes and more luxurious surroundings now, I would never forget what it was like to worry about where the next paycheck was coming from. Bob and I felt so much gratitude for our situation, and we reminded ourselves how important it was to share our good fortune by giving back and helping others.

I had always appreciated my loving husband, but after this trip we grew even closer. We had just celebrated our third wedding anniversary, and it felt like we'd been together for a lifetime. In my mind, he was the most exceptional man and husband; I was absurdly happy with him. I didn't need to travel in space, I was already in orbit and back whenever I was around him, and I couldn't imagine being apart. More in love than ever, we were finally in sync with the rhythms of each other's lives. We came home from Paris with a spring in our step and a song in our hearts.

The summer of 2003 flew by. There was football practice, summer activities with grandchildren and golf on the weekends. On Sundays after church, we often went to a movie or cooked at home. Those days offered the rare opportunity to idle our engines. Bob had returned home rejuvenated and dived back into work. For him, running his company was never work—work and fun were the same.

A big-picture person, Bob loved coming up with deals. He was, quite simply, happiest when drilling, so I knew he would never retire. In my mind, that was a good thing because, as I used to tell him, I wasn't the "let's do lunch" kind of woman.

Our home continued to be a somewhat exotic fishbowl, with an ever-increasing number of interesting visitors, friends, Cameron's buddies and dogs coming and going. Our dog family had mysteriously expanded to include four male King Charles spaniels, Dickens, Happy, Charles and Chesley (named for our dear friend Chesley Pruett). The vet once commented to me that I was brave to have so many alpha male dogs. Because I was the lone female in my house, I had to laugh. Was she referring to the four-legged kind or the two-legged kind? I wasn't entirely sure. Life at *Reflections* was truly never dull.

In the fall, our busy schedule began to move even faster. Football games, charity galas and dinners, board meetings and weekend house parties punctuated the season. The days rolled into weeks and, before I knew it, Christmas was here again.

At our annual family Christmas Eve celebration, we gathered together with his four children, spouses and grandchildren and sang Christmas carols and gave thanks for our blessings. Surrounded by family, Bob (the benevolent dictator as we sometimes called him) was especially happy. Christmas morning 2003 dawned bright and clear. Bob was up early, eager to cook our customary omelet with caviar before starting the day. It would, as always, be a day filled with visits to family homes, presents and good cheer.

CHAPTER EIGHT

RACING AHEAD

IT WAS A NEW YEAR, and once again we were off to the races. Bob's ever-expanding business continued to demand his time, as did our other commitments. By now, I was used to the routine and knew how to handle it without making myself crazy. What's more, Cameron was driving (every parent's nightmare!). Somehow, we managed to fit in our obligations and still be there for each other.

Not long after the new year kicked off, I got a call from out of the blue. It was Governor Rick Perry's wife, Anita Thigpen Perry. She wanted to come visit me at home; I was flattered, of course, and immediately agreed, curious to know what she had on her mind. We scheduled a date, and she arrived right on time with a mutual friend, Glenda Kane of Corpus Christi.

My first impression of Anita Perry was of a personable, sincere, well-spoken woman on a mission. We bonded right away. By the time she explained her new role—helping the Texas Association Against Sexual Assault (TAASA)—I was charmed. Bob had not been involved in state politics, except to support his son, Rob, who had run for statewide offices. He had never met then Governor Rick Perry and was intrigued by my meeting, which I refused to let him join. It was a "girls only" affair, I reminded him.

As it turned out, Anita (as she insisted I call her) was helping to raise funds for TAASA, and she was passionate about her involvement. I found it hard to refuse her, especially since she asked in such an agreeable, non-imposing way. Before I knew it, I had told her about my experience as a victim of sexual assault.

Soon thereafter, I agreed to chair an inaugural fundraiser for TAASA at River Oaks Country Club. I think I would have done anything for this incredible woman, so long as it was legal. She has a soft touch and a special way of connecting with people. It was clear that she wanted to make a difference and to change people's lives for the better.

That night after she left, our home was all abuzz about our special visitor. In the kitchen, Cameron and his girlfriend, Brittanie "Bo" Hoster, a student at St. Agnes Academy, were all ears. In a moment of pure coincidence (or, as I prefer to think of it, a moment when God gets involved), Bo told me that a classmate of hers, Lorin Leatherwood, had been date-raped during spring break in New Braunfels.

Stunned that this problem was once again hitting close to home, I asked how Lorin was recovering. Apparently, she was doing more than recovering; she was speaking out at the Houston Area Women's Center (HAWC) and at her church. Bo put us in touch, and I invited her to participate in the luncheon. She went on to participate in the TAASA Speak Up/Speak Out campaign.

Meanwhile, I started putting together a fundraiser. Knowing that sexual assault is a tough, sometimes grim, subject for a luncheon, I invited the Children's Chorus of Houston to sing at the event. Lorin agreed to speak, as did Sister Jane Meyer of St. Agnes Academy and Father Daniel Lahart, president of Strake Jesuit. At the luncheon, Lorin gave an honest, impassioned account of what she had been through. Anita Perry, a stalwart TAASA supporter, also spoke, as did TAASA executive director and tireless advocate Annette Burrhus Clay. Afterwards, several guests came up to me to recount their own stories or the experience of a family member or friend. It was like a meeting of a secret sisterhood, dressed to the nines, baring their souls.

I went home that afternoon feeling that we needed to raise the flag on awareness of this underrated, underreported crime. Bob understood my pain and was, as always, extremely supportive. I have to admit that, after the event, the pain I endured so many years ago felt like it had happened yesterday.

While the luncheon was a huge success, I cried myself to sleep that night. The next day, I vowed to help as an advocate in any way I could; I eventually connected with Ellen Cohen, former director of the Houston Area Women's Center, who was a state representative at the time. We were intent on making a difference. My daughter-in-law often says that I like to make waves. So does Ellen! Together we united to create a tsunami. A vocal defender of sexual assault victims, Ellen spent part of her freshman term as a state representative helping to pass legislation requiring the fees collected from adult entertainment clubs to be used to fund assault prevention programs. Ellen and I worked together on that and, to this day, it's one of my proudest accomplishments. We fought the adult entertainment lobby—and prevailed.

Then, suddenly, it was May, and we were on our way to Madrid to attend the wedding of Crown Prince Felipe de Borbón, now King Felipe VI, who was marrying television journalist Letizia Ortiz at the Catedral de Santa María la Real de La Almudena. We were delighted and honored to be invited. I recall hundreds of people lining the streets and later found out that there hadn't been a royal wedding in Spain since 1906.

Of course, I had agonized over what to wear; I had never been to a royal wedding. I finally settled on an ice-blue dress and jacket designed by John Anthony, complete with a matching hat from Suzanne Couture. My dress had some lovely couture details, but it wasn't cutting-edge. It was simple and in good taste.

The day of the wedding, we left the hotel and drove to the cathedral. All along the way, we could hear the crowd voicing its approval. Cameras were snapping, people were calling out *"Guapo y guapa!"* to Bob and me. It was clear the royal family was very popular.

With an estimated twenty-five million people watching the televised ceremony in Spain alone and millions more watching around the world, the beautiful Letizia Ortiz arrived at the church in a gorgeous Manuel Pertegaz gown accompanied by young male attendants wearing breeches. More than 1,500 guests attended the wedding, including a who's who of royal families: Prince Charles; Japan's Crown Prince Naruhito; Greek Prince Pavlos, his wife, Marie Chantal, and his parents King Constantine and Anne Marie; Queen Rania of Jordan; Queen Beatriz of the Netherlands; and South African President Nelson Mandela.

It was a splendid ceremony, one that marked a middle-class "commoner" proving she was worthy of a prince. Letizia Ortiz represented the future of Spain in a progressive world. The wedding reception was held at the Palace, with a formal receiving line and a seated lunch. King Juan Carlos was so happy to see Bob in the receiving line that he invited us to dinner that night at the Zarzuela Palace with just the family.

We left the next day for Houston feeling very happy for our friends, whose new daughter-in-law was not only wonderful but equal to the task of her demanding role. Just as we landed, my cell phone rang. It was Cameron telling me that he had been injured and was in the emergency room at St. Luke's Hospital. There was blood everywhere, he said, but he wanted to reassure me that he was fine.

Needless to say, that statement was anything but reassuring.

We arrived home and, sure enough, there were streaks of blood leading from the front door to the living room area. Upset and anxious, I got my mother on the phone and learned that Cameron and Bo had been at home, when he'd gotten upset about something and pounded the floor-to-ceiling plate-glass window in the living room. The window apparently wasn't up to code and had shattered, and he cut several nerves in his hand.

Bo had driven him to the emergency room, as he was bleeding profusely. (We later learned he'd cut a radial nerve.) It turned out he needed surgery. Once again, I went from royalty to reality. Cameron was hurt, but safe, and I needed to consult with the doctors. He did wind up having the surgery, and, as he was young, the prognosis was good for a full recovery. I will never forget the sight of my son's blood on the floor of our home. I went weak in the knees when I saw it. It was one of the scariest moments of my life, but thanks to Bo's quick action, he was spared his life. He would need surgery but he wouldn't lose use of his hand.

It seemed like I spent my life bouncing from one emergency to another. Out of one frying pan and into another. It was always something. I'm guessing that it's like that for most people. Life is never neat, orderly or predictable, no matter how organized we are. I swear it took six weeks for my blood pressure to return to normal.

Cameron improved slowly; thanks to his need to use a PC, his dexterity also improved. To this day, my memories of attending the royal wedding are juxtaposed with my son's horrific injury. I suppose that's what reality truly is: a dream-like experience shattered with the clanging of an emergency. No wonder we lose ourselves in fairy tales. Maybe what we really need is to seek out a little reprieve from the endless demands of being a mother and wife. Nobody said it would be easy, so we should give ourselves a break every now and then. I retreated to the Golden Door Spa to indulge and let my hair down.

On June 12, 2004, former President George H.W. Bush was celebrating his eightieth birthday with a party at Minute Maid Park. The following day, he would sky-dive at the Bush Presidential Library in College Station. To kick off the festivities, Bob and I had planned a smaller, more intimate event at our home on June 11th for out-of-town guests and heads of state. Plans had been underway at our house for several weeks to orchestrate security and logistics. Evan Hughes, a former staff member when Bob was Secretary of Commerce, was helping to coordinate all the moving parts.

Given the circumstances, I wanted to be involved in every detail. After all, the party was taking place in our home; I wanted to leave nothing to chance. That's when the unexpected once again intervened. We got a call that Ronald Reagan had died on June 5th in Los Angeles, and we made plans to attend the funeral in Washington, DC. Scheduled for June 11th, the funeral was being held at the National Cathedral. I recall being dropped off within walking distance amid a sea of protesters. I admit I was nervous—the protesters seemed very hostile—but I was also upset. While they may not have agreed with Reagan's policies and actions as President, making a scene at his funeral was, more than anything, disrespectful.

Inside, the Cathedral was packed with an impressive array of politicians and world leaders—from Mikhail Gorbachev and British Prime Minister Tony Blair and his wife, Cherie, to Jordan's King Abdullah, German Chancellor Gerhard Schröeder and President

George W. Bush—as well as former Presidents Jimmy Carter, Gerald Ford, George H.W. Bush and their wives.

We were seated next to Caroline Kennedy Schlossberg and some of Liz and Dick Cheney's family. Former British Prime Minister Margaret Thatcher, wearing a grand black hat, delivered a commanding eulogy with the gravitas of a true leader. Supreme Court Justice Sandra Day O'Connor also gave an impressive eulogy, as did Canadian Prime Minister Brian Mulroney and both the former and then-current Presidents Bush.

Irish tenor Ronan Tynan sang "Ave Maria" and "Amazing Grace" so beautifully that I thought an angel had descended from heaven. His voice filled the cathedral and comforted all of us gathered to honor former President Reagan. At one point, all I could think of was that I was hosting a party that evening in my home and that several guests who were attending the funeral would be joining us tonight. A moment of panic set in, but there was nothing I could do about it. I was in Washington, DC, not Houston. Things would sort themselves out.

The Bushes, Saudi Ambassador Prince Bandar, Ronan Tynan, and Bob and I flew back to Houston together. We all toasted the former President and his eightieth birthday, and we toasted to the memory of Ronald Reagan. When we landed in Houston, Ronan realized that he'd left his tuxedo in Washington. Mild chaos ensued, as he was scheduled to sing at Minute Maid Park the following day. Emotions were running high in the wake of the funeral and the forthcoming celebration.

Bob and I made it home just as several out-of-town guests were arriving. Security was doing "walk-throughs," and Evan Hughes, former aide to Bob when he was Secretary of Commerce, greeted us at the door, reassuring us that everything was in order. As hostess, I was nervous about receiving several heads of state. I said a little prayer and hoped for the best.

In the end, it was a wonderful event. Guests included Mikhail Gorbachev, who had an impromptu meeting with Dick Cheney early in the evening at our dining table; former British Prime Minister John Major and Chris Evert; singer Clint Black and numerous heads of state. By the time we brought out a small chocolate cake to wish former President Bush a happy birthday, I was relieved and elated. The wonderful catering staff and Evan had handled the evening better than I possibly could have.

July came around, and I was truly ready for a vacation. Bob and I planned a sailing trip to New York to celebrate the Fourth of July. We met *Rhapsody* at Seawanhaka Yacht Club where Bob had raced as a child. It was an exceptionally hot day. We saluted Lady Liberty and watched the fireworks display from the water near Rye, New York.

The fireworks did not disappoint. Cameron's June 10th birthday had gotten lost between a funeral and a President's birthday, so we celebrated onboard. That weekend in New York was relaxing and special. We barbecued, pulled out paper plates and had a real American picnic with Bob's cousin, Stanley Stern, and others.

We also saluted our country, which we both held most dear. It was hard not to be affected, after having so recently said good-bye to an American President beloved by many. I remain impressed with Ronald Reagan to this day. He was able to connect with people and bridge differences. In this era of partisan bickering, our country could use someone like him.

Sailing on *Rhapsody* was a favorite summer pastime.

CHAPTER NINE

CAUGHT IN THE HEADLIGHTS

BY AUGUST, Bob and I were feeling a little depleted. In the past three months, we had been to a royal wedding, buried a former U.S. President, celebrated the birthday of another, and suffered sleepless nights after Cameron's injury and resulting surgery. We needed some quiet days. On the water, everything seemed less complicated, so we headed to our sanctuary, Rhapsody, once again.

We decided to make a familiar cruise that was becoming another summer tradition. We would start in Boston, sail to Newport and then to Nantucket, Martha's Vineyard and finally onto Kennebunk in Maine. Bill would continue as captain, and he agreed to bring a mate/chef. All Bob wanted to do was stand behind the wheel with the wind as his only boss.

I needed to unwind. With that in mind, I brought along a stack of unread best-sellers, including several James Patterson books. I had been hooked on the author and his Alex Cross character since former President George H.W. Bush first mentioned them to me a year or so earlier.

Bob didn't seem quite himself. Ronald Reagan's death had shaken him up. He had a wonderful memory and photo of himself with this incredible man, sharing a cookie at the White House. As President, Reagan had had a significant impact on Bob, and he couldn't believe that someone who seemed larger-than-life was no longer with us on earth.

Cameron joined us on the cruise from Martha's Vineyard to Maine. He had grown up so fast and had become a pretty good sailor himself. Dodging lobster pots, we picked our way up to Kennebunkport, where we anchored at Chick's Marina. I recall it was cold enough for us to go out and buy several windbreakers after docking.

The next day, we visited the Bushes at their home at Walker's Point, and were treated to a ride on their boat, *Fidelity*. She went fast enough that we held onto our hats—literally! Ever the gallant man, the former President carried our bags into one of the guest rooms. It struck me then that few people are more down to earth—and yet more imposing—than George H.W. Bush.

Smart, engaging, charming and guileless, he was in a class by himself. That day, their home was full of grandchildren, extended family, friends, dogs and something else: love. That's what I saw. Love in every corner of that gorgeous home. The real key to the Bushes was the longevity of their marriage and loyalty to and love of their family.

All too soon, it was time to go home. We knew what awaited us: a ton of mail and a long to-do list. Bob was eager to find out what was going on at work. We missed the dogs and our own beds, as many folks do when they've away from home a while.

I was still suffering from periodic, unexplained dizzy spells. Sometimes, one would come over me when I was driving, and I had to pull over and wait for it to pass. I saw several doctors. One of my cardiologists was convinced it was heart-related. I had several tests, the diagnosis was SVT—a fast heart rate. I went back to an exercise program of walking at Memorial Park and Pilates. Bob and I played golf on weekends and went for bike rides whenever we could.

We both had some aches and pains. Bob's back was a constant sore spot, and I was having hot and cold flashes. We went to war over the air conditioner: I would set it at sixty-nine degrees, and he would push it up to seventy-five degrees. We laughed about our ailments and tried to live life one day at a time. At least we were still standing.

We had some fences to mend. Bob hadn't spoken to his sister, Barbara, in years, and his brother, Bus, had died estranged from him. I recalled that my grandmother, Dorothy Jolley, and her brothers had died estranged from one another. It all boiled down to money, the so-called root of all evil. I will never know what exactly precipitated the breaks in my family, but I know that my grandmother was sad toward the end. She didn't know where her brothers and their families were and what had happened to them, and she seemed very alone.

The McCutchen/Jolley family was evidently the type to hold grudges and so apparently was the Mosbacher family. In my opinion, life was too short to hold a blood relative at arm's length, unless they'd done something heinous like commit murder. We can all commit murder with words, it seems; rivalry, jealousy and envy have started many wars. Taking the high road isn't easy, but the view is better. Sitting alone in a corner basking in one-upmanship isn't noble, it's a lonely road to travel. And in the final analysis, what is the fight really about? Pride? We all have faults!

I don't know exactly when or how it happened, but in therapy I had begun to let go of past grievances and forgive all those who had hurt me. I decided along the way that we're all flawed. Does it matter if Dad seemed to love you more than your sister? And so what if your other sister went out with your boyfriend? She probably did you a favor if he was that easy to sway. Did Mom really favor your brother over you? If we were really honest with ourselves, wouldn't we admit that our parents, too, had their disappointments and maybe they only seemed to ignore us? Maybe they were just tired and having a bad day. I don't mean to minimize the pain children of abusive or alcoholic parents feel; I only mean to point out that most of us do the best we can.

It occurred to me that I needed to make peace with those around me who had caused me strife. I apologized to my ex-husband, Donald, for any pain I caused him. I made peace over some past issues with my mother, and I somehow made peace with myself. At first, Bob couldn't understand why I would forgive and forget, especially since some of my wounds from family and ex-family members still stung.

But the very act of letting go set me free. Miraculously, I wasn't angry anymore. I stopped yelling at every red light and at every clerk who put me on hold. It was as if I'd shifted gears and things no longer aggravated me. Even though I was going through menopause and taking nothing, it felt like I had been given a magic potion. I would eventually have a complete hysterectomy due to fibroids and an enlarged uterus, and the hormonal changes at that time should have made me more volatile. But they didn't.

Looking back, I think just learning to weather the storm of life made me more mellow. There were constant reminders that life as we knew it could change on a dime. We were also losing friends, and that was, in itself, sad and sobering.

On October 8th, Bob and I headed to Saint Tropez in the south of France. He was competing in the seventy-fifth anniversary of the Dragon fleet. Having previously won a world championship in this class of boats, he was ecstatic. Constantine, former King of Greece, and his wife, Queen Anne Marie, had invited us. Joining Bob as crew was former teammate George Francisco and his son, George. Bob's son-in-law, Downing Mears, and his daughter, Lisa, were joining us, as were Trebie and Lisa Francisco.

The race in Saint Tropez proved to be a magnet for boats from around the world; more than 260 were expected to compete. Classic dragons, built before 1972, would race in a separate division. Olympians and world champions were attending, as was Her Royal Highness, Princess Anne of England.

The races began on Monday, October 11th. The day dawned cold, rainy and dreary.

Queen Anne Marie and I boarded a dry spectator boat to watch our husbands compete. Bob's crew looked cold, wet and serious; Bob, on the other hand, was in his element.

I didn't need to feel guilt watching from my warm perch. My husband was exactly where he wanted to be.

We had rented a house for the duration, and one night we invited King Constantine of Greece and Queen Anne Marie to join us for dinner. Racing spawned close friendships, and there was a lot of merriment among these kindred spirits. The other ladies and I went shopping one day, and, as it was the off-season, there were a lot of sales. Unable to resist a sale, I loaded up with Christmas presents and lots of sweaters.

On Thursday evening, there was an anniversary regatta dinner. I was honored to be seated with King Constantine and his cousin, Princess Anne. An Olympian herself, she is an extraordinarily interesting dinner partner; she's also very down to earth.

After a marvelous week, we headed home. Sadly, my luggage never made it. Months later, Ambassador Howard Leach called Bob to tell him that he had my suitcase at the U.S. embassy in Paris. It was completely empty, but he was happy to return it to me. I guess my clothing was sold on eBay.

For Halloween that year, we decided to dress up and greet trick-or-treaters at our door. I love Halloween and was pleased that Bob agreed to dress as Superman. I would be Wonder Woman, the Amazon. We didn't have many kids come to our door, but we enjoyed feeling like kids ourselves.

Christmas came and went again, and suddenly it was New Year's Eve. Our preference was always to celebrate at home. We often joked that, just for grins, we should one day celebrate on top of the Empire State Building. Instead, we did the next-best thing: we opened champagne and watched one of our favorite films, *An Affair to Remember*. We always got teary-eyed when Deborah Kerr's character Terry is hit by the cab and she can't meet him six months later at the top of the Empire State Building. He was her destiny, however, so it worked out in the end.

Neither of us particularly wanted anyone to know how sensitive and sentimental we were. We would cry easily listening to any Sinatra or Gershwin tune. We were both crybabies when it came to old classic films. When we had a few free evenings, we would hold hands and get misty-eyed watching *Gone with the Wind, Love in the Afternoon, Sabrina, Breakfast at Tiffany's* or *Singing in the Rain*.

On those rare occasions, we would share a bowl of popcorn and lose ourselves in classic Hollywood romances. Sometimes we would get up and dance to the theme song. I have a million memories of Bob, and these movie nights remain some of my most sacred. They still tug at my heartstrings.

In no time at all, it was summer. That July, Bob had something very special planned. I never thought he could top my fiftieth birthday, but he did. This year, we were going buffalo hunting in Africa with Jimmy and Susan Baker. I had literally dreamed of going to Africa; so had my mother. For years. *Out of Africa* by Isaak Dinesen, a luminous book written about the author's years on a four-thousand-acre coffee plantation near Nairobi, was one of my mother's favorite books. Mom was living vicariously through me at the time, and she couldn't wait to hear about my adventures in Africa.

Our plan was to fly to Tanzania, where we would stay on a coffee plantation near the town of Arusha not far from Mount Kilimanjaro, and then fly to the edge of the Serengeti National Park the next day. There were several families staying in the small coffee plantation hotel who were planning on climbing Kilimanjaro. I was struck by a beautiful, young teenage girl who had been walking in town with her mother. Apparently, she was very distressed because a local tribal leader, who was searching for a wife for his son, had offered up a cow in exchange for the girl; incredibly, a cow was considered the more valuable property. Her mother teased her that she was seriously considering taking him up on the offer.

We took a small plane from Arusha—beautiful, backward, haunting, unpredictable Arusha—to our safari location the next morning. On landing at our first stop, there was a group of at least forty people there to greet the plane. I had brought coloring books and crayons to give out to local children, but the pilot took one look at the gathering crowd and advised against it. A small act of generosity, he said, could start a riot. I was disappointed not to share my coloring treasure trove, but it quickly became obvious that I was a more interesting object of fascination.

Several people touched me as I approached the plane to re-board; they were especially interested in my blond hair. I obliged them—after all I was a guest in their country—and let them tug at my bracelets and my hair. I wanted to be friendly, but I have to admit that I felt somewhat like an exotic bird in a cage! The pilot seemed happy—and relieved, honestly—once I re-boarded.

Not long afterwards, we landed at our tented city in the wilderness. Or at least that was my impression, that is, until my cell phone rang and it was Cameron calling from Texas. It looked to me like we were in the middle of nowhere, but apparently even nowhere has cell phone service. The connection was so good, it sounded like Cameron was right next door.

Once again, the locals turned out to greet us. "Jumba," they said, meaning hello. Someone showed Bob and me to our tent, which was more than adequate, with cots on stilts and an attached bathroom and shower. I was worried about lions and other predators wandering into the camp at night, but Jimmy had assured me that there were hired guards whose job was to stay awake all night and ward off any dangerous wildlife.

At the safari camp, I felt like even more of a strange species. The staff seemed to stare at me everywhere I went. Unfortunately for me, there was no running water. I shouldn't have been surprised—we were out in no-man's land, after all. But when I expressed an interest in showering that evening, a staff person appeared with hot water he had heated on the campfire. I stepped into the shower and immediately felt a sharp pain in my foot. Looking down, I saw a bite and the spider that had inflicted it.

I started shrieking, and Bob came running. I was—and still am—allergic to most bee, spider and insect bites, and I was concerned about the possibility of having to be flown to the nearest hospital. Really, I didn't even know if that was an option, and that made me even more anxious. Bob was nervous, too; he remembered my run-in with the brown recluse spider a few years earlier.

We waited a few minutes and then a few more, until we realized that I was fine. Thankfully, there was no emergency. Later, as we were heading to the dining tent for dinner, we heard Jimmy shout. He had been attacked by some nasty ants and would likely be in for a long night. After a delicious dinner and fascinating conversation, we settled into our luxurious tents on wood floors.

Sleep didn't come easily. The African wilderness is full of mysterious sounds. I heard monkeys shrieking and other animals snorting. At one point, an animal (or two) pushed its nose into the side of the tent, much too close to me and my cot. I tried to wake Bob, who was blissfully snoring away. Terrified, I pushed my cot into the middle of the tent and tried to go back to sleep.

The next morning, I told one of our guides what had happened, and he said that a pair of leopards had wandered into the camp. "They can be quite aggressive," he said. The baboons were sounding an alarm of sorts. On hearing the story, Bob was upset that I hadn't moved his cot into the center of the tent along with mine. Instead, he pointed out, he was left to fend for himself (or so the story goes).

We left the following day in separate trucks to begin stalking water buffalo. Despite the abundance of flies, we really enjoyed the countryside. It was like something out of a movie—until we ran into an angry elephant protecting her offspring. We were in trucks, although at one point, our driver looked set to abandon his vehicle. The elephant seemed very unhappy and ready to charge, but she finally backed down at the last minute.

Every day, Bob returned to the campsite empty-handed. He was a very competitive person—especially with Jimmy and especially on the golf course with one dollar at stake—but he couldn't seem to find anything mature enough to shoot. But, our days were long and pleasant. We awoke every morning at sunrise and had a cup of rich African coffee. We would then get dressed and head off in search of a trophy. Bob and I stalked water buffalo every day, only to come back with nothing but sunburn, bites from flies and sore feet.

Meanwhile, Jimmy managed to track down everything he had a permit to hunt. I joked and told him that I would lock up our dogs the next time he came to visit, just in case he mistook one of them for a wildebeest. To me, Jimmy Baker is larger than life; a John Wayne-style hero, he commands attention but without arrogance. I can't think of a smarter, more brilliant tactician, orator and wordsmith.

Every night, we ate what Jimmy had shot. A chef, hired for the duration of the safari, prepared delicious meals. One night, a lion roared loudly enough—and was obviously close enough—that I said, "Bob, did you hear that?" Bob, who was deaf in one ear and didn't answer me, was obviously sleeping on his good ear.

"Yes, dear," Jimmy answered from a tent farther away. We had a good laugh over that the next morning, even as we were thankful the lions didn't come into camp.

The gorgeous countryside and its gentle human inhabitants were enchanting. I could finally understand why people lost their hearts—and sometimes their souls—to Africa. It was a memorable trip, one of the most magical times in my life. The African people I met on that trip were so special. We discovered that many were keen to improve themselves, so we sent books to our gun bearer when we got home.

We returned with a disappointed game hunter (Bob), but also a happy one, as he too lost his heart to Africa. Never mind that he didn't shoot anything; that wasn't really the point of our trip. We had taken dozens and dozens of photos, enjoyed a wonderful picnic in the bush, and visited Ngorongoro Crater, a conservation center where we'd seen all kinds of animals that don't migrate. I recall being shocked when several lions passed nonchalantly within inches of our truck.

After leaving Africa, we enjoyed a few blissful days in Paris—eating, walking, enjoying each other's company. For the first time in so long, there were no business meetings and no commitments. We just enjoyed reading the papers, drinking coffee and walking without purpose. It was sheer heaven to be so free. For years, I would dream of Africa.

We came home to no crisis for a change, and settled back into the routine of work, weekend golf and quiet dinners at home. By September, we were savoring life and taking things in a more orderly fashion than in the past. The respite was short-lived.

In October, Bob's son, Rob, was sworn in as the ninth president and CEO of the Overseas Private Investment Corp. (OPIC), and Bob felt an increasing responsibility to be in Houston to oversee Mosbacher Energy. On the one hand, he was thrilled for and extremely proud of his son; on the other, he had a nagging, growing concern about his business. Before long, he was in overdrive again.

With Cameron off to school at Fordham University, I was now an empty nester. One minute, I was worrying about raising a six-year-old; the next minute, he was in college and gone. I missed him and his friends. Fortunately, I had different projects—with TAASA and statewide political candidates—to fill my days. I needed to keep busy, or I would start worrying about things that really didn't matter. We all need to wake up with a purpose in mind, or we wind up creating drama to relieve the boredom.

I took up riding again, this time at the Houston Polo Club, and was on my horse, Perfect Gentleman, several times a week. He was cheaper than a therapist and just as effective. Riding helped me forget about anything that was bothering me, even if it was just for a couple of hours. I often felt that life was moving too fast and I had to run like crazy to keep pace with it.

Over the previous several years, we had lost more good friends. I always enjoyed looking at our wedding photos, but it was getting harder to page through them and see so many wonderful people who were no longer with us. I had never thought of Bob as being the same age as his contemporaries because he looked and acted so much younger. He was energetic and in good health; while I knew he would not live forever, he seemed young enough that I wasn't concerned about losing him imminently.

We never brought up death as a topic of conversation, but that year we began to feel that life was increasingly more fragile. One of those dear friends we lost was Chesley Pruett, who founded his own oil exploration and production company in 1946. Chesley was a tireless Republican Party fundraiser and one of the few people on earth who brought an immediate smile to my husband's face and a twinkle to his eyes. Fun and mischievous, he had once rounded up all the stray cats at the pound on Halloween and dropped them into unsuspecting children's trick-or-treat bags at his home in El Dorado, Arkansas! He was a "one-off," as Bob was fond of saying.

As I began to bracket time—indeed, to try and freeze every moment in our days—I became more aware that we were living on borrowed time. It wasn't the result of any current crisis in our life or any other close calls. It was more something we brought home with us from the Reagan funeral: the realization that we really were finite. I never thought about my own health, and I had no clue what the coming months would bring. At the time, it felt that we could somehow defy the odds and outrun death. He would not catch us in his headlights because Bob was immortal.

It was an honor to be sworn in by Governor Rick Perry as the 2007 Inaugural Chair.

CHAPTER TEN

FULL THROTTLE

LEADING BY EXAMPLE, Bob was living life to the fullest, and so was I. In a flash, it was December 2006, and Governor Rick Perry had asked me to chair the 2007 Inauguration. After I was sworn in by the Governor, I spent the better part of the Christmas holidays that year raising money for the January 16th ceremony, which included the swearing in, the Texas Ball, parade, barbecue and the like.

Fortunately, we had a great team, which included attorney Colleen McHugh; University of Texas Board of Regents Chair James Huffines; and Lyndon Rose, an attorney and former University of Houston Regent. Longtime Perry senior staffer, Teresa Spears, was designated the inaugural officer and Austin-based Wayne Hamilton as director. Together, Teresa and Wayne assembled a first-rate team, which included Lia Zaccagnino and Hugh Sidey, to organize a parade, luncheons, a barbecue, the swearing-in ceremony and the ball. Teresa also brought in other seasoned consultants, along with a large group of capable young adults.

Evan Hughes volunteered to come to Austin from Houston and help me as a "chief of staff." An unflappable, flexible and detail-oriented person, Evan had expertly handled Bob's every need as aide when he was Commerce Secretary as well as presidential and vice-presidential security details at our home for multiple events. I knew he could handle any problem that might surface, and do it with a smile. He turned out to be a godsend.

At our first Inaugural Committee meeting in Austin, there were inexplicably dozens of dead grackles littering Congress Avenue. We went through a blockade to get to the hotel. I didn't think anything of it at the time, except that it was strange, but looking back, it was an omen of how this inauguration was going to proceed. Soon, record freezing temperatures forced us to cancel the parade. After that, it seemed like we were running into one snafu after another. We were snake-bitten!

At first, I think I was viewed with suspicion by staff, but I was only there to help out. Besides, my name was on all the documents as Inaugural Chair. The buck stopped with me. I moved into the Four Seasons Hotel in Austin and went to our temporary offices every day to pitch in and do what I could to continue raising money and provide moral support. Teresa and Lia, real pros, had their team moving in perfect lockstep time, but we kept marching one step forward, two steps back. For the barbecue, we had tents pitched on the Capitol lawns, only to watch them blow over in a rainstorm. I remember driving over to survey the damage; a small lake had sprung up under the tents, and ducks were happily paddling around in it.

Several frantic discussions with Wayne and the team ensued, as it appeared the barbecue would have to be cancelled. First the parade, then the barbecue. I wasn't having any of it. The barbecue was steeped in tradition—at least, that's how I saw it—so that show would somehow go on. Hugh Sidey suggested that we could have a street closed and I jumped on the idea. The alternative to the downed tents on a soggy lawn was to close the street and relocate the tents onto Colorado. Little did I know how a simple request like "Do what you can to close it" was actually a very complicated process. I had no idea how many parties had to agree to close the street until I signed thank-you notes expressing my gratitude to dozens of folks for their compliance.

With that fire doused, I then proceeded to break a tooth. I flew back to my dentist in Houston to have it fixed. I was burning the candle so much at both ends that one morning I woke up so dizzy that Evan took me to the emergency room. I had had a heart ablation the year before for the arrhythmia that had been causing me to faint. It seemed that atrial tachycardia was the culprit. Another arrhythmia. The doctor at Seton Hospital in Austin told me to slow down and take some time off, until I pointed out what I was doing for the governor's inauguration.

"Well, get plenty of rest afterwards," was his response.

Richard Flowers and Daisy White of Houston-based and Tilman Fertitta-owned Event Company agreed to work their magic and transform the Austin Convention Center into an elegant ballroom. They were planning to bring in huge towers of roses and other scenic backdrops to give the convention center an air of intimacy. Workers continued to erect bleachers on the south steps of the Capitol grounds in freezing conditions. I started making runs to bring hot coffee back to these unsung heroes. We couldn't control Mother Nature, but we forged ahead.

Finally, on the eve of the inauguration, the staffers and I saw that the bleachers were covered in ice. It was clear something would have to be done. The final decision was made early that morning to move the ceremony indoors. It was the first Texas governor's inauguration to be held indoors since Price Daniel Sr.'s ceremony in 1957.

Friends often joke that I act as a kind of lightning rod, meaning that if lightning struck, I would be the target. I had a knack for being in the middle of the action and in the wrong place at the wrong time. Perfect example: The morning of the inauguration, we bundled up and went to the church service, where I was told that several buses weren't going to make it because of icy roads. What's more, the staff would have to stay downtown that night in order to make it to work at the inaugural ball. It was incredible! It would later be known as the Ice Inauguration.

Thanks to the weather, the Ross Volunteers of Texas A&M University couldn't make it. As a result, the Governor and the First Lady would not be walking through the traditional saber arch. Flights were cancelled; the city of Austin virtually shut down. Even The University of Texas Longhorn band couldn't perform. Fortunately, Bob had driven in and was by my side.

I prayed hard in church that morning that there would be no car accidents and that the guests who were able attend would have a wonderful time. By the time country legend Larry Gatlin belted out *Amazing Grace,* I finally started to relax. Bob held my hand and calmed my nerves. The traditional nineteen-gun salute by the National Guard greeted the Governor and guests as we made our way to the Capitol and into the House Chamber. Several hundred legislators and other dignitaries were there to witness the oath of office. When the House Speaker banged his gavel, the head flew off. When we played a recording of the Longhorn band performing the national anthem, the tape player malfunctioned. Instead, the crowd began singing a capella.

"What else could go wrong?" I whispered to Bob. He almost burst out laughing.

Still, despite all the cancellations and last-minute changes, both Governor Perry and Lieutenant Governor Dewhurst took their oaths of office without a hitch. Rick Perry, the longest-serving governor in Texas history, gave a speech devoid of fanfare and frills. The ceremony had been reduced to the basics and was, as a result, much more intimate. Sometimes less really is more.

Bob and I stopped at the barbecue and were relieved to find it bustling with activity. The tents were both dry and heated, providing a welcome refuge for the hundreds of guests who had braved the weather to attend the inauguration. The luncheons for both honorees were also well attended; slowly, I started to exhale. By the time I had to get dressed for the ball, I was in a celebratory mood. There was music, food and much merry-making—it was obvious that everyone enjoyed the event. Entertainer Ted Nugent's appearance was controversial, but it went well.

The next day, we rented a car to drive home, as the airport was still closed. Bob teased me for a long time after that experience about my debut as an event planner. Even the staff got in on it, making t-shirts that listed everything that had gone wrong on the back. It was funny and heart-warming. Wayne, Teresa and their team had been exemplary in every way. And despite the missteps and snafus, we were all honored to be a part of history.

Texas is such a great state with a special, unique culture, and that was evident during the festivities. I had paid my dues and now felt like a seasoned event planner. Having to improvise and not sweat the small stuff really taught me what I was capable of doing. I felt like I could plan a party and plan for any weather contingency.

Later on, King Juan Carlos of Spain called Bob to tell him that he was meeting President George W. Bush in Texas and wanted to stop by for a visit. Queen Sofia would be with him, so Bob invited them to come for dinner at our home. I pulled out all the stops. We had a wonderful French chef, Jean-Pierre, who we'd met during our stay in St. Tropez. He concocted an elegant dinner menu, while I invited old friends—George and Trebie Francisco, Dr. Denton and Louise Cooley, Kathi Mosbacher—who had met the King with Bob in the 1960s. Cameron and Bo also made a trip home to meet him.

Our honored guests arrived a couple of hours late. Not surprisingly, as their schedule wasn't entirely their own. We were secretly pleased they were late because earlier that evening we'd had an electrical fire in the laundry room. I'll never forget the look of shock on Jean-Pierre's face when he walked out of the kitchen and saw flames leaping from behind the laundry room door. The fire department came and put it out. According to the captain, the fire could have traveled through the ceiling to other parts of the house, which would have been a real disaster.

King Juan Carlos and Queen Sofia arrived hungry, so we all sat down to dinner while the King entertained us with sailing stories. When it came to entertaining, I'd learned to expect the unexpected. The inauguration experiences had forged an unflappable hostess.

We continued to host fundraiser after fundraiser at our home that year. After our misadventures, nothing threw me. Among my favorite events was a seated dinner honoring the World War II Museum in New Orleans and George H.W. Bush, a veteran of that war. It was a moving moment to see so many veterans in the room that night, including my uncle, Harold Seckinger, who had served at Normandy. Richard Flowers had set up large screens for the video about the museum, and there were American flags on every table. The camaraderie in the room was palpable.

Former President Bush charmed the crowd with stories about his first parachute jump during the war and subsequent jumps on his birthday. He joked that nobody understood why he would jump out of a perfectly good airplane. Modest and self-effacing, he was my favorite war hero that night. Bob was too young to have served in World War II, and I think he wished that he'd been able to join the action. He was never one to sit on the sidelines.

The landscape of our home seemed to constantly shift, as party tents were set up and taken down on a regular basis. In June, we hosted a twenty-first birthday party for Cameron. Richard Flowers and Daisy White, our event planners extraordinaire, created a night-club in a clear tent for Cameron and his friends. It was a 1980s-theme party, and it was great fun to see how their age group interpreted that decade. Many of the girls wore costumes from television shows like *Dynasty* and *Dallas;* a few of the boys wore leisure suits. My costume featured enormous shoulder pads and Texas-sized hair!

Politically speaking, things were heating up. Candidates were jockeying for front-runner positions in the primaries leading up to the 2008 presidential election. Bob felt compelled to get involved and eventually became totally immersed in Senator John McCain's campaign. He had promised Senator McCain that he would help him raise money. That spring, our home became a kind of McCain head-quarters. We hosted numerous breakfast and lunch meetings to orga-nize a Texas finance committee. Dallas resident James Huffines, CEO of Plains Capital Bank and two-time chair of The University of Texas Board of Regents, became a statewide chair. Capable, highly effective and a veteran fundraiser, he brought a lot to the table.

As a mentor, James taught me a great deal about fundraising. I pitched in and was later designated a national co-chair of Women for McCain, along with lobbyist Judy Black, whose husband, Charles, was a campaign chair. Bob began traveling back and forth to cam-paign headquarters in Washington, DC; money was trickling in. People were reluctant to commit before the primaries. Bob, with the help of fundraising professional Susan Nelson, worked the phones; they were, indeed, a finance staff of two.

From Susan's perspective, it was a fascinating experience, even for a seasoned fundraiser like herself. She sat next to Bob in her office and was always surprised when he called a CEO, and the CEO actu-ally took the call. Bob would first laugh and tease and put the other person at ease, then he would list McCain's qualifications and talk about his impressive Navy record and how he survived prison camp as a POW in Vietnam. I wasn't surprised when the checks started arriving. Persuading people to part with their money for the right cause—and charming them along the way—was one of Bob's great gifts. He always told me that it was hard to get the first olive out of the jar, but once the first one was out, the others came easily.

I was also volunteering for the Republican National Committee, so I started fundraising for McCain in earnest. We went to strategy meetings at the McCain ranch in Arizona and planned a fundraising event in our home. But Mitt Romney seemed to have all the momentum at the time. We were having trouble getting friends to commit to serving on the host committee, and I worried that nobody would attend. We needed a plan. I suggested to Bob that we host a tea and invite Cindy McCain, with no donation required to attend. In my mind, once the guests had a chance to meet and visit with Cindy, they would gladly join the campaign.

A huge crowd turned out for the tea, and Cindy, in her earnest way, began to win people over. Accomplished, yet humble about all of her professional and charitable accomplishments, she was the quiet light in the room. Few realized how much she had achieved; even fewer knew that she'd brought their daughter, Bridget, home from an orphanage overseas. An infant struggling to survive, Bridget had captured Cindy's heart, so Cindy surprised her husband with the baby. That is just one example of her extraordinary compassion and capacity for love.

Bob and I spent most of our time discussing politics and polling, and his concern about the direction the country was going. He was worried that certain freedoms, as we know them, might be threatened if the wrong candidate took office. While Hillary Clinton appeared to be the front runner, the playing field was too unpredictable to call. The fact that Bill Clinton had defeated George H.W. Bush after just one term really rankled Bob. He personally didn't want another Clinton in the White House.

During this time, the Bakers often came over for quiet dinners, and the discussions nearly always turned to the campaign. It was clear that the country's mood had shifted; many Americans were looking for a change. Given the circumstances, most Republican candidates would have an uphill battle.

In June, we attended the annual luncheon for the American Hospital Foundation at the U.S. embassy in Paris and then headed south to St. Tropez for a few days of relaxation before continuing on to London. There, we ventured to Woodstock to attend a lovely ball at Blenheim Palace, thanks to fellow Houstonian and great friend Peder Monsen. Hosted by the Duke and Duchess of Marlborough, the ball was an evening of superlatives at one of the most gorgeous palaces in England. Bob and I had been shooting with Peder and the Duke previously, and it was always thrilling to visit Blenheim Palace.

The event itself was spectacular. The moon was full, the temperature perfect, and hundreds turned out. Tables for ten were set in the great hall. Moreover, it was a white-tie event, so the ladies—the American women, in particular—wore their finest jewelry. Wearing a white satin gown designed by John Anthony, I felt like a princess. The guest list included Luce and Winston Churchill, Stella McCartney, Viscount and Viscountess Linley, Jade Jagger and other luminaries.

Over cocktails, my dinner partner accidentally bumped into me and spilled his glass of red wine on my gown. Covered in wine, it looked like it was tie-dyed. We were too far from London to dash out for a change of clothes—all I could do was air dry. He was mortified and asked me to send him the dry cleaning bill. I didn't have the heart to tell him that it would never get perfectly clean. I just laughed and acted like a good sport. What could I do? We spent the night dining, dancing and having a ball. I later discarded the dress. It was a mess.

While we were away, our housekeeper called the office to say that we had had a home intruder over the weekend. Nobody was home, and when she walked in on Monday morning, she found my master bath and dressing area had been ransacked. Apparently, someone had rummaged through my things, including my lingerie drawer. My mother met the police at our home. Based on the state of affairs, a Houston Police Department homicide detective had been called in. Cameron was away at school, and no family member had been at the house.

Nancy Crawford had been in jail, and after a few years, we hadn't heard a peep from her. We had relaxed and had only part-time security. Bob consulted with the lead homicide detective once we returned home. He was deeply concerned. I appeared to have someone fixated on me.

A series of hair-raising incidents occurred after that. We found notes, a splayed dead rat and doors left wide open at random times. Sadly, we resigned ourselves to more security, and I was asked not to go anywhere alone. It was disconcerting and frightening.

CHAPTER ELEVEN

PRESIDENTIAL RACE

AFTER WE RETURNED TO HOUSTON, I had a series of rolling allergic reactions that ultimately required hospitalization and steroid injections. I would be released after a few days, only to return again with another serious reaction. Finally, I was admitted to Methodist Hospital, where I stayed for several weeks.

Back home for Thanksgiving, I woke up in the middle of the night in agony. My knees were on fire. Bob drove me to the emergency room, where the doctors discovered that my blood pressure was so dangerously low they couldn't administer pain meds. I was later admitted to Intensive Care.

As it turned out, I was diagnosed with avascular necrosis of the knees and hips. It's a breaking down of bones and was probably caused by the steroids I'd had while pregnant and, more recently, for allergic reactions. It's a little-known side effect and can result in complete hip and knee replacement.

By Christmas, I was sleeping in every morning and napping (something I never did). I was exhausted all the time. Finally, Bob recommended that we fly to New York and see a specialist at New York Presbyterian Hospital. Dr. Mezitas told me I was suffering from Addison's Disease and prescribed Cortef. He did not want me to return home for Christmas. I pleaded and went home with the promise that I would come back on the December 26th so that he could monitor me closely. I had cheated death, but I still had to be careful.

I went home to Houston for good at the end of January and was sworn in for a six-year appointment as a Regent for the University of Houston. About a week later, Cameron called me from school and said he wanted to come home and chat with me. "Mmm-hmm," I thought. He arrived with Bo Hoster, who looked somewhat nervous. Haltingly, he started to tell me what was up.

"She's pregnant," I said. Mother's intuition.

He was so relieved that I had beat him to the punch. Her parents, it seemed, were pleased too. We had a grandchild on the way. Yes, it was the cart before the horse but even Bob was thrilled.

Family wedding plans weren't the only surprise we got during the 2008 campaign season. On the presidential election front, Mitt Romney had placed first among Republican voters in a poll; we all knew that already. But on January 3rd at the Iowa caucuses—the first contest of the Republican primary—Romney placed second behind former Arkansas Governor Mike Huckabee. Then, two days later, Romney won the Wyoming caucuses.

Despite those results, we weren't counting out McCain; his campaign was gathering momentum. Republican donors were still largely divided between Romney and McCain, but the next three primary elections would tell the tale. New Hampshire and Florida would inevitably be the trial by fire, as they often are.

Over drinks one night, Bob and I looked back at how far Senator McCain and his campaign had come. Considering that during the first quarter of 2007 the campaign had spent more than $1.6 million and was deeply in debt, the miracle was that it had come back against those odds to remain strongly in the race. Gone were the expensive private airplane rides. Budgets were tightened, and people were laid off.

Rick Davis had taken over as campaign manager following Terry Nelson's resignation. As a result, Senator McCain had been dismissed by pollsters as "roadkill." By late 2007, the campaign was strapped for cash and just limping along. The media largely overlooked him; fundraising was at a virtual standstill.

But Bob had other ideas. As General Chairman of the campaign, he spent his time on the phone wooing party leaders and potential donors. Every time a check came in, Rick Davis had someone walk it over to the bank and deposit it. At one point, things were so tenuous that Bob jokingly said he was going to stand on a street corner and sell pencils to raise money for his candidate.

All kidding aside, the Senator loved a good fight and so did Bob. It wasn't over until it was over, and it was open season. Then, all of a sudden, things shifted dramatically. McCain, the ultimate "comeback kid," won the New Hampshire and South Carolina primaries. On January 29th, he won in the battleground state of Florida; Romney came in second. As Super Tuesday loomed in the not-too-distant future, hope became a real possibility. All was not lost.

On the Democratic side, some polls showed a dead heat between Senators Hillary Clinton and Barack Obama. But in the Iowa caucuses, Senator Clinton came in third. Despite some pessimism from media outlets, she prevailed in New Hampshire. The Secretary of State for New Hampshire ordered a recount, but the election results stood.

The following month, on February 5th, McCain won the majority of delegates and states in the Republican primaries, which made him the presumptive lead as the Republican candidate. Rick, Susan, Fred Malek, Wayne Borman, Bob and others were ecstatic. The night the results were declared official, many staff members got emotional. We popped some champagne, and I toasted my husband, who had become McCain's "wing man."

On February 7th, Romney dropped out of the race and later endorsed McCain. At that point, there was a general regrouping as former Romney staffers were "absorbed" into the McCain camp. This type of merging created a few tense moments among those who had been working for Senator McCain since the beginning and Romney's new kids on the block. For us to win, however, we needed to join forces.

The next evening, when we began our nightly "quarterbacking," Bob told me privately that he was concerned that a Republican candidate couldn't win the election. Depending on the polling source, Senators Clinton and Obama appeared to be neck-and-neck. Bill Clinton was campaigning hard for his wife, but sources inside both campaigns told us that the Obama machine was formidable. Moreover, he was having historic success raising funds over the Internet. Bob felt that Obama posed the greater threat to Republican success.

Indeed, the junior Senator from Illinois was active in courting younger voters and those not normally engaged in the political process. His slogan, "Change," was everywhere—on billboards, on television and in print. It was also all over social media, which at the time was cutting edge. The McCain campaign was lagging on this important digital front, as well as on outreach to minorities and other groups.

In particular, Bob was frustrated that the campaign wasn't actively engaging Hispanic voters, and he was vocal about it. While McCain's position on immigration wasn't popular with many Republicans, he had a real opportunity to bring traditionally Democratic-leaning and voting Hispanics into the Republican camp. Bob met with leaders in the community and with campaign staffers brought on board specifically to spearhead an effort in that arena. The problem, they said, was a lack of traction due to a lack of support from campaign leadership.

Another thing Bob wanted the campaign staff to do was reach out to CEOs and engage them in economic discussions with Senator McCain. Over and over, he made his point during the morning leadership sessions.

"What am I?" Bob would say. "The village idiot?"

I just listened quietly. In many ways, he had more campaign experience, more business leadership experience, a longer record of public service and a longer lifetime of experiences than those making some of his campaign's strategic decisions. I urged him to call the Senator and speak with him directly.

"Mica mouse, I have to do something to help this man," he said to me one day, his intense blue eyes reflecting an earnest frustration. "I need to spend more time in Washington, D.C."

Uh-oh. That was my first reaction. It was another defining moment for us in a long line of defining moments. Bob would be turning eighty in March, and we had planned to spend some time together, just the two of us, in the Bahamas, Paris and the south of France. We had put off cruising the Mediterranean to work on this campaign, and I was looking forward to having him all to myself. After all, I had been sharing him with everyone! I didn't feel neglected, but I did have an odd feeling that we were living on borrowed time. Maybe it was his age, or maybe it was all the health ups and downs we'd been through in the previous few years. We were a team—there was no question that I would support him—but I admit that I was conflicted. Momentarily.

His focus wasn't on the home front. Bob was a patriot, and like every good soldier he would die with his boots on. Public service is a noble calling; it was as natural to him as breathing. He wasn't driven in this instance by ambition or reward or the promise of recognition. He had told me before that he had no desire to serve as an ambassador or as a Cabinet member. He had been there and done that.

So one night, after I'd been encouraging him to call Senator McCain, he got up from the dinner table and announced that he would call him "right now." It meant a lot to me that he valued my advice, and he had often used me as a sounding board over the years. I was his audience when he was writing a speech; we were each other's confidantes. A straight-shooter by nature, I rarely sugarcoat the facts. And I didn't then. Bob didn't need flattery; he needed the truth.

"I hope that you'll join me in Washington after the wedding," he said to me before he went to call the senator. I smiled, knowing it was a *fait accompli*. There was no way he wasn't going.

"What kind of clothes do I need?" I quipped. We both laughed. My wardrobe was a running joke. In many respects, my clothes went with the job. While I wasn't paid, I did work—at philanthropic endeavors, hosting events, raising money. I didn't need a ball gown to work the phones, but I did need clothing appropriate for public appearances. Jeans and t-shirts weren't an option.

On March 11th, Bob turned eighty, a milestone he was particularly proud of. He didn't look or act his age, and I often felt he could pass for sixty. Nevertheless, he was eighty and would have taken out a billboard to announce it if I had agreed to it. He was proud of what he'd achieved, happy in his life and a loving husband, father and grandfather.

To celebrate the occasion, he threw himself a festive birthday party at the 21 Club in New York City. This elegant restaurant had been a speakeasy during the era of Prohibition, but for Bob it was a place of childhood memories. His father, "Pops," had a special table there. Bob recalled meeting George Gershwin and Ethel Merman for lunch with his father. He planned the menu and the invitation list, looking forward to his special evening.

My present was a video tribute to my husband, with photos dating back to his marriage to his first wife, Jane, and his childhood. Granddaughters Meredith and Jane gave a special speech and toast, as did others, including his sister, Barbara (they had repaired their relationship). Some of his favorite Frank Sinatra songs played in the background. It was a wonderful evening all around. Bob went back to our apartment feeling contented and at peace with the world. That was all that mattered on this nostalgic day. Like Ol' Blue Eyes, Bob had done it all his way.

As for me, I had an unwelcome premonition that I was celebrating one of his last birthdays. I couldn't explain it. Suddenly, I wanted time to stand still. I knew that campaign-related activities would take over every moment in the coming months. We would have to "sleep fast," as Bob was fond of saying.

After the birthday dinner, we returned to Washington, DC, where Bob was staying at the Willard Hotel. We had dinner on the terrace, and walked to the White House and the Department of Commerce. I reminded him that I had never been inside or seen his office. He laughed, remembering that during the Clinton administration we had sat on a park bench beneath the window of his former office and shared a hot dog. He told me that I could have a guided tour after McCain was elected president.

The next morning, after yet another discussion on strategy, he stole a quick kiss and disappeared into the campaign trenches. He had work to do, and so did I. I returned home, where there was a wedding to plan.

Over the next several weeks, Bob serial-called me during the day, sharing triumphs and stories about coaxing and cajoling friends to give to his candidate. While he no longer sweated bringing in campaign donations, he didn't take campaign dollars for granted. He also started working with the Republican National Committee to form a Victory Committee, a critical finance operation. Granite Capital

Holdings Chair Lew Eisenberg would be the next national Victory chairman. Statewide chairs would be designated later; my name came up for Texas.

While he was helping to shore up the McCain campaign, I was immersed in wedding details. Bo and her mother, Lynn, had miraculously secured a Catholic church for June 7th, 06-07-2008 or 6-7-8, was a popular date for weddings that year. Bo found her dress, a gorgeous Vera Wang, at Bergdorf Goodman in New York, and selected navy blue frocks for her bridesmaids.

At Easter, Bob, Cameron, Bo and I went to the Bahamas for a weekend sail on *Rhapsody*. Cameron had selected the engagement ring, and I was in charge of bringing it to the Bahamas. He hid it inside a magazine and gave it to Bo on the beach. When she flipped through the pages, the ring popped out. She was delighted. That weekend, during a day sail, we discussed the groom's wardrobe. Cameron wanted East Coast preppy—white slacks and navy blazers—for his groomsmen. A hands-on groom, he custom-designed a tie from Vineyard Vines for each of the male wedding party members to wear.

The rehearsal dinner would be held at the Bayou Club, where Bob and I had first met. The plan was for a Scottish-themed seated dinner, with the Duncan tartan featured prominently. Bob and I talked privately about staging some fireworks after the dinner. He loved a good party, so he was all for it. That Easter, we went to St. Paul the Apostle in Lyford Cay and prayed for the bride and groom and for our country.

Then it was back to Houston for us and back to Washington for Bob. Meanwhile, Cameron, now a gourmet cook, met with the head chef at the Bayou Club to plan the menu. He and Bo chose the cake, the flowers (wildflowers) for the reception and decided on a Tex-Mex buffet. They even found the band. Richard Flowers had it all under control.

It has been said that the mother of the groom wears beige, smiles and says nothing. Basically, my job would be to seat more than 150 guests at the rehearsal dinner. Here's the thing: emotions are already so frayed during weddings, and the "list" can always be source of stress or a bone of contention. Rooms can only hold so many people. At one point, I had more attendees for the rehearsal dinner than I had room for them. There were a few uncomfortable moments (I thought I might need to un-invite extended family), but it all worked out fine in the end.

Bo, on the other hand, suffered one glitch. She went to try on her gown at the dressmaker, and the tulle had been cut too short. While the seamstress was able to steam and stretch it, the bride-to-be was in a panic. I, on the other hand, was so busy with details that I didn't realize until a week before the wedding that I had no dress to wear. Fortunately, I found something lovely to wear at the last minute—a cornflower blue Carolina Herrera skirt. Still bloated from the steroids, I wasn't my usual size but I was too happy to care.

Before we could blink, the morning of the wedding was upon us. I have never seen a more relaxed bride and groom; this was clearly a good match. All the parents and step-parents teared up during the ceremony. Bob held my hand and got choked up. Like many of the other guests, we were reminded of our own wedding day. The reception went smoothly, and most of us danced the night away. Everything seemed perfect. I went to bed feeling like I truly, finally had a daughter.

Bob took an early flight to New York the next morning to meet with potential donors. I packed my bags, including a few suits, as I was planning to meet him in Washington a few days later. He was still camped out at the Willard and driving to and from campaign headquarters in Arlington, Virginia.

After leaving instructions for the care of our four dogs, I flew to Washington. Bob was still in New York, so I took a taxi the next day to meet with the Women for McCain staff. Judy Black, our very smart and capable co-chairwoman was out of town. I introduced myself around and went by the finance office to meet Susan.

Her office was in high gear, a far cry from the ghost town I'd seen on my last visit. There were staffers everywhere, working the phones and planning fundraisers all over the U.S. I asked her how I could help, and she handed me a call list and pointed me to Bob's office. There were only a handful of offices with doors, and the others had four and five staffers crammed inside. I laughed when I saw Bob's cozy little space. As Secretary of Commerce, he had one of the largest offices of any Cabinet member; here, he was in a bare-bones shell of a large closet, camped out and loving it.

I was soon introduced to Dianne Kube, a veteran fundraiser who had previously been administrator of an oncology center. Bright, outgoing and engaged, she volunteered to join forces with me. We set up some tables outside of Bob's office and started working the phones. She enlisted a few more people to help, including an intern named Elizabeth Berry. Things were crowded, so I moved to a desk in the far right-hand corner of Bob's office. I hung a Women for McCain sign on the wall. I wasn't exactly unobtrusive.

The next day, Bob arrived sometime after lunch. Imagine his surprise when he saw that we were sharing his office.

"Well, you said you wanted me to come and help out," I smiled innocently. He just shrugged and went to work making calls.

At first, it wasn't easy sharing that space. We would both speak loudly into the phones. He would shush me, and I would say "Shhh, back at you!" Eventually, the irritation gave way to camaraderie, and we high-fived any time we got another financial commitment.

Tired of living in a hotel, we spent the following weekend looking for an apartment to rent. Both of us wanted our own space. Fortunately, we found a charming temporary rental, where I could set out a few family photos and other personal items. We were adaptable, but it was nice to be in a homier place.

Bob clearly enjoyed being back in Washington. Over many late-night dinners, we shared our triumphs of the day and rehashed the good, the bad and the sometimes ugly aspects of the campaign. He said that the beauty and history in Washington inspired him and helped buoy his spirits.

As the campaign built up momentum, it sometimes felt like we were on a runaway train. Ever the morning person, Bob always left early. I joined him by midday to give him space in our crowded office and frequently stayed as late as I could to make calls to the West Coast. Susan continued to give me lists of key female donors to cold call. I slowly began to connect with women all over the country; at some point, I could barely keep up with returning calls and emails.

Judy and I had divided our tasks. She was a respected lobbyist at Brownstein, Hyatt, Farber and Schreck; she had also served as a Special Assistant to Ronald Reagan when he was President. Her schedule didn't permit her to fundraise full-time, so we agreed that she would handle the grassroots, and I would handle women in finance. This arrangement suited us both and allowed us to use our talents and time wisely.

In June, Barack Obama was declared the front-runner for the Democrats. Senator Clinton dropped out, and the real competition began. It was going to be a nail-biter for Republicans. We had our work cut out for us.

With Bob's blessing, Dianne and I began planning Women for McCain fundraisers in Newport and San Diego. As the majority of voters, women are key in any election. We needed to court their votes. It was summer and most people were on vacation, so we decided to do our fundraising in popular destinations. We chose Newport because the *Rhapsody* was moored there. Dianne, her intern Elizabeth and I had developed a Sailing for McCain theme. The plan was to harvest as much money as we could from Romney supporters.

Mitt Romney and Roberta McCain, the senator's mother, agreed to be guest speakers in Newport. After fundraisers at the New York Yacht Club and at one of the lovely Newport mansions, we planned to take high-dollar donors out on the *Rhapsody* the following day. The fundraiser was well attended. Will Walker, a grandchild of Dr. Denton and Louise Cooley who had been working for Romney, had thrown his lot in with the McCain team after Romney dropped out and worked hard to get guests there. Anita Perry came from Texas, adding more star power to our event.

We went for a sail the next day. Roberta was engaging and fun to sail with. An incredible woman with a sharp mind and amazing spirit, Bob and I adored her. We gained additional insight into who and what had shaped John McCain. His family was unique.

Right after that sail, we flew to San Diego to hold a West Coast fundraiser. Through Elizabeth Berry's family connections, America's Cup skipper, Dennis Connor, had offered to host us on his boat. Meg Whitman, who was CEO of eBay at the time, was the guest speaker and a big draw, as she was reputed to be an excellent speaker. Bob and I had printed *"Sailing for McCain"* t-shirts and belts as party favors. None of us were surprised by the great turnout.

For Bob, these events were a welcome break from working the phones. He rarely attended campaign-related functions, as he felt better able to help McCain's effort by making calls. Excitement was building, and we were looking forward to the convention in September.

Meanwhile, Judy was working hard on the grassroots effort. She and her staff planned special after-work-hours events for women supporters. She also put together a national network and began holding conference calls to further engage women, which proved to be very effective. I thought Judy was a great partner to Charlie, who was working long hours traveling on the road with Senator McCain. Charlie had made a major career sacrifice to help the campaign; Judy was warm and friendly and doing a great job of capitalizing on her Washington area connections as well as those in other key states, such as Colorado.

The hours were long for all of us. Several campaign staffers had started a weekly Bible study get-together, which helped a number of people stay centered. In politics and especially in a campaign, there are often internal power struggles and overblown egos. Long days fueled by nothing but caffeine can make people behave less than diplomatically.

Here's the other thing: There is no "I" in team. We were all a team, but there was a clear hierarchy. All correspondence, including emails, had to be approved through the legal staff. We couldn't afford a gaffe. During this hectic time, I learned to word my voicemail messages very carefully. One day, for instance, I left a heated voice mail message for Judy. I felt left out of the loop, but it all turned to be a miscommunication. Judy, however, didn't take kindly to my loud, emotional message on her cell phone.

Of course, I apologized, and we eventually worked it out. But I realized that I needed to watch my tone and calm down instead of flying off the handle. I wasn't angry with her, just with the circumstance. I thought I was merely venting my frustration, but I had come on too strong. More often than not, voicemails and emails are at the root of misunderstandings and miscommunications in today's technology-driven world. Like Bob, I can be a bit too honest. If something bothers me, I speak up. Bluntly. It takes discipline to cool off first before letting it rip.

Fortunately, Judy was a good sport and accepted my apology. I learned to bite my tongue (or at least try to). Most of us have sent off a sarcastic or angry email in the heat of the moment, but it's hard to un-ring a bell. It took me a while, but I finally figured out to "think twice before saying nothing."

The finance team was kept in a separate area from the main part of the campaign. Every day, I was struck by how smart and professional the young staffers were. In the process of planning fundraisers in their regions, they frequently encountered some high-maintenance people. I was amazed at how well they kept their cool in a high-pressure environment and continued to do their jobs—and do them well.

Right before the convention, we traveled to the McCain's retreat in Sedona, Arizona to strategize with the team. Cindy was a gracious hostess. Clearly exhausted, one morning she confessed that she'd fallen asleep in her clothes. She had been campaigning hard and fast with practically no break. The Senator was rebounding; it seemed that his town hall meetings were working. He was also doing well in the debates. Bob continued to voice his opinion that weekend, but it often fell on deaf ears. He kidded that he had earned a few gray hairs and was entitled to speak his mind.

The campaign staff was fortunate to have a former Cabinet member who was willing to put in the time in an office filled with young people. He truly was the voice of experience, and I felt many times that he wasn't fully appreciated. "No one likes a crybaby," Bob often advised me. He truly believed in McCain and was not going to be deterred from what he saw as his mission.

The convention rolled around, and we headed to Milwaukee. Bob loved conventions. This one was like old-home week for him. He ran into countless friends and exuded a confidence in his candidate that he didn't always feel. Beau Eggert had joined him as acting chief of staff, and he escorted him to countless news interviews in the media area. I had been approached to be a delegate from Texas, but I had so many other responsibilities that I felt I could better serve by networking with donors.

Unfortunately, Hurricane Gustav blew in, and the first day of convention activities were cancelled. Finance Chair Susan Nelson organized an impromptu phone bank, asking for volunteers to make calls and solicit donations to help hurricane victims. Bob and I joined in. It was clearly the right thing to do, and we managed to raise some significant dollars for the hurricane relief effort.

Bob and I also organized a small fundraiser for that evening, and brought in country -western singer Clay Walker to entertain. At our invitation, Anita Perry flew in to help with our nighttime fundraiser.

President Bush and Governor Perry were unable to attend the convention due to hurricane relief efforts.

Our little event wasn't so well attended. Clay, being a good sport, teased us that he had never played to such a small audience. I told him not to worry and that he would play another gig. Meanwhile, I invited him to join us for the convention's evening sessions. It was his first convention, and he was excited.

Later, when Sarah Palin was announced as the vice-presidential candidate, there was a real bump up in the polls. Afterwards, Dianne and I met many of her family members in the lobby restaurant of our hotel. They had not anticipated the buzz from her selection and were a little lost in the fray. Nobody had really briefed them on what to expect and how to handle it. To be honest, it was bedlam; both Governor Palin's husband, Todd, and her brother needed a little extra support.

I asked Todd where his wife was, as I wanted to meet her, but she had gone to bed. It took a little coaxing to bring her back downstairs to meet the staff. As soon as she appeared, she was mobbed. I found her warm and razor-sharp; we thought she added significant personality to the ticket. Honestly, she was a surprise to most of us, but Bob and I thought she was a solid choice.

The next day, Senator McCain asked me how I felt about the decision to bring Sarah Palin on as his running mate. I was enthusiastic and told him I thought they'd made the right decision. "She is refreshing," I said in an interview with *USA News*. Privately, Bob and I thought she would connect well with a broader range of people and with women.

Dianne and I focused our efforts on the luncheon for Cindy McCain. A professional group had been retained to organize it, but Dianne and I were in charge of bringing co-hosts and sponsors on board. Clay Walker was honored to stay and sing a medley of patriotic songs at the lunch. It was a complete sellout.

That day, Cindy was radiant. She and the Senator were greeted with thunderous applause by their supporters. Several family members were there, including Meghan McCain, who had developed a large following thanks to her sassy, pull-no-punches blog. A video tribute introduced guests to all her philanthropic achievements, which she rarely mentioned. By the time Clay sang "I'm Proud to

Be an American," the room was alive with patriotic pride; the atmosphere was electric.

We got through the week on sheer nerve and adrenaline. There were breakfasts, luncheons with state parties and receptions with high-net-worth donors. By the time we arrived at the Xcel Center every night to hear an impressive lineup of speakers, we were all running on fumes. I stifled many a yawn and prayed that I didn't look tired while on camera. My mind was always racing ahead to the next day and the next to-do list.

After the evening sessions, Dianne and I went to the lobby bar at the hotel. It was chock full of staffers too excited and keyed up to go to bed. It was here that we found out what had transpired, and everyone could let their hair down. Shoes and ties came off. There was an atmosphere of trust, and even a few staff members who needed consoling. Bob joined us once or twice. It was actually great fun because we formed lasting bonds with many of our colleagues.

All too soon, we were back in Washington. It was the final lap, and there was no time to slack off. Steve Schmidt had been brought on as a campaign adviser. We attended several staff meetings, and he did his best to keep morale up. There was some concern that staffers were leaking articles and information to the press. He wanted a ship-shape, disciplined organization.

About this time, the campaign suffered a few missteps. I had asked a Houston couple to host a fundraiser for the Senator. Well-regarded and respected, they were top citizens whose fundraisers always drew a crowd. The hostess and I had been working long-distance on planning it. Then, out of the blue, Bob got a phone call requesting that he not move forward with this fundraiser.

"The people have a sterling reputation in our state," Bob said. He argued until he was practically blue in the face. Eventually, he volunteered to make THE call. I was appalled; there was absolutely no reason for these neighbors of ours not to host their event.

I began hearing rumors that Governor Palin wasn't being managed well. The blowback from the purchase of her expensive campaign wardrobe for the convention was just the tip of the iceberg. I thought it was strange that the staff seemed to want to make her over into someone else. We were already concerned that McCain was looking less and less like the maverick he was.

Whether Sarah Palin was difficult is a matter of perspective. I had seen first-hand that she was thrown in to sink or swim and that she wasn't really being listened to. Playing the blame game never accomplishes anything. It was no time to start pointing fingers.

Bob also felt strongly that they were missing an opportunity to make a tough stand on the economy. In the absence of a strong statement from the McCain campaign, Barack Obama gained real momentum. It appeared to Bob and me that the wheels might fall off.

I named our beautiful home *Reflections*
because of the special way light bounced
off the walls of glass.

CHAPTER TWELVE

HAZARDOUS ROAD CONDITIONS

WHILE JOHN MCCAIN continued to weather the demands of campaigning, a real storm was brewing. Hurricane Ike, a Category Four storm, had made landfall along Cuba on the heels of the convention. We had already seen the devastating effects of Hurricanes Gustav and Hanna; Ike was even bigger, at one point stretching more than six hundred miles in diameter.

On September 8th, Governor Perry issued a warning for eighty-eight Texas counties; President Bush followed by making an emergency declaration for Louisiana, Mississippi and Texas. The National Weather Service in Houston and Galveston warned residents on the west side of Galveston Island and other low-lying areas to evacuate or prepare to risk their lives. Galveston has more than a passing familiarity with killer storms. In 1900, a hurricane hit the island, killing thousands and virtually wiping out the city.

Residents of the Gulf Coast region were still smarting from Hurricane Katrina in 2005, which had left New Orleans submerged in water and caused billions of dollars in damage. More than one million people from the central Gulf area were relocated to other cities. Many New Orleans residents came to Houston; children were absorbed into schools around the city including my son's school—Strake Jesuit. One of Cameron's classmates from Strake Jesuit, Patrick, had just moved into his dorm at Tulane University only to be told he must evacuate. As the area was reeling from the effects of Katrina, Hurricane Rita appeared as a Category Five monster threatening to slam into the Texas Gulf Coast. Before it made landfall, over two million people from metropolitan Houston evacuated. Traffic on the highways was backed up for miles; cars ran out of gas, and people were forced to abandon them. It was absolute chaos.

At the time, Bob and I were attending an Army-Navy football game in New Orleans. We managed to catch one of the last planes out and flew to New York. With Katrina on my mind, I was not going to ride it out. My mother and I had ridden out two hurricanes before and wound up without power for a while, so we weren't taking any chances. We were staying away. Fortunately, Rita weakened before making landfall. While Houston was spared any significant damage, many neighborhoods lost power for several days. Even so, if that was the worst of it, that was fine.

I didn't feel quite so easy about Hurricane Ike now. On September 11, 2008, the National Weather Service forecasting model put Texas square in the hurricane's path. Storm surges between Morgan City, Louisiana and Baffin Bay, Texas, were predicted to be as high as twenty-five feet. In preparation, I called Sunset Animal Clinic about boarding the dogs, but was told that no staff would be on hand to care for them. We didn't have live-in help, and I was worried about our furry family members. The howling winds and driving rain would likely frighten them.

Finally, Nate Gancher, an off-duty Houston police officer who provided security for us, promised to check on the dogs. Our housekeeper, Dora Carter, left extra food for them. Unfortunately, we hadn't had time to board up the large wall of panes in our glass house. On September 12th, I convinced my stubborn and fiercely independent mother to seek shelter in a downtown hotel that had a generator. She lived alone, and I was concerned about the possibility of her home losing power. It would also be difficult for her to get to a hospital in the event of an emergency.

I stayed in Washington. Bob was traveling, so I kept a hurricane watch at our apartment. Nervous, I called both my mother and Nate several times. It goes without saying that I didn't sleep at all that night.

Ike pummeled Galveston and the Texas coast, becoming the most expensive natural disaster in the state's history. When it was safe to get out and drive, Nate checked on our property and the dogs. The news wasn't good. Trees were down everywhere, and our home looked like it had been bulldozed. A large oak tree had fallen on the roof of the library and knocked a large hole in the ceiling. There was water everywhere. Apparently, several tornados had followed the storm, and our home had taken a direct hit.

Nate climbed over the fallen trees to check on the house and dogs. They were scared, but in good shape. Our home, however, was not. Over eighty-nine trees were down. Water had washed in and my living room furniture was destroyed, along with my son's room and the adjacent guest rooms. Dubbed the Cameron wing, his side of the house would need new floors, new curtains and new furniture. The house would also require a new roof and other extensive repairs.

Heartsick as I was, I was also grateful that we had insurance. Others weren't so fortunate. Friends in Florida had warned me about mildew and mold damage. All I could think of was that I had a grandchild due in October, and Cameron was graduating in December. His little family planned to spend Christmas with us and would likely live with us while he waited to hear about law school acceptances. Now, I had no place for them.

Bob returned to Washington, and we came up with a game plan. Dwight Fields, who had worked for our family on and off for years, would help manage our contractor, George Gazis, during the period of house repairs. Over dinner that night, Bob told me he'd been feeling uncharacteristically tired. I pointed out that he had been burning the candle at both ends, and then repeated what I'd said to him when we were dating and he had developed prostate cancer: "If you slow down and get some rest, you might feel better."

The next day, he made an appointment with Dr. Massumi in Houston, intending to get there as soon as he could. In the meantime, we returned to campaign headquarters and made plans to attend fundraisers in Florida at the end of September. I remained behind, as there wasn't much I could do at home without a roof over my head. Literally. I knew that if I saw the state of my house, I would just pace the floor and cry. My mother had always told me to "never cry over things that can't cry over you." I was having a difficult time following her sage advice. It would do to remember, I told myself, that families across Houston had damaged homes and no power. We weren't the only ones who had suffered a loss.

Bob flew home as soon as he could. Power was out everywhere, but people were staying put in their homes. The Texas Medical Center had been badly hit. I wasn't sure how Bob was going to get around, but he wanted to check on his offices and our home.

Back in Washington, tensions were mounting in the campaign office. Staffers were bickering, and tempers were flaring. Needing a break from hurricanes and political campaigns, I headed off to San Diego to visit Cal a Vie Spa, owned by our friends and neighbors, John and Terry Havens. Hiking the hills in the early morning and eating healthy food—I had been living on pizza much of the time—was rejuvenating. I returned to Washington a few days later rested, more relaxed and ready to face whatever was headed my way.

In late September, Bob and I met in Palm Beach to attend a McCain fundraiser. I woke up the next day with a throbbing headache that seemed immune to Advil. The pain was excruciating. Once again, I found myself in a doctor's office being handed yet another prescription for medication. A few days later, the headache had worsened. I asked the hotel for the name of another physician and went to see him right away. After examining me, he said that I had a serious, but unidentified, infection and would need sinus surgery.

As he couldn't operate right away—he didn't have a team of cardiologists and internists needed to clear me for surgery—I called Dr. Stewart, one of our doctors at Weill Cornell Medical Center in New York City. He ran the necessary tests and scheduled me for sinus surgery the following day.

While the surgery went well, I found out during the follow-up that I would need more surgery. The infection had gotten worse. I had the second surgery the next day; it was staph, which could be life threatening. Then, four days later, the doctor told me that the infection had moved too close to my brain, and I needed emergency surgery as a result. There's a saying that bad things come in threes. Bob and I could not believe it.

That night, while we were out to dinner at Fridays on Lexington Avenue, Bob tripped on something and fell, hitting his knee. The next morning, he could hardly walk. I limped into the hospital pushing Bob in a wheelchair. "What's wrong with this picture?" I asked. "I thought I was the patient!"

He arranged to have an X-ray taken of his knee, but not until I had been wheeled into surgery. I was nervous—who wouldn't be after two surgeries?—and wanted him to stay with me. I was right to be nervous; the third surgery was worse. I woke up feeling very disoriented, only to find that Bob was in a cast. He had broken a bone. What a pair we were! This time I stayed in the hospital. It turned out that I had a staph infection and was lucky to have such an attentive physician.

Benched for the rest of the season, I stayed in New York to convalesce while Bob returned to campaign offices in Washington. In October, my grandson Donald "Donnie" Duncan IV was born in New York. Nothing prepares you for the overwhelming feelings that come with being a grandparent. I was beside myself with joy and love for this new little life. Holding him for the first time, I thanked God for such a sweet gift. It was hard to tear myself away from the hospital after he was born; I wanted to camp out in the lobby.

Meanwhile, I was on the phone with our contractor almost every day. He was trying to find a roofer, without much luck. They were all backed up, as were the mold and remediation companies. I began calling out-of-town companies and found a vendor from Tennessee to come in and help. We also needed flooring in Cameron's wing, but the floor companies were log-jammed. Finally, I threw myself at the mercy at the owner of Clouse Floors, a local flooring company and told him about my new grandchild and my desperate plight. My story resonated with him, and the flooring was laid in time. Thankfully, I also had a good, reliable contractor. George understood the situation and managed to accelerate the work schedule, assuring me that my grandson would have a place to live at Christmas. We were lucky to have such terrific people in our corner.

In the midst of my decorating and construction project, I continued to keep a close eye on the presidential campaign. John McCain was losing ground. The campaign staff had tried a few Hail Marys, but Senator Obama had the lead. Bob called me every day to tell me that morale was down among staffers; he was also deeply disappointed about some of the decisions by senior staff.

On election night, Bob joined the McCains, the Palins and staff members in Phoenix. Still recovering in New York, I watched the election returns on television. Senator McCain gave an eloquent concession speech, and the family put on a brave front. They had given it their all, but it just wasn't meant to be. Bob and the team were heartbroken, of course.

I watched Barack Obama's election speech and was touched that our nation had elected its first African-American president. For those of us who didn't grow up facing discrimination, it's harder to identify with what many minority families in this country have been through. The crowd surrounding Obama was emotional, and their reaction tugged at my heartstrings. Despite a grueling campaign—and even though my candidate did not win—I felt firmly that we all needed to stand together and support the President. At the end of the day, we are one nation. It was time to be hopeful that the U.S. Congress would unite and support good legislation.

Bob joined me in New York. He was clearly worn down, while I was feeling better and eager to get out for meals and other activities. He kept making excuses about not eating. At times, he said he had indigestion; other times, he just wasn't hungry. He was also having trouble sleeping, so I urged him to see his doctor. He refused. It was almost Thanksgiving, but the house still wasn't ready. Bob, however, wanted to go home, so he did. He was sleeping in our bedroom, one of the few rooms in the house that hadn't been damaged. The fact that there wasn't any furniture in the main living areas wasn't an issue for him now, just as it had not been when we first moved in.

Finally, it was time for me to come home, too. I walked in, took one look at what had been my beautiful home, and burst into tears. It was heart-wrenching, and there was still so much to be done. I raced around town, buying beds and other furniture for the empty bedrooms, and supervised the work being done. It took an army to get the house ready for my son and his family. I bribed, cajoled and begged every step of the way—and nobody let me down. But

GALLERY

Exhibiting at the Dallas State Fair on J. Miller. This was my first time in the show ring, and much to my surprise, I won.

Working in advance at the GOP convention in Houston with a delegate.

I was thrilled to visit the White House in 1986 and meet Nancy Reagan—an amazing person. President Reagan popped into the Republican Regent tea and joked with us.

My fearless mother, Jane Seckinger McCutchen, learned to fly and was my dad's co-pilot.

My father, John J. McCutchen, M.D., J.D. (right) receives the gavel and is honored to be inducted as president of the American Heart Association Houston.

Dressed up for a Texas party at the Inauguration of George W. Bush in 2001.
Credit: Getty Images

Bob with close friend Don Bren in the South of France. Bob once promised to dance on a coffee table if Don would donate to the RNC Team 100 donor program. He did, and Bob danced.

Turkey hunting in south Texas was great fun with Ambassador Rockwell Schnabel and wife Marna.

Shooting at the gorgeous UK estate owned by Wafic and Rosemary Said.
To my left is the prominent Canadian businessman, Paul Desmarais.

Bob and I at *Reflections* with our rambunctious King Charles
Spaniels. I was the only female in the house.
Credit: Alexander's Fine Portrait Design

From the left, Berdon and Rolanette Lawrence,
Lisa Mears and Downing Mears in Italy on
a cruise on the *M/Y Hallelujah*.

Bob and I shared a dance at the
White House at the 60th anniversary of
George and Barbara Bush.

The only time Bob sat still was on his boat.
Look at that infectious smile! He was a happy guy.

At the Bush Library with former first lady of Texas Anita Perry, to my left, and Neiman Marcus CEO Karen Katz, to her left, who was given an award by Drayton McLane, to her left.

From the left, Shahla Ansary, Laura Sweeney, actress Carlin Glynn, director Pete Masterson, Mike Sweeney and I celebrate Bob's birthday at the Bayou Club.
Credit: www.AlexandersPortraits.com

We were sharing a laugh with H.M King Juan Carlos on his beautiful yacht *Fortuna*.

From the left, Placido Arango Arias and Barbara Walters
with Bob and I at the Queen Sofia Spanish Institute Gala.

From the left, Margaret
Alkek Williams and Joanne
Herring at a Grand Prix F1
party held in my home,
co-hosted by Michael Mithoff.

It was a joyous day when Kathi Mosbacher married Mike Wheeler.
Here we are with the family supporting our beautiful bride.
We hosted her reception at our home.

From the left, Katie Mears, Lucy and Peter Mosbacher,
Bo and Cameron Duncan celebrating Bob's birthday party.
Credit: www.AlexandersPortraits.com

We were always happy to
support friends in a good cause
and the Houston Opera Ball is
a truly special night (here in
Oscar de la Renta—we all miss
our friend Oscar).

With H.M. King Juan Carlos in the Isle of Wight.
We were attending the Governor's Ball with the sailing team.

Representing Iceland at the Consular Ball as an Honorary Consul
with escort, former Secretary of State Geoff Connor.
Hosted by Mayor Anise Parker, it was an extraordinary evening.

At the Consular Ball in Houston
with my great new friend, Icelandic
film producer, Margret Ericsdottir

Bob and I with a wonderful friend, Consul Charles Foster, center, and other
party goers at the Asia Society gala that honored Bob.

Donnie Duncan was swept up in Governor Perry's
arms at a Christmas party at the Mansion.
His mom, Bo, was on staff at the time.

The 2007 Texas Inaugural "Ice" Ball was a celebration
as we had survived a week of logistical challenges
thanks to Mother Nature. Patty Huffines of Dallas,
John and Weezie Steen (not pictured) and
Bob propped me up. Credit: Globe Photos

Bob was happiest when he shared a birthday toast with granddaughters,
Jane Mosbacher Morris (left) and Meredith Mosbacher.
Credit: www.AlexandersPortraits.com

A portrait taken for the Museum of Fine Arts Houston for an
installation of owners with their pets. Straining at their leashes are
from the left, Charlie, Dickens and Chesley. (Happy was a bad boy
that day and had to sit this one out.) Credit: Timothy Greeneld Sanders

The New York Times

I was surprised to be featured in the Sunday special Inaugural
edition that featured the Inauguration of George W. Bush in 2001.
Credit: Fred R. Conrad/The New York Times/Redux

With Barbara and George H.W. Bush and
Prince Bandar at King Fahd's palace in Riyadh.

"You are the rose between two thorns," joked George Bush.
Denton Cooley, left, was a dear friend of my dad's.

At Walkers Point in Kennenbunkport with the Bushes.
Bob and George H.W. Bush were always kidding around.

Embarking on a day sail in beautiful Bermuda was bliss.

Life was always a breeze on *Rhapsody*. It was the only place Bob silenced his persistently ringing cell phone.

Toasting each other and life at the famous Le Club 55 in Ramatuelle, France.

Bob windsurfing in the South of France. He later taught me to windsurf but I had to be rescued because I couldn't get back to shore.

I was in heaven anytime I was on a boat (big or small). Dickens and I are enjoying the summer breeze in the Abacos.

On the left, Bob, Bob McNair and Downing Mears, far right, and other sailing buddies aboard *Rhapsody* which we co-owned with the McNairs.

Bob was so handsome and hale.

I was the luckiest girl on the planet to get to sail
with Bob in so many idyllic settings.

With the handsome prince, now H.M. King Felipe of Spain, with his father (H.M. King Juan Carlos) in Spain.

In Spain, with H.M. Queen Sofia, who recalled a lighthearted moment when she once playfully threw a pitcher of water on Bob as a joke.

Bob, Cameron and I shared a wonderful afternoon in Lyford Cay with George H.W. Bush and our neighbor Sean and Micheline Connery. 007 movies were our favorites.

Life
&
Arts

Austin American-Statesman

statesman.com

Sunday, January 14, 2007   Section **J**

The 2007 Inauguration was during freezing
temperatures. We had to cancel the parade!
But the photo shoot at the Blanton was fun.

BRINGING
THE PARTY
TO LIFE

Bob and Mica Mosbacher found their love overseas quite literally. They met ten years ago at a sailing party given by the Boston Club for America's Louis Vuitton Cup. Bob was a two-time world champion Olympic-class sailor, and Mica was working for Louis Vuitton Houston and co-hosted the party. "We were initially attracted to each other because of our love of sports. We both love to sail," she says. Bob's charismatic and kind-hearted ways led them to marriage in 2000, on Mica's birthday.

Bob is the founder and chairman of Mosbacher Energy and Mica is currently the chairman for the 2007 Texas Inaugural Committee. Together, the Mosbachers share their strong commitment to helping others and supporting philanthropic causes.

They enjoy cooking, spending time with their family, playing with their four dogs and relaxing at home when they can. They also both love sailing in the Bahamas and relishing a peaceful walk on a moonlit beach. "Our relationship works because we are both so much alike that when we lock horns over an issue, we often end up retreating and laughing about how alike we are," says Mica. She adds that being honest with each other is very important and love will always find a way to pull itself through.

The couple enjoys dining together at home, but some of their favorite restaurants include Tony's and Mark's, where they celebrate special occasions. On Valentine's Day, they exchange cards and reminisce about their years together while enjoying caviar and champagne. "It sounds corny, but with true love you don't have to do anything special to feel special," says Mica.

MAKEUP BY EDWARD SANCHEZ

MICA & BOB
Mosbacher

Bob takes me for a twirl in our home during a Valentine's Day photo shoot.

From the left, Patty Cisneros, me, Barbara Bush and Susan Baker in Canada at the beautiful home *Charlieu* with hosts Jackie and Paul Desmarais (not pictured).

Standing next to a true American hero, General "Stormin Norman" Schwarzkopf and wife Brenda, during the 10th anniversary in Kuwait of the Gulf War. He was larger than life.

Christmas Eve at home with our family included a festive dinner and singing Christmas carols. I looked forward to it every year.

We attended many charitable events as Bob felt strongly that giving back to our community was so important.

Bob and I were always relaxed and happy around water. Here we share a laugh at the Royal Bermuda Yacht Club.

Bob and I take in the sights of romantic Paris from the balcony of the Crillion Hotel.

Bob sharing a giggle and a "see thru" cocktail with Secretary
James A. Baker and Dr. Denton Cooley.
Credit: www.AlexandersPortraits.com

I was honored to serve as National Co-Chair of Women for McCain.
Bob was General Chairman. We were excited to attend the opening of the
Guthrie Theatre during the 2008 Convention. *Credit: Getty Images*

Bob with former NCI chair Andy Von Eschenbach, to his right, and Dr. Tripp
Casscells (who lost his life to cancer) both gave invaluable advice.

I was elated to be the winning bidder of Clint Black's guitar at the American Heart Association Gala in Austin. My brother John, to my right, plays the guitar and was itching to play it.

The 2008 GOP Convention in Minnesota was country-western music star Clay Walker's first foray into politics. He later sang for a sold-out crowd including actor Jon Voight at the luncheon for Cindy McCain.

Country Music legend, Clint Black, later signed my guitar at the American Heart Association Gala.

Proud to be a honorary Cougar and to serve with former board chairs, Carroll Robertson Ray, center, and Nelda Blair. *Credit: Jeff Sutton*

Lynn Wyatt and I share a laugh at Cameron and Bo's rehearsal dinner. *Credit: www.AlexandersPortraits.com*

With Joanne Herring after receiving the title of Dames, Order of King Francis I, Joanne quipped, "There ain't nothing like a dame." *Credit: Dave Rossman*

Dedicating a statue in Dr. Ali Masumi's honor at the Ansary Atrium of the Texas Heart Institute.
Dr. Massumi, second from left, saved Bob's life by identifying a pulmonary emboli.

Speaking at the funeral of
Kameron Rahming in Nassau was
the hardest thing I have ever done.

Speaking about Bob at the
Bush Library at Texas A&M
University while launching his
biography *Going to Windward*,
co-authored by Jim McGrath,
was a poignant evening for me.

Former Presidents George W. Bush and George H.W. Bush pay their respects to Bob as he is transported by the Texas A&M Ross Volunteer Honor Guard. *Credit: PHOTO: Michael Paulsen/©Houston Chronicle. Used with permission.*

Performing with the extraordinary cast of Mama Mia including ABBA Dancing Queen Judy McLane at the Winter Garden Theatre was an item on my bucket list.

The first time I saw this ruby red Ferrari steed, I knew that racing was in my blood. *Credit: John Pesina*

Talking to Mario Andretti at the launch event for the F1 inaugural race in Austin in 2012 was exciting.

At the dedication of the Plensa sculpture installation, "Tolerance" generously underwritten by the Aga Khan Foundation. Both Mayor Parker and former Mayor Bill White spoke. *Credit: CultureMap*

While surveying the eruption of the Eyafjallajokull volcano in Iceland from the air, it exploded and halted air traffic in Europe for days. The shocked expression on my faces says it all.

UTO | GOP PLAYERS IN FLORIDA

Appearing live on Fox News Neil Cavuto's show "Coast to Coast"—filming in Orlando. Neil likes to kid me about supporting Senator Ted Cruz. I was torn between candidates.

A "pinch me" moment with Ferrari F1 driver Mark Webber.

From left, racing aficionado Lisa Niemi (Swayze-de prisco), me, Eilleen Littlefield, Karen Garrett and racing king Davy Jones at the Rolex 24 hours at Daytona.

Donnie cheers the Ferrari car as it passes turn 1 during the 2014 F1 Austin Grand Prix

Senator Ted Cruz, wife Heidi, and I
share camaraderie in Colorado during
the 2016 presidential election.

From the left, brother John and sister-in-law Karen Garrett with
NFL legend Tom Brady at Becca Cason Thrash's charity dinner for Best Buddies.
Becca's soirees are always special! *Credit: Fulton Davenport*

John McCutchen races the "Heart" car
at COTA in United series as we cheer him on.

Karen and I always have fun at the Heart Ball in Austin. Our team enjoys racing to promote heart health and CPR.

We dubbed ourselves the Widows of Eastwick. Eileen, left, me and Lisa (right) lost our husbands to pancreatic cancer. BFFs.

In Minnesota with former President of Iceland, Vigdis Finnbogadottir. She was the first elected female head of state in Europe.

With my movie-star handsome son, Cameron, and wife, Bo at the 2014 Grammy Awards.

My precious girlfriend, Kristen Perry, said that the Grammy Award ceremony was at the top of her bucket list. She didn't get to meet Paul McCartney but we saw Yoko Ono at our hotel.

I did come away from that experience feeling that with my blonde hair and blue eyes, the contractors and subs were underestimating me. It made me feel like Reese Witherspoon's character in the movie *Legally Blonde*.

During the process, I learned to negotiate some construction-related contracts. And even though people could have taken advantage and overcharged me, I found our workers to be reliable, reputable and honest. Perhaps the fact that Bob was lurking in the background helped. At any rate, it took a village to get our home together.

In the middle off the chaos, a lovely invitation arrived from President George W. and Laura Bush to join them at the White House for a Points of Light charity celebration. George H.W. and Barbara Bush would also be attending, and Ronan Tynan was scheduled to perform. Longtime supporters would have the opportunity to give both pairs of Bushes a proper send-off.

The appointed afternoon came, and we headed to the White House. We arrived early, so we waited in the car for ten minutes before Bob said he would go to the guard house to ask if guests were allowed in yet. I waited in the car. Ten minutes went by, then ten more, then thirty. I was getting hot and antsy. Finally, I got out of the car and went into the screening station. I asked one of the agents if he'd seen my husband and was told that he was inside. Furious, I stormed in and checked in with an aide, telling her, "My husband left me in the car." She just laughed and said, "I bet he hears about that for years."

I finally spotted Bob and sidled up to him. "You forgot me!" I said. He looked a bit perplexed, but he apologized. Somewhat mollified, I settled down to enjoy the ambience of the White House. No matter how many times I had been, every time was a "pinch me" moment.

In December, Cameron arrived in Houston with Bo and Donnie. He was thrilled to be home, and I was thrilled to have him and his family there. It was just a few weeks before Christmas, when Bob began complaining about indigestion and a gnawing pain in his stomach. He made an appointment with a gastroenterologist, who ran some tests and didn't find anything serious. Bob thought it was probably reflux or GERD (Gastroesophageal reflux disease). I wasn't so sure.

We pulled out all the stops for our Christmas Eve family gathering. There were twenty-four of us. We ate caviar, turkey and beef. Granddaughter Jane Mosbacher played the piano, while we sang carols and had a wonderful evening. After everyone left, I sat on the sofa and cried. Bob had never seen me overwrought. "What's wrong?" he asked. "My darling, it's Christmas."

He thought it was exhaustion and a reaction to the hurricane-related damage. But I knew intuitively that it was more, and I trust my intuition. It was my radar warning system. I knew in my heart that this would be the last real Christmas we would all have together.

We took a Christmas vacation in the Bahamas with our family. The first day there, Bob felt terrible. I called our internist, Dr. Muntz, and he arranged for Bob to have tests done in Palm Beach. He flew with his daughter, Lisa, and his grandson, Bayly. When he returned a couple of days later, everyone wanted to go out to dinner, but I explained that he needed a night in. Something wasn't right. Meanwhile, I called Dr. Masri in New York and asked him to urge Bob to fly up there for more extensive tests.

Bob had also been making some calls. He spoke with one of his friends, a doctor at M.D. Anderson Cancer Center in Houston. I could tell he had a hunch, but neither one of us wanted to give voice to our fears. We weren't ready to face it. As my mother often said, the definition of fear was Failure Expected and Received. Together, Bob and I were going to stare down this illness, whatever it was, and defeat it.

Before we left the Bahamas, I visited with a young Bahamian named Kameron Rahming. He not only shared my son's name, but he was also the same age. Kameron had been treated for cancer in a Texas hospital and was now in remission. During my recuperation from Addison's disease, he and I had started corresponding. I was lying in bed, and so was he. Somehow we connected and became email pals. I was happy to finally meet him. He turned out to be a handsome, charming and delightful young man.

Bob and I celebrated New Year's Eve that year at a supper club in New York. We shared caviar and champagne, and toasted the new year. As hard as we tried to be festive, Bob was a little on edge and

I was anxious. I couldn't shake off the nagging feeling that something was seriously wrong. He continued to be exhausted and not quite himself.

I was so distracted that while walking back to our apartment that night, I managed to drop my purse without realizing it. In it were my keys, credit cards, driver's license, cash and, most importantly, my cell phone. I had been holding Bob's hand, and my purse was tucked up under my arm. I didn't even notice that I'd dropped it until we were back in our apartment. We immediately retraced our steps.

Halfway back to the apartment, Bob's phone rang. A stranger identified himself and said that he had my purse. He returned it to me with everything in it accounted for. We were speechless. He refused a reward and instead wished us a very happy new year. For those who think New Yorkers are jaded and won't stop to help a man on the street, this man represented redemption. Perhaps New York was a kinder, gentler city after September 11, 2001.

The next day, Bob didn't feel like going to lunch. I had been pestering him to see another doctor, but he dug in his heels. His symptoms worried me. In addition to the fatigue and the stomach pain, I saw that he was at times forgetful. The incident at the White House was still fresh in my mind. But he refused to see a doctor, partly because of our overcommitted calendar. First, we were due to attend the christening of the George H.W. Bush aircraft carrier, and then we were off to San Francisco for his daughter, Dee's, sixtieth birthday.

We went to Washington to spend the night before continuing on to the shipyard in Virginia. That evening, we went to the emergency room with Bob suffering from terrible stomach pains. The attending physician thought he had pancreatitis and gave Bob special instructions to watch his diet. He also prescribed some medications. It was well after midnight when we left the hospital, so we went back to the Willard to grab some sleep. We were due to leave early the next morning for Virginia.

Needless to say, I didn't sleep at all. Instead, I stayed up most of the night watching a movie. Bob slept fitfully. We were both tired the next day, but excited about the occasion. We knew it was be a special celebration. First, we stopped at the pharmacy to fill the prescriptions. I waited in the car for over forty-five minutes. When I finally went in to see what was taking so long, Bob was on the phone. His son-in-law, Downing Mears, was asking him to take care of himself.

I gathered that some of the family had noticed that he wasn't quite himself. I practically dragged Bob to the car; he seemed disoriented. I said he should skip the San Francisco trip and go straight home to his doctor, but he wouldn't hear of it.

"It's Dee's big birthday, and I have a special surprise for her," he told me. I bit my tongue and started praying. Then, in a case of serendipity, his cell phone rang. It was Dee. She was calling to tell her father that the best birthday present he could give her was to stay home and take care of himself. I overheard that part of the conversation. Relieved, I dialed Dr. Spyros Mezitas, my endocrinologist, who told me that Bob's symptoms sounded like cancer symptoms.

Without asking Bob, I made travel arrangements while he was on the phone. I directed the driver to take us to the Delta shuttle; we were going to New York. Of course, Bob tried to protest, but this time he had no choice. He knew that I could be equally stubborn and had been known, on occasion, to take no prisoners. This time, I was getting my way.

We saw Dr. Mezitas late in the day. After examining Bob, he took me aside and told me that the symptoms definitely seemed like cancer. He urged me to contact Dr. Masri and get a referral to a specialist who would do a biopsy. I didn't share his concerns with Bob. Instead, I told him that Dr. Mezitas wanted him to see another specialist and have a few more tests. Again, I didn't sleep that night.

The next morning, I called Dr. Masri. He had seen the results of the tests Bob had had in Palm Beach and told me that he didn't like what he saw. He referred us to a top gastroenterologist and arranged for us to see him that morning. The new doctor was kind, caring and concerned; he scheduled Bob for an outpatient biopsy at the hospital.

Bob completed the tests and was told that it would be a few days before the results came in. Barely a day went by before Dr. Masri called us. We were eating lunch at the New York apartment. I answered the phone, and he asked us to come into his office. I looked over at Bob, who shook his head, no. I used hand signals to see if he wanted to speak with Dr. El Masri. Again, he shook his head, no.

I told Dr. Masri to give it to us straight. He didn't want to deliver the bad news over the phone, but I insisted. As gently as he could, he told me that Bob had pancreatic cancer. I was in shock, but not completely surprised. Carefully, I broke the news to Bob. This time, he felt like he'd been punched in the gut.

It was probably early, I told him, and we could treat it. He made a few calls, and we arranged to return to Houston that night. He made an appointment at M.D. Anderson Cancer Center for the following day.

Again, I couldn't sleep. No surprise there. I prayed to God for a miracle. I prayed for it to not be Stage Four cancer. That was a long night for us. The next morning, we saw a surgeon who told us the disease did not look contained. That was bad news. Dr. John Mendelsohn, then president of M.D. Anderson, and his wife, Anne, came by that night to offer moral support. He recommended that we see Dr. Robert Wolff, calling him "a top doctor and the best in the country."

Dee flew in on Sunday, and while she stayed with her father, I went for a long walk. I have always enjoyed walking, meditating and praying. I knew I would need that now more than ever. I was concerned about the family and hoped that we could all pull together. Tragedy often brings out the worst in people. Illness can make in-laws feel like outlaws. Everyone handles grief and bad tidings in their own way, and everyone often has a different idea on what course of action the patient should take. There were definitely family tensions.

That night and every night after that, I spent hours on the Internet, reading anything and everything I could about the disease. I learned there were few cases that were caught early enough to treat. There were no tests for early screening, and the disease was brutal.

We finally saw Dr. Wolff, who ran more tests. I remained hopeful that it was in the early stages. When he delivered the dreaded news that it was Stage Four, all I could do was cry. I tried to cry away from Bob. He was having a tough time coping with it, and I was trying to be brave. I was cautiously optimistic.

My son and his family were still living at the house, and little Donnie was a source of sunshine during the early bleak days. Cameron loved Bob like his own father and was trying to handle it the best he could. I cleared my schedule, knowing that days at M.D. Anderson could be long. A friend and former patient, Rosalba Gutiérrez, used to say that you could fly all the way to Paris for the amount of time you spend at the clinic per visit. (Sadly, Rosalba died of breast cancer at a young age.)

Bob was prescribed Tarceva by mouth and chemotherapy. I questioned why he needed chemo if it was Stage Four, and Dr. Wolff said that it would give him a better quality of life. We followed his orders, and the family all agreed to take turns sitting with him during the chemo treatments.

One night Bob lashed out at me, seemingly childlike and almost panicked. We were like two people drowning. Even though we prayed together, we needed professional help. That help came from a phenomenal therapist at M.D. Anderson. Slowly, she prepared us for family members' possible reactions and for what the next few months would look like. We saw her together and independently. She was a lifeline for both of us.

She also helped me pull it together, as I was the primary caregiver. I attended some cancer workshops; I knew I was kind of a control freak, and I needed to make sure I didn't get too worn out. My health was still fragile. I had to take care of myself, for Bob's sake.

That first month was a total blur of blood tests, doctor's appointments and chemo. I spent every evening continuing to research alternative treatments—and praying for a miracle. Bob remained strong and went to the office as much as he could. His sense of humor returned; I marveled at how well he was handling it. He was a fighter, and he wasn't going quietly.

Bob with young Kameron Rahming at
M.D. Anderson Cancer Center. They drew
strength from each other that day.

CHAPTER THIRTEEN

RACING FOR TIME

IN BETWEEN DOCTOR'S APPOINTMENTS, testing and treatment, we both endeavored to live our lives in a normal fashion. While this random terrorist named Cancer had attacked, crawling into a foxhole to avoid the enemy wasn't an option. There was nowhere to hide, so we soldiered on. We had a battle plan and an arsenal of physicians, medicine and knowledge. Our commander was Dr. Wolff. At the time, it really did feel like we were going to war. I recalled some of the writings in the ancient manuscript, The Art of War, by Sun Tzu:

> When ten to the enemy's one, surround him;
> When five times his strength, attack him;
> If double his strength, divide him;
> If equally matched, you may engage him;
> If weaker numerically, be capable of withdrawing;
> And if in all respects unequal, be capable of eluding him,
> For a small force is but booty for one more powerful.

and

He who wishes to fight must first count the cost. When you engage in actual fighting, if victory is long in coming then men's weapons will grow dull and their ardor will be dampened.

There was no doubt in my mind that victory, if possible, would be long in coming. We had to prepare for a long-distance race, indeed a marathon. From the beginning, it was clear that we weren't going to surrender until we had exhausted all the possibilities that modern medicine had to offer. After all, we had God on our side. We didn't question God at that time; neither of us were angry with Him. Faith means having trust, and that's what we had.

While it is tempting to say, "Why me, Lord?", it's just as easy to ask, "Why not me, Lord?" We were not the only ones affected by this situation. Too many of our friends and relatives had been diagnosed with cancer. I had lost my father and my uncle, both of them struck down in their prime. Bob had lost a spouse. We were both grateful for the lives we had, so we figured this trial was another test of our mettle.

I had kept a gratitude journal for years. During this frightening time of uncertainty, I routinely gave thanks for the many blessings in my life. I had a beautiful family with a precious grandchild. Unlike many in this world, I wasn't hungry; I hadn't been wounded in war, and I had a roof over my head. My mother reminded every day to look for beauty in the world—and enjoy it.

M.D. Anderson was busy and hectic; the hallways and waiting rooms were crowded with patients, relatives and medical staff. At times, it felt like we were in an airport terminal or Grand Central Station at rush hour. The lab where Bob had his blood drawn was so congested—they drew blood from hundreds of patients every day—that we often waited in the hall.

Despite this activity level, there was extraordinary beauty everywhere, particularly in the camaraderie among patients and families. People were kind to one another. While we were all strangers, there was an unspoken understanding that we were all on this big cancer-fighting ship together. I saw compassion in the faces of our caregivers; I witnessed a stranger helping a patient who was throwing up by the elevator. That compassion and kindness helped fill the hospital with beauty, amid the sorrow and suffering.

Like so many newcomers to the clinic, we were a little overwhelmed at first. As Bob had served on the board, the hospital provided an escort to help us get around. The courtly gentleman that he was, Bob didn't want any special treatment. Cancer is a great equalizer and does not discriminate; we were as special as any other patient.

There were many challenges during the first few months. Bob was on a strict treatment regimen, and we had to learn about medications and dosages. It was like learning a foreign language. As his nurse at home, I had to familiarize myself with side effects and what adverse symptoms to look for. His nutrition was important as well. I received clear instructions to make sure he followed a healthy diet. At one point, he started feeling nauseous, so I bought whey protein to make shakes.

At some point into the treatment, Bob also started to feel weak. Fiercely independent, he didn't want help getting dressed. However, it soon became clear to him that he needed to rest. Before cancer snuck up on him, Bob was going all the time. Now, he had to learn to idle his engine a bit and read a book or watch a movie. We began having more frequent movie nights, during which we would watch any of our favorite films, including all the James Bonds.

One pressing need was how we would handle the numerous inquiries about Bob's health. He was, after all, a public figure. Jimmy Baker suggested we issue a press release, informing the public that he had pancreatic cancer. But Bob was having none of that. He valued his privacy and wanted to tell people on a "need-to-know" basis only.

At the time, most of his peers weren't going to be satisfied with being directed to a blog. Bob was of a different generation, so posting updates on Facebook or on one of the cancer update websites wasn't a practical solution or even an option for him, really. His secretary, Becky Lundmark, and I spent countless hours fielding questions. His mobile and mine rang incessantly. Friends were reaching out with heartfelt entreaties, and it was challenging to balance the concern of Bob's many long-time friends with his current desire for privacy and keep our lives as normal as possible.

Whenever possible, I tried to keep our closest friends apprised via email. However, when former President Bush called, I wasn't comfortable with merely sending him an email. On those days when Bob was home resting, we had a steady stream of visitors. Friends and family obviously boosted his morale, and during those first trying weeks I was happy to welcome them. Church became an especially important part of our routine, too. I often attended mass during the week. Bob resumed work on his memoir, *Going to Windward,* and looked forward to his meetings with co-author Jim McGrath.

Striving some normalcy, we attended parties when we could. A gregarious person, Bob enjoyed these events; they also provided a much-needed distraction. It was at one such event that an acquaintance came up to Bob and asked, "What's your prognosis?" The insensitivity of the comment seemed to rock Bob's composure. "I might be around next week," he said without much bite. We left right after that.

I quickly learned that people, confronted with the fact that someone has a terminal illness, just don't know what to say. Unsure whether or not to mention the elephant in the room, they become tongue-tied and say all the wrong things. It's only human nature to explain that you lost a relative to the same disease or that a friend also has it, but the war stories just made the situation more painful.

We also received unsolicited medical and dietary advice, and other helpful hints on treating his disease. While all advice was given with the best intentions, we had faith in our doctors. It's so easy to inadvertently say the wrong thing to people who are ill. At the time, the best approach was a simple hug. That says it all.

Bob continued to weaken, and I became hyper-vigilant at night. I would stare at him at all hours, looking for any alarming symptoms. It got harder to sleep. My physician thought I would benefit from anti-anxiety medication, but I was reluctant to take anything. I wanted to stay alert and be able to watch over him.

His birthday was coming up in March, and I planned a seated dinner at the Bayou Club. It was, after all, where we first met. In my heart of hearts, I was concerned that it might be his last birthday. So was he. We never spoke of our fear, but it was a possibility that couldn't be ignored. We were both realists.

His small party was very festive, and Bob was in high spirits. There were toasts from family members and friends. It was a love fest. I kept stealing glances at him all through dinner. Bob had been so good to me; I loved him now more than I had when we were first married. His concern was clearly more for others than for himself. I was proud of the way he was handling his situation: he kept going and never complained. The example he set for all of us was truly inspirational.

We remained cautiously optimistic, and my prayer warrior friends continued to pray for a miracle. God, the ultimate healer, said: "For I will restore health to you and heal you of your wounds" (Jeremiah 30). Another personal favorite is from Psalms: "Lord my God, I cried out to you. And you healed me. O Lord, you brought my soul up from the grave; you have kept me alive that I should not go down to the pit" (Psalm 30: 2-3).

By the end of April, Bob started having what is commonly referred to as "rolling infections." Trips to the emergency room became more and more frequent. I kept a bag packed for him. It seemed that there was a crisis every other day. It was clear that his health was declining. I felt sick at heart.

About that time, I reached out to Andy Von Eschenbach, one of Bob's former doctors who had treated him for prostate cancer. He was the twelfth director of the National Cancer Institute and the former Commissioner of the U.S. Food and Drug Administration. I called him and told him the situation. "We need to do all we can to fight this disease," I said. "Is there a trial going on somewhere else? Is there another physician I might consult with?"

On his recommendation, we wound up in the offices of Dr. Daniel Von Hoff at the Translation Genomics Research Institute (Tgen) in Phoenix, Arizona. Dr. Von Hoff had conducted national clinical trials with more than 200 new antineoplastic and biologic agents. His clinical research had led to new agents that were approved for cancer treatment, including gemcitabine (the drug Bob took during chemotherapy).

Dr. Von Hoff had more than thirty years' experience and was serving on President Bush's National Cancer Advisory Board. His cutting-edge work was on the development of molecularly targeted therapies for individuals with cancer. The study of pancreatic cancer was one of his areas of expertise.

Dr. Wolff had given us his blessing and agreed to cooperate in any way he could. The pancreatic cancer medical team across the nation is small and collegial. Dedicated to his patients, Dr. Wolff was willing to help facilitate any course of treatment that made sense. He had also been quick to dissuade us from other treatment options that I had brought up periodically. We didn't have time to go on wild goose chases.

At Tgen, Dr. Von Hoff patiently outlined several options, including palliative care. After several tests, analysis and discussions, he told us that Bob qualified for a trial. He emphasized that it would not cure his cancer, but it might extend his life. Bob's quiet response: "I will take five more years."

With renewed hope and a real shot at our miracle, we began commuting weekly to Scottsdale, Arizona. We camped out at the Ritz (not bad quarters) and often walked across the street to the shopping mall. It was beastly hot, but we were glad to be there. We had spent quite a bit of time in Arizona during the election; the irony of being here because of cancer several months later wasn't lost on us.

The facility at Tgen was tranquility itself. Bob usually went to sleep during chemo, and sometimes I would slip out and try to clear my mind. A manicure or anything self-indulgent relaxed me, if only for a little while. I would return to find him still sound asleep and well cared for. This was a very special place. Dr. Von Hoff always made us feel safe—he was like a guardian angel.

The first few times we were there, Bob felt well enough to go to dinner. I snapped photos of him drinking a margarita at a favorite restaurant, and sent them out to friends and family with the caption, "Texas chemotherapy." We shared a lot of laughs, trying to make the best of a tough situation.

Gradually, the commute began to wear on Bob. He went through the airport in a wheelchair, and I had to diplomatically ask the TSA screeners to be gentle when they patted him down. It was painful to watch him untying his shoes and patiently going through the process. I had a letter from his doctor, but it was frequently ignored. Other times, the male attendant would help Bob take off his shoes and belt. He was treated kindly by most screeners and never made a fuss. Naturally, I was like a mother hen, clucking away at all of them.

One night I had to rush Bob to the emergency room at M.D. Anderson. He wasn't feeling well, due to an infection. They admitted him to the hospital. In the hall the next morning, I ran into my friend, Karen Rahming, from the Bahamas. I knew that her son was fighting cancer, and she had brought him to Houston again for treatment.

There are no coincidences in life. Kameron's hospital room was next to Bob's. I couldn't believe it. A year earlier when I met Kameron at our home in Lyford Cay, I never dreamed that we would all be in a cancer center together. We traded hugs and cheered each other up.

When I got home, I told Cameron that our friend Kameron was at the hospital with Bob. Both boys shared the same name and were the same age, yet one was gravely ill and the other healthy. Life was not fair. Bo baked cookies with Bahamian flag decorations. She and Cameron brought the goodies later in the day, and we all piled into Kameron's room. We hadn't been there five minutes when the doctor came in. The grave expression on his face spoke volumes, so we quietly slipped out.

Karen came bursting out of his room a few minutes later. She was crying. Bob had waited in the hall and enveloped her in his arms. The news was bad. It was, in fact, the worst news any parent could get. I cannot imagine losing a child; I didn't want to imagine it. As I stood nearby with my healthy son, I became emotional, too. So did Cameron. I realized *There but for the grace of God go I.* Our sons were on loan to us from God. All I could think was Kameron was needed in Heaven.

A woman of tremendous faith, Karen dried her tears and went into Kameron's room. Her concern was her son. He was holding up remarkably well. I think it was part of God's plan to place us all together at such a tragic moment. My husband didn't say it, but I could tell what he was thinking: "God, take me not her son."

I have always been told that I like to make
waves—in fact, sometimes it's the only way
to affect change.

CHAPTER FOURTEEN

TEN-CAR PILEUP

BOB AND KAMERON were both released a few days later. Kameron went to stay with relatives in Ft. Worth. Bob returned to work for half days, while I marveled at his stamina. We also flew back and forth to Tgen a few more times. On what would be our last day there, we were told that his bilirubin was too high for chemo. I tried the grapple with what the nurse was trying to tell us. Finally, she reached out, hugged Bob and told him good-bye.

Oh no. No, no, no, I thought. She was telling us the trial hadn't worked. Bob put up a brave front and thanked everyone for the great care. I felt like I'd been sucker-punched. This was bad. In the car, I told Bob it wasn't time to surrender yet. There were other physicians who might have a few tricks up their sleeves.

I suggested we take a few days off and go to Palm Beach. The sea water was restorative to us both, and he could have chemo there. His treatment protocol was back to the standard chemotherapy. I located a reputable clinic, and we headed to the coast and the sea air.

Bob perked up once we were in our hotel room. Although it practically knocked the wind out of him, he jumped into the ocean with the joy of a child. He parked himself in a beach bungalow and dozed in the sun. It was doing him a world of good.

This excellent little Florida oncology clinic was quiet and peaceful, which was exactly what we needed. Bob joked that "Palm Beach was God's waiting room." We were both a little shell-shocked and welcomed the tranquility. Bob injected humor into each day and made me smile through my tears.

We returned to Houston, feeling somewhat better, and I jumped back into my research on treatment options. Bob went back to working on *Going to Windward,* and running his company. Our pastor, Dave Peterson, came by, as did scores of friends. Despite his cheery demeanor, I could tell that Bob was starting to tire even more easily, so I took on the role of gatekeeper as well. I often turned off the ringer on his phone while he slept. He needed rest, and I wanted to make sure he got what he needed.

Sadly, we lost Kameron Rahming in July of that year. He had spent his last few weeks in a hospice in Texas. Such a positive young man, he had even gone shopping for new glasses shortly before he died. The world had lost a bright light. As we watched the fireworks from our back yard on the fourth of July, we hoped he was able to see the fireworks all over Texas.

Bob rallied, and we agreed that I needed a break. I went back to Palm Beach with the plan that we would meet there in about a week. From there, we would go on to Lyford Cay and celebrate our wedding anniversary in our honeymoon cottage. In addition, Karen had asked me to speak at her son's funeral, which would held at about the same time. I felt deeply honored and humbled to be asked. And while I wasn't sure that any words would appropriately honor Kameron, I was going to do my best.

One day while I was in Palm Beach having an afternoon walk along the ocean, my cell phone rang. It was Dr. Wolff. "Mica, it's going to get rough from here on out," he said. Alarmed, I found a bench and sat down.

"But our wedding anniversary is coming up," I said. I felt like a prisoner begging for a lighter sentence. Your honor, may we have leniency as an important occasion is forthcoming—as if I could bargain with the doctor and God, and not have the time we had together overshadowed by the specter of cancer.

I hung up in tears. There was my intuitive feeling again, telling me that it would soon be time to surrender. "Please, please don't take him from us!" I cried. My heart started pounding; I felt my face flush red. This was how a panic attack must feel. "Lord I need more time with him," I said to nobody in particular. "I will never love any man as much as I love my husband. He is everything to me. He is the love of my life. I can't live without him." And on and on I went.

If my heart didn't break that day, it came darn close. I ended up the following day at the cardiologist with a case of congestive heart failure. I didn't tell Bob. Instead, I holed up in my hotel room and wailed. Later on, I called my therapist and learned from her that the news from Dr. Wolff had started a pattern known as chronic grieving. The next day, I got on the treadmill and tried to meditate and pray.

Two days later, I had an emergency root canal. Many people believe that "dis-ease" causes disease. They may be right. I had not been taking care of myself. I had been eating too many hospital hamburgers and French fries, and I was out of shape. Like many caregivers, my health had been compromised. It's a sad fact that many also don't survive long after the loss of a spouse.

Frankly, Scarlett, I said to myself, I don't give a damn about me. We were in a struggle between life and death. I mean, really, who cared what I looked like? I was normally meticulous about my appearance, but I was letting things go. My gray roots were starting to show; I had dark shadows under my eyes.

Bob flew in and together we continued on to Nassau. I had an ice pack for my cheek and a throbbing tooth. The air pressure didn't help, but I was determined to be at Kameron's memorial service. That night, at dinner in our home, Bob gave me such a loving look that I cratered. I had held it in for so long in front of him, trying to put on a brave face, that I couldn't hold it in anymore. I let out a sob and then another. Embarrassed to have lost control, I ran out to the driveway and collapsed. I lay there and howled.

He came outside and held me close. We exchanged several "I love yous" before I finally calmed down. We talked about our love for on another, our marriage and our upcoming anniversary. He had rented the cottage we honeymooned in and was planning to an intimate dinner for two. Bob was nothing if not romantic. I was especially touched by his gesture.

The next day, I walked into a packed church, holding my ice pack. I walked to the front for the viewing and choked up when I saw Kameron. It was a joyous, uplifting occasion of faith and a celebration of his life. He was in a better place and well again. When it came time for me to speak, I summoned all my inner strength. It was important to me to be as brave as Kameron had been that day in the hospital when he got the bad news.

I drew the comparison between my son, Cameron, and Kameron—same age, same name. Drawing from Scripture, I said that Kameron was extra special because he had been called back by God. Death was just a passage to a hereafter more glorious than anything we could imagine. "We cannot understand the mystery of death because the knowledge hasn't been given to us," I said. "We must rely on faith and endure many tough trials. God would hold us in the palm of His hands."

I was speaking to myself as well as the people in the church. I was preparing and reassuring myself that if it was Bob's time, then God would grant me the strength to endure losing him. Surrounded by such God-loving men and women that day helped to comfort me. Kameron was reaching out and helping me cope. That was his last gift to me: the reassurance that all would be well, that he was whole again.

I came back to Bob that day with a smile on my face. In trying to uplift Kameron's grieving family, I had been uplifted myself. We looked forward to our anniversary and a walk on the beach, to remember. From this point on, we had to live each day as if it were our last together. We had to say everything we needed to say to one another. That night, we looked at the stars and marveled at the beauty of the wind ruffling the palm trees.

"There's Venus," Bob pointed up, where the night sky was brimming with stars. We walked on a short distance, hand in hand. "It will be all right."

On our tenth wedding anniversary, Bob wasn't feeling well and neither was I. In fact, I went with him to the Lyford Cay Clinic, as I was feeling dizzy. After a quick examination, the doctor said that I was having another bout of congestive heart failure. We didn't want to disappoint each other so we got dressed and went by golf cart to our honeymoon cottage for dinner. He opened the wine, and we toasted. Bob's face was drawn and pale; I was feeling worse, too.

Feeling frustrated and sad, we abandoned our romantic dinner plans and returned to our home. I called Dr. Dean Tseretopoulous, the local cardiologist, and asked him to make a house call. He came right away. Bob was severely dehydrated and needed fluids, so Dr. Tseretopoulous inserted an intravenous drip and set up an improvised pole.

We flew back to Florida the next day and then on to Houston. It was apparent to us both that we needed night nursing care. Bob was suffering some pain and discomfort, and I was utterly exhausted. We hired some very competent nurses through a reputable agency. Some he liked more than others. I wanted nurses who had a take-charge attitude and were not intimidated by him. He wanted pretty ones. While the idea of sharing our home with strangers wasn't a pleasant one, it was time. I was still hyper-vigilant at night, as these nurses' skill levels were all over the map. Most were caring and experienced. I gradually gave over more and more trust to those I got to know and see on a regular basis.

We decided to go to New York and visit with renowned specialist there. We'd heard about a new trial that might be beneficial, so we went and met with some leading oncologists. Dr. Wolff wasn't convinced that the trials would help; he had sound reasons to support his skepticism. But Bob was the one calling the shots. He always said that even though he didn't have control over his cancer, he most definitely had control over his medical decisions.

Things were rocky and unpredictable from that point on. We had good news, too: Cameron had been accepted to law school at Washington and Lee University. I would be sad to see him and his family go, but they would be home for Christmas.

In fact, when Parents Weekend rolled around, I decided to fly up to Virginia and visit Cameron and meet his classmates. My first night there, I got a call from Dr. Wolff. Bob had a serious infection and some possible complications. The doctor was concerned and said I'd better get down there. Terrified and fearing the worst, I flew home in the morning. Bob had been admitted to the hospital again. He was on antibiotics and very weak. Fortunately, he rallied after that incident, but from then on I was afraid every time I had to leave him.

In January, I received an unexpected letter from the Foreign Ministry of Iceland as well as Hjalmar Hannesson, the Ambassador of Iceland to the U.S. It was an invitation to consider the post of Honorary Consul General of Iceland, Texas. If I were interested, he would forward my name as a candidate. An Honorary Consul has similar responsibilities as a career consul, except it's a volunteer position. There's no money involved, but it was more than a title. The role had multiple official functions.

Bob explained to me that they had already vetted me before sending the letter. I accepted and received a call asking me to come for an interview in Washington, DC. The interview and the prospect of a job—even uncompensated—really appealed to me. Being assured that the nurses and Bob's family would be with him, I flew up to Washington and met with the Ambassador and his staff, including Hjordis Gunnarsdottir.

In the middle of the interview, Bob called me sounding panicky. He was home alone.

"Mossy, isn't one of your daughters with you?" I asked.

"No, Dee is sick and I sent the girls home." He called three more times during the interview. It was all I could do to get through it and the luncheon. Things were piling up. One shock followed another and then came the aftershocks. It was like a head-on collision with no way to stop the oncoming car.

I had an earache and a low-grade fever, and felt like I was coming down with an infection. All I wanted to do was get off the line of duty and get some rest. Instead of explaining to Bob or to a family member that I was burned out and needed a few days off, I flew home. The flight was extremely turbulent, so I took one of the Ativan that had been prescribed in case of anxiety.

As soon as I landed, I phoned the nurse several times, but she didn't return my calls. When I finally got back to the house, I was irritated and agitated. Bob was asleep when I arrived, so I poured myself a glass of wine. One glass led to another. Not used to taking the Ativan, I didn't understand how the wine would amplify the effects.

I sat on Bob's bed and gave voice to my anger about cancer in general, and his in particular. I was sharing my feelings with him as I always had, but this time I wasn't calm. Truly, I wasn't myself. When I called my mother, she said I didn't sound like the daughter she knew, and she came right over. That night, I passed out for the first time in my life.

The following day, I went to see my therapist, who said I was traumatized and suffering from PTSD again. She suggested I take some time to regroup. Bob had many people caring for him, and he could cope without me for a few days. More importantly, I shouldn't feel guilty about leaving. She offered to explain that I wasn't abandoning him; my body just needed rest.

Caretaker burnout is a risk for all long-term caretakers. By trying so hard to be a good caretaker, I had pushed myself beyond my limits. I knew I would never intentionally harm someone I loved; but I had lost control of myself, and I was embarrassed by my emotional outburst. I wouldn't take Ativan again, as I learned the hard way never again to mix sedatives and booze. It makes for a scary cocktail.

The next several days were quiet and introspective. I realized that I had to surrender to Bob's disease; it was running its course, and we could no longer outrun it. Instead of praying for a miracle, I began to pray for strength. I needed to be at my best so that I could help Bob begin his long good-bye.

Honor guard salutes Bob and our family as
we leave Memorial Drive Presbyterian Church.

CHAPTER FIFTEEN

HEAVEN BOUND

ALTHOUGH IT REMAINED UNSPOKEN, our journey's destination had changed. Never one to be in denial, I was no longer kidding myself. Bob's condition was precarious, and I had to brace myself for the worst. My therapist tried as much as possible to prepare me to accept the truth.

During the sessions, I voiced my fear of a future without him. She encouraged me to articulate my feelings: my concerns, angst and pain. We discussed the need to come up with a game plan. I would have to plan a funeral and make preparations for handling my financial affairs. Bob had taken care of everything through his office; I was clueless. I didn't even know how much our property taxes were. I had no relationship with a CPA or a business attorney.

Friends like Johnny and Kris Perry, Laura and Mike Sweeney, Anne Mendelsohn and others propped me up. They took me out to lunch and dinner. Father Lahart remained a source of strength for me. He had a perpetual, beaming smile on his face and an infectious laugh. Over lunch one day, Bob asked him to speak at his funeral.

I felt very helpless during this period, but easing Bob's suffering and providing good medical care gave me a sense of purpose. I wanted to create a stress-free environment for him. Although there was no roadmap to follow—a kind of caregiver's manual for spouses—there were friends walking parallel paths. The husband of a friend of mine from the Bahamas had also been diagnosed with pancreatic cancer.

While I was in New York City to attend a special All Saints Mass with fellow members of the Sacred Military Constantinian Order of St. George, a friend of mine, Patricia Kennedy of Los Angeles, introduced me to her friend Lisa Niemi Swayze, a widow about my age, who had just lost her husband to this disease monster. After lunch, Lisa and I traded emails, and she offered insights and support. I was lucky to have her help navigating those uncertain times.

Many friends reached out to me, but it was hard for some to relate to what I was feeling. Unless you've walked that rocky road, it's difficult to understand the emotional rollercoaster I was on. There was so much cumulative fatigue. Trying to explain to people how I felt and what I was going through was exhausting. It was taxing enough to walk them through Bob's prognosis. It all took energy that I didn't have to spare. I became all too aware that one disturbing side effect was that for some couples, we were a reminder of the terrible possibility of losing a spouse. As a result, some people were uncomfortable to be around me.

Prayers remained my lifeline. My prayer warrior buddies like Paula Douglass and Susan Baker sent me scriptures that I saved on my Blackberry ™ and read during desperate hours. I reflected often on the temporal versus the spiritual realm. One of my favorite scriptures was Matthew 11:28. "Come unto me, all ye that travail and are heavy laden and I will refresh you."

Jimmy Baker came by frequently for a visit and a drink. He was a bright spot in our day.

"I know what you're going through, Mica," he told me.

And he did. He had lost a wife to cancer. Whenever he was around, laughter echoed through the house. His light-hearted kidding was the best medicine for Bob.

At night, I read to Bob from the New Testament. A man of deep, quiet faith, he welcomed the good news in Christ. We were in the middle of a mighty storm, and God was our rudder. Our faith anchored us. The cancer might own his body, but it didn't own his soul. Though we were facing a shipwreck of sorts, cancer could not steal Bob's immortality.

That said, he wasn't ready to go yet and, at times, the inevitability of it made him angry. A terminally ill patient goes through several stages of grief. Most of the time, Bob accepted his fate. However, he was competitive and a fighter. He wasn't going to just curl up and die. Bob's indomitable spirit never ceased to impress me. He was weathering the storm with grace and unfailing faith. He never directed anger at God; more than anything else, he was frustrated. He liked his life and wanted more time.

Sleeping at night became virtually impossible for me. I was on red alert and could not relax. Home alone with Bob, I was waiting for the next crisis. He would fall asleep early, and I would try to lose myself in a good movie. If I didn't fall asleep on the sofa, I would lie next to him and sleep fitfully.

One night at around one o'clock in the morning, I started looking for my purse. To this day, I don't know why. I walked into the kitchen, spotted my purse on the countertop, and walked towards it. I heard what sounded like heavy breathing. Chiding myself for having an overactive imagination, I dismissed my inner radar warning system, and picked up my purse. Then I heard the distinct click of a revolver. Steadying my nerves, I nonchalantly walked out of the kitchen.

I wanted to run to the bedroom on the opposite side of the house and push the panic button. Yet I felt a divine presence telling me not to. There was no guard, and the panic button made an audible sound. I finally reached the bedroom, went in, locked the door and prayed. Of course, I was tempted to wake up my protector—Bob— but he had had a rough day and had taken a sleeping pill. Of course, I didn't sleep.

The next morning, I knew I needed to call the police, but decided to first see if anything had been taken. I had left my keys in the kitchen. They were gone. I became frantic. I went to search for them in the car. What I found sent a chill down my spine. I had a distinctive key chain consisting of three tortoise shell rings. They were fanned out on the console of my car—without the keys.

We were not sure if this was a random intruder or a stalker. We had no security at that point and no reason to assume that anyone was fixated on us. We called our old friend in homicide at the Houston Police. He observed that we had been away for the better part of a year, and now that we were back, so was my stalker. The keychain, he said, was displayed to convey a message: "I have your keys, and I can return any time I want to." It was a chilling taunt.

Once again, we re-keyed the locks and hired full-time security. "Here we go again," I said to Bob. If my nerves weren't already frayed, I was now terrified—of Bob's prognosis and for my life, or at the very least my sanity. My PTSD returned as did flashbacks.

Gradually, we moved to twenty-four-hour nursing care. Bob needed pain medication, as pancreatic cancer can be especially painful. The chemo had caused him to tire easily. As much as he hated it, he resigned himself to nurses. Finding the right agency and the right nurses was a process of trial and error. Some had never taken care of a cancer patient; others had no experience caring for someone who was terminally ill. If I was ever going to let go and get some rest, I needed to have complete trust in the nursing staff.

"Find a cute one," he joked. We did, but I largely requested experienced, mature nurses. They were wives and mothers who could better relate to our situation. There was no substitute for maturity, either.

In general, there seemed to be a lack of awareness that the "Mosbacher Urgent Care Clinic" was also a private home. It felt like our house was overrun with medical personnel, and for them, this was a workplace. For me, it had to be a home and a retreat. Sharing it with strangers meant that there were few safe zones for me. They were in our bedroom and bathroom, and in the kitchen. I walked into the kitchen one morning and counted five people. Bob had lab sticks, infusion and a team of specialists. The nursing agency had disregarded my directives. It was not a good fit.

My mother suggested I talk to my aunt, Sheila Seckinger, a hospice nurse. She advised me to call the hospital and ask for nursing agency recommendations. I did, and we ended up with Ultra Staff Nursing and some of the top, private-duty nurses in Houston. Sheila also suggested that I have a frank talk with the case manager and discuss my previous experiences with private-duty nurses. It was critical that I outline my expectations regarding skill levels—in other words, no more LVNs—as Bob required more than just a babysitter. He needed experienced registered nurses, preferably with oncology experience.

I contacted Ultra Staff Nursing and laid things out clearly for the case manager; I was trusting my husband to these nurses, and I had to feel one-hundred percent confident in their abilities. She agreed that there would also be clear instructions for me to be awakened if Bob took a turn for the worse. We also discussed his personality. Charming and delightful, he was also headstrong. Bob was a major force and needed nurses who would be kind, but firm. I wanted competent professionals of a mature age who wouldn't be impressed with his persona.

The agency sent top professionals to care for him. They became my heroes. Many were sensitive to my grief as well and found time to give me an extra hug. I gradually got to know a little about their personal lives. One was recovering from breast cancer; she was pro-active and a godsend.

It was difficult for me to hand Bob's health care over to someone else. I wasn't a nurse, but I had taken care of him all our married life. He'd had some close calls, and I had recognized the symptoms of several serious conditions. We had been in the trenches together, and we had each other's backs. In my opinion, a professional caregiver, no matter how experienced, is no substitute for someone who truly loves you.

My role as caregiver came with the territory. I took our marriage vows seriously—"in sickness and in health"—and knew that if the roles had been reversed, Bob would have looked after me. Bob needed me. Of course, he was also concerned about my welfare. He could understand what I was going through, as his first wife had been taken by cancer.

My therapist cautioned me to pace myself. Symptoms of caregiver fatigue included irritability, depression and feelings of worthlessness. I had already shown some symptoms of grief and extreme stress. For months, I had been living in an emotional pressure cooker; now that I had gotten the nursing situation to the level that made me comfortable, I had to take care of my emotional well-being. Bob needed a healthy wife with her wits about her to navigate the next part of the journey.

I forced myself to go for long walks and to Pilates class. Remembering how manicures and pedicures had provided a rest in

Phoenix, I would schedule one occasionally. I kept my cell phone on at all times and told the nursing staff to call me immediately if an emergency situation arose. Nurses from the agencies we had used in the past had frequently ignored my express wishes. But Ultra Staff's nurses actually listened to me. They kept me in the loop, took my opinions into consideration and never discounted my concerns.

We all wanted Bob to remain on earth as long as he had some quality of life. There was no reason for him to die because of a complication. Those of us who are mothers had to learn at some point to trust a babysitter to care for our child. Having an especially conscientious team in charge, one that also understood that I knew my husband/their patient best, allowed me to relax my grip.

As I learned to trust the nurses, I also had to learn to accept that, despite the quality care we were providing him, Bob's health was deteriorating on a daily basis. As Jim McGrath put it, it was like watching a slow train wreck. It was excruciatingly painful. At times, the grief seeped into my pores, and I ached all over from the pain. Grief had its teeth in me and wouldn't let go.

When the emotional pain washed over me, I was powerless to stop it, so I went wherever it took me. There were times I felt I would implode and shatter into a million tiny pieces. Intense emotions of love and impending separation would well up out of the blue. Hearing a favorite song like Clay Walker's "Chain of Love" or "Unchained Melody" would trigger crying jags. It was agonizing.

I couldn't see a bright and happy future anymore. There was no light at the end of my tunnel. Simple tasks like going to the bank became harder. I became forgetful. I remember once going to the bank to deposit some checks, only to find that I'd forgotten them. I dissolved into tears in the parking lot. The disease that had taken over our life and its attendant grief required that I summon all the inner strength I had.

At some point, the cancer finally brought out the warrior woman in me. I have Celtic and Viking blood, and it began to stir within me. I declared war on cancer. I would not allow myself to have an emotional meltdown. My trust was in the Lord; He would send his angels to protect me.

My courageous husband just forged ahead. When he could, he worked from home or even went to the office. He reviewed pages of his autobiography and met with Jim. I had been working on my public art project to be located on Allen Parkway called *Tolerance*, and Bob met with me and David Jones of Dini Partners to come up with a fundraising strategy. Functioning like a husband and wife on non-cancer-related projects helped us both.

We managed to stumble through the days, but the nights were harder. Bob's health problems seemed to flare up after dark. A nurse would frequently wake me up to express her concerns. I would throw on my clothes, grab my purse and drive him to the emergency room. The song, "Help Me Make It Through the Night," took on new meaning.

One evening in mid-October 2010, we again rushed to the hospital, where Bob was admitted. Dr. Wolff came to the hospital room and told us that Bob's liver was shutting down. This turned out to be a defining moment.

"How long do I have?" my husband asked very matter-of-factly.

"A week or two," Dr. Wolff answered. Then he said those dreaded five words. "Get your affairs in order."

Taking the bullet, Bob turned to me and said, "We don't even have funeral plots."

"I'm on it," I choked.

Dr. Wolff gave him the choice of having stents put in his liver; it was a stopgap measure, but it would prolong his life. While he was in the procedure the next day, I called Geo. H. Lewis & Sons to discuss funeral plans. Director Tom Jones and I visited at length on the phone.

I knew a burial in Washington, DC would suit Bob. He had put off buying funeral plots. Every time we attended a funeral, we looked at the cemetery to see if it felt right to us. We came close a few times, but he resisted. He just didn't seem that keen on any Houston cemetery.

While in Washington, we had often driven by Arlington National Cemetery. Bob would comment on its significance and what it represented. He also liked the idea of being buried in a historical place in one of his favorite cities in the world. As he never served in the military, he couldn't be buried there.

Still, Washington had many other options. Tom Jones recommended the historic Congressional Cemetery and told me a little about it. The idea was appealing. He arranged for me to meet Terry Shotkowski, a funeral director and a colleague of his, in Washington the following day. I chartered a plane so that I could return quickly if Bob took a turn for the worse.

I flew up in the morning. It was a gloomy day; the damp, dreary weather matched my mood. I went straight to the Congressional Cemetery to meet Terry. The minute I met him, I relaxed. Friendly and radiating positive energy, he was like a beacon of hope. The Cemetery's director, Cindy Hayes, gave us a brief introduction to the hallowed grounds.

Situated on thirty-five acres, Congressional was established in 1807 and became a national landmark. More than 65,000 individuals—many of them our nation's founders—were buried or had been memorialized there. Also buried there were Native Americans and young mothers who had died in childbirth. Veterans from every war were interred there, as were former FBI Director J. Edgar Hoover and composer John Philip Sousa. I even found descendants of family members—Downing Mears' relative, former Secretary of State Abel P. Upshur, was buried on the property. There was one vice president, a Supreme Court justice, six Cabinet members, nineteen senators and seventy-one Congressional representatives. Bob would be in good company.

More importantly, docents led numerous tours every year. Destination graves had been carefully chosen, and the tours were theme-driven: Women in the Arts, Men of Adventure and Civil War tours were popular. One local theatre company even re-enacted the assassination of President Abraham Lincoln. His assassin, John Wilkes Booth, was buried there in an unmarked grave.

Cindy showed me the four plots she had selected, which were in the 'patriot' section near former Vice President Geary, a relative of Bob's stepson, Bobby Geary. I took this as another sign. Cindy took me over to see the Public Vault, where a large number of bodies had been held during winter months, when the ground was too frozen for the grave diggers. I went inside and was amused to see Halloween decorations. Cindy snapped my photo. In it, I was smiling.

We also looked at the beautiful, historic little chapel. I trusted my instincts and wrote a check. When I returned to my hotel to collect my luggage, I was at peace. The bellman loaded my bags into the car, and I went inside to call Bob. I planned to meet Dianne Kube for dinner at Café Milano and then fly home.

I spoke to Bob and went back outside to find a policewoman unscrewing the license plate on my hired car. I asked her what was going on.

"This car is being impounded," she answered briskly. "He had no proof of insurance."

I told her that my luggage was in the car and that I needed to get it out. Incredibly, she was reluctant and had to be persuaded. She finally let the bellman take it out. He put my bags and me in a cab. It was still raining.

By the time I met Dianne for dinner, I was laughing and crying. The day had been surreal. The juxtaposition of ridiculously sad and funny made us both roar with laughter. It was a release of so much emotion.

During dinner, I asked Dianne if she would be a consultant for us and help coordinate Bob's memorial services. Her family had owned a funeral home, and she understood the nuances and protocol of funerals. She also knew and cared about Bob and understood my high expectations. I wanted his last party to be the grand one he deserved, with all the pomp and circumstance of a state funeral.

Bob meant so much to so many. His send-off was going to be among my last loving gestures to my husband. It was important that friends from Washington and the Northeast could come to one of the two services. I envisioned a large funeral and reception in Houston and a private interment in Washington, followed by a reception large enough to include all those who cared about him.

Dianne suggested the Commerce Department building. It was the perfect choice. She was also planning her daughter's wedding in London. I laughed and told her that a funeral is kind of like a wedding in that both have thousands of details. She had good connections and promised to follow up with Terry and the funeral homes, and to fly to Houston when she could. Dianne had good judgment and would make sure everything was done right. We were in good hands.

I went back to Houston that night and shared the photos of the "events" at Congressional. Bob smiled when he saw dogs running across the grave sites and laughed when I told him about the destination grave tours. I could tell he was pleased with my choice. He said he would break the news to his family.

Despite being a Houstonian, he liked the idea of resting in Washington. He began sharing with me his thoughts on his funeral.

We discussed hymns and Scripture. Bravely, he described the grave marker. He wanted a more modern version of the traditional obelisks at the cemetery. "Pink granite," he said.

I showed him the photo of me in the Public Vault, and he laughed. "I might end up there," he teased. "Washington winters can bring snowstorms." Pragmatic and filled with good humor even in these circumstances, he cracked several more jokes.

It was a bittersweet time. Bob was admitted to the hospital again around Halloween. His daughter, Dee, brought him a ghoulish mask. He took great pleasure in playing this trick on unsuspecting visitors: He would hide under the sheet and then pull it off his face, exposing the mask. It especially tickled Jimmy Baker, who got quite the surprise during one visit. On seeing Bob's face covered with a sheet, he thought his friend had already died.

The path we were on now was the last we had ever imagined taking. But we had no choice; we were on a pathway to heaven. I so hoped young Kameron would be among those to greet him at the pearly gates. He was such a joyous spirit.

As our small ship was tossed to and fro in the sea of cancer, God watched over us with His promise of glory.

Bob is sailing in paradise. I wish him fair winds and following seas.

CHAPTER SIXTEEN

IMMORTALITY

DIANNE CAME INTO TOWN and met with the principals at Geo. H. Lewis & Sons. She stayed with us and gave me much-needed emotional support. I often had late-night, long-distance chats with her, I had been telling her that my home was like a fishbowl, with medical staff camped out in various rooms. She thought I was exaggerating, until she counted nineteen people in the kitchen on her first day there.

She knew I was fiercely private and that I felt outnumbered in my home. Visitors came and went. My phone rang non-stop. I was having to fight to have even one private moment with Bob. I needed to hold him and tell him how much I loved him. His emotional support was vital to my very existence. Dianne took it all in and validated what I was feeling.

The situation was getting harder by the day. It seemed like everyone wanted to come by and pay their respects to Bob. He only wanted his closest friends and family. I frequently had to be the bad guy and explain that he really wasn't up to having visitors. I was being pushed and pulled by so many people, and I recognized that I needed some support. I contacted the therapist who had once helped me through my divorce. Dr. Gray knew all my history. He recognized abandonment issues and understood the family dynamics. He also knew how hard I could be on myself.

"You are not trying to win a popularity contest, Mica," he counseled.

There was some apparent family tension and I tried to avoid getting involved. I didn't have the energy to be confrontational. I didn't want to end up being a kind of scapegoat for strong emotions, such as anger at the situation. Dr. Gray said that it was imperative for my own mental health to talk with impartial people in a protected, safe emotional environment.

So as Bob imparted his wishes to each of his adult children, I took a backseat to the discussions. He was still in charge of his life and his medical decisions. My role was to follow his wishes and not boss him around.

In November, George H.W. Bush surprised Bob with the announcement that a Mosbacher Institute would be established at the Bush Library at Texas A & M University. Bob was thrilled beyond words. We began implementing a plan to take him to College Station for the dedication; the plan involved nurses and medical equipment.

Ultimately, however, it became clear that any kind of travel would be too complicated. Anything could happen, and we didn't want to be far from Houston. We planned a dinner at River Oaks Country Club. Close friends came in for it; I brought Bob, who was in a wheelchair, along with a pretty, young nurse named Laura. Former President George W. Bush, who hosted the event, spoke, as did Governor Perry. I also said a few words, including "This is our last public appearance." It was my way of letting our closest friends know the truth without sending out a press release. There wasn't a dry eye at dinner that night. Barbara Bush told me she felt so sad, yet Bob was elated and honored.

As it was certain to be Bob's last Christmas, I recalled the premonition on Christmas Eve from the year before. Determined to celebrate with a bang, I went overboard decorating our home. I left no area untouched; the house was turned into a Christmas store. I almost had fake snow blown, but drew the line at that extravagance.

I also planned a cocktail party for family on Christmas Eve. Bob's own goal included going into the office for his annual company Christmas party.

When that date rolled around, a nurse went with him. I honestly don't know how he was able to go. He was painfully thin and wan; it took sheer willpower for him to be there. But he pulled it off and returned home with a big smile on his face. He had wanted to say good-bye to his valued employees.

Early on Christmas Eve morning, Bob's nurse, Laura, woke me up and said he wanted to talk to me. He had been awake all night debating with himself. Apparently, the pain was worse. He had decided to go to the hospital, knowing he might never leave.

We had previously discussed the possibility of going to the hospital toward the end, especially for pain control. It was time. When we got there, they did some tests and discovered that his liver was shutting down again. Another LVN later joined us and made an honest comment to the doctor. It was a frank—and I think insensitive—comment. "His liver is shot," she said. I bristled.

"That's my husband you're talking about," I said firmly and walked away.

I went down to the chapel and prayed. I was going to need God's help to get through the next several weeks. Despondent, I went home in time to eat Christmas Eve dinner with my son, Bo, Donnie and my mother. Alexander Rogers, our family photographer, had been hired to take photos of the whole Mosbacher-Duncan family. I had forgotten to cancel him, so we posed for photos on the saddest day of my life.

The premonition I'd had at Christmas the year before had been fulfilled. I was devoid of tears that night and just tried to make the best of it. My mother and I went to midnight mass at St. John the Divine. Donnie was old enough to enjoy the presents under the tree, and I wanted to make the most of Christmas morning. Bob had even bought me some gorgeous pearl earrings from Laurie and Terry Taylor of Tayco Jewelry that he had designed.

On Christmas Day, I went back to the hospital, and Bob put up a brave front. He still had his faculties. I found him sitting in bed, reading a newspaper. He was also watching the Weather Channel, a lifelong habit of his. We soon moved him to Palliative Care. I came mornings and evenings and stayed up late. A kind doctor warned me not to keep up that kind of schedule. He advised that he'd seen families wait day after day to be with their loved one when he/she died, only to have it happen when they went to the bathroom. The doctor wanted me to conserve my strength, as the end could take days, even weeks. Every evening, I was reluctant to leave, but I finally stopped staying in the hospital after midnight. We had private-duty nurses, and Bob's family took turns sitting with him. The girls were amazing; he was well cared for.

Before leaving, I usually stopped by the hospital chapel. A Christmas tree was by the door, with a sign each night asking worshippers to write their prayers on the notecards provided and pin them on the tree. My prayers were for Bob to remain alert and pain-free and to go peacefully.

His family shouldered the responsibility. Dee, herself a physician, interacted with the doctors and brought me up to speed. We discussed changing what would have been a large internment in D.C. to a much more intimate one. She was very gentle and kind to me just when I needed it most. Bob had the very best care and was in a world-class hospital. We did all we could to make him comfortable. The floor nurses were fantastic.

On New Year's Eve, Father Lahart joined us. I brought a bottle of champagne and together, he and Bob popped the cork. Father Lahart said he had administered to many a dying man, but he had never toasted with champagne. He had a philosophical discussion about the fear of dying. He had known a man of the cloth—a very devout man—who was afraid to meet his maker. Judgment Day can seem daunting to us mortals, but Father Lahart had something to say about that, too. "No one is good all the time," he said. "We are all sinners. That's why there is forgiveness."

A few more weeks went by, and it seemed the appointed time was approaching. Bob remained alert. Cameron flew in to say goodbye; their last kiss tore at my heart. Bob was trying to be stoic, but I couldn't stand it. I left the room in tears.

Dianne came to Houston and helped me select clothes for Bob's funeral. I wore mostly sweats these days, however I needed appropriate clothing at what would be two extremely crowded memorial services and receptions. So I called Ann Sappington at Stanley Korshak in Dallas to help find two black suits.

On Saturday, January 23rd, I kissed my husband good-bye and told him I loved him. On Sunday morning, my Blackberry™ vibrated. I looked at it and saw a Google alert about Bob; he had died that morning and nobody from the hospital had called me! I had spoken to our private-duty nurse earlier, but he was still alive at the point.

I ran to tell Dianne, who called the funeral home. They had not been informed, either. There had been some sort of mix-up in the chain of command at the hospital. More than likely, each had assumed that someone else had called me. Although never pleasant, notifying the next of kin is part of the job. Someone had probably dropped the ball. M.D. Anderson had given Bob such fine care that I realized this small misstep wasn't intentional. I was furious at first, but I was also in shock, upset and badly shaken. Nothing prepares you for the finality of death.

Assuming I knew, the family had given Jim McGrath permission to send out a news release. As it was Sunday morning, all I could think about was going to church. Lynn Hoster, Bo's mother, offered to go with us. In the car en route to St. Michael's Church, the King of Spain called me to offer his condolences. I was deeply touched by his magnanimous gesture. In addition, one of Bob's daughters called to ask me what day and time I wanted to hold the funeral. "Whatever y'all want," was my response. Sad, drained and empty, the details didn't seem to matter. Bob's children would do a good job organizing everything.

After church, my mother joined us for lunch at Olivette Restaurant in the Houstonian Hotel. I had no appetite and picked at my food. During our meal, Dianne fielded media requests. A local channel wanted to do an on-camera interview; I nodded, but then immediately realized how disheveled I looked. My hair was dirty, and I had obviously been crying. Teresa Ramos, a stylist I used at the Trellis Spa, just happened to be at the Houstonian Hotel for a bridal party. A staff member got word to her, and she came to my rescue.

Teresa had lost her husband to cancer and knew exactly what I was feeling. She had done my hair several times during the past few months and had counseled me. She told me that she liked to write letters to God and place them in her Bible. I began to do the same.

The camera crew met me at the house. I gave a few telephone interviews as well. All the reporters were respectful and had kind things to say about Bob. It was hard to pick up the newspaper on Monday morning and see his name in the headlines; I was numb with shock and functioning on auto-pilot. I got word to mutual friends of Bob's previous two wives and let them know that they were more than welcome to attend the funeral. Sandy Geary Smith said she would come; I knew Bob would have been touched.

One of his daughters mentioned that I might want to host a reception at our home for friends. I hadn't planned for it but, after our private visitation with Bob, I decided it was a good idea. I remember standing at the front door greeting friend after friend that night. It was odd not to have Bob sharing my hostess duties. Several people asked if I was going to sell the house.

Sell my home? That would be like leaving Bob twice. I got prickly every time someone asked the question. It was an especially sore subject. But it occurred to me that people didn't know what to say. "I'm sorry for your loss" or "I'm here if you need to talk" were the best things I could hear.

On the day of the funeral, I arrived at the church early to thank the Texas A&M Choir for attending. Susan Ford was already there. Later, I was greeted by President George W. Bush and his father, George H.W. Bush. Governor Rick Perry and Anita also attended. I was very touched that the Governor had ordered flags to be flown at half-staff in Bob's honor.

Bob had invited both Dave Petersen and Father Lahart to speak at the service. The church was packed; the music was uplifting. President Bush and Jimmy Baker spoke; Bob's children, Rob and Dee, gave funny, touching remarks. Dave preached about the glory of God and gave an impressive sermon. Father Lahart told about Bob's request for last rites.

An honor guard of Ross Volunteers escorted Bob's casket to the hearse. After the service, we greeted close friends at River Oaks Country Club. My mother, Dianne, Father Lahart and I flew on to Washington later that day with Bob's casket. It was placed in the passenger section of the plane, and I stared at it during the entire flight. When we landed at dusk, I could see a rainbow in the distance.

We were staying at the Jefferson Hotel. That night, we sat around and sang songs. We were a noisy crowd, but Bob would have approved of our brand of an Irish wake. Later, Senator McCain spoke at the private service in the chapel at the Congressional Cemetery. Richard Flowers and Daisy White were there overseeing the last details, down to an arrangement of my favorite music.

That day had dawned clear and cold. En route to the cemetery, I had received an email from the Ambassador of Iceland—the State Department had confirmed my appointment. It was a sign from Bob! I summoned my courage and made it through. At the graveside, I pointed out some of the historical graves to the grandchildren. They grasped the sense of history in this special place. I greeted Bob's sister, Barbara, who lived in New York and had been unable to come to Houston. Other friends traveled to pay their respects, and we exchanged heartfelt hugs.

Dianne and Daisy had thoughtfully made a CD with a compilation of music from the album *Nation Under God* performed by the U.S. Air Force Band. The moving song, "Goin' Home" was also part of the soundtrack from the film, *A Clear and Present Danger*—a favorite. I pulled up a chair and listened to the beautiful music. For a few minutes, I shut out the endless chatter around me. Closing my eyes, I felt Bob's presence. I tried to say my goodbyes. Finally, I tore myself away and went back to the hotel.

Later that afternoon, Commerce Secretary Gary Locke met me at the side door to the Department of Commerce building. A consummate host, he walked me to the reception, expressing his respect for Bob along the way. Bob's portrait had been brought down and was prominently displayed in the large reception hall. Before Bob died, I had shared with him our plan to host a reception at the Commerce building. He had been so pleased. On this day, friends traded hugs and memories, grateful for the opportunity to celebrate Bob's life.

We left that night. Two days later, one of the worst snowstorms of the season shut down Washington. Bob was sending me a message. While he wasn't lying in the Public Vault, his prediction of a storm had come true. He was clearly still watching the Weather Channel—only this time from Paradise.

From the left, Karen Garrett, production crew member, Ally and I filming a PSA for Hands Only CPR in Atlanta.

CHAPTER SEVENTEEN

GODSTONES

AFTER THE INITIAL RUSH OF SERVICES and receptions, things never settled down. I was paralyzed. Internally, I felt like an emotional earthquake was rocking me to the core. I was reeling from the aftershocks of Bob's death and feeling totally bereft. I could have passed for one of the Walking Dead because grief was practically sucking the life out of me.

I couldn't just sit in my room and cry. I feared that if I did, if I fully gave into my grief, I would end up in the grave alongside Bob. Instinctively, I realized that my survival was linked to moving forward, a kind of grieving forward. If I let his death box me in, all would be lost.

My brother, John, was racing a Porsche in the Rolex 24 on January 30th at the International Speedway in Dayton Beach, Florida. The Grand-Am class endurance race was not for the faint of heart. It was a twenty-four-hour race requiring great skill and stamina. John's day job was as an executive with Hunt Construction; racing was his hobby. He had always been an adrenaline junkie, but a careful one. I used to watch him sky-dive. He was fearless.

Recently, he and his wife, Karen, had established a 501c3, Godstone Ranch Motorsports, with a mission to race for charity. In this particular case, they were racing for the Texas Heart Institute to raise awareness of heart disease and raise funds for research. The concept and name of Godstone was Karen's brainchild. Years before, she had taught art classes to adults at St. Martin's Episcopal Church in Houston. While there, she had envisioned a kind of arts-related camp where participants could share their God-given talents. The idea later morphed into motorsports racing.

The idea of "racing for a cause" was unique at the time. I knew absolutely nothing about motorsports racing. I didn't watch NASCAR or Speed TV. I wasn't even sure I liked it, but I needed something to look forward to. My mother was thrilled at the prospect of watching John race, so we had planned on going after the funeral services.

We arrived in Daytona Beach on a rainy Friday. John sent a golf cart and, together, we all went to the pits. He showed me the car and introduced me to the team manager and other pit crew members. Karen's mother, Mary Kay Garrett, was there with her friend, Ron. I felt like an alien who had landed on another planet. In some photos that Karen took, I saw myself and didn't recognize the tired face, etched with lines of grief, staring back at me.

My mother was excited and as frisky as a puppy. She was an adventurous soul and couldn't wait for the action to begin. I, on the other hand, sort of stared at the track and out into space. My heart wasn't in it at all. Then they started the car's engine. VROOM. VROOM. ROAR! I felt the surge of adrenaline. Clapping my hands over my ears, I left the pit to find earplugs. I had no idea how thunderous and loud a race car engine could be.

Returning with my ears properly insulated, I sat transfixed on the "block" while John made a practice run. I felt a rush. The car went around and around as it completed laps. I was suddenly flooded with passion—a new convert. As the engines roared, I felt alive again.

That night at dinner, John shared his strategy and began to educate me about technique and racing terms. This was the forty-eighth running of the Rolex 24; this particular year, there were two Chip Ganassi racing cars, and famous drivers like Mike Rockenfeller, João Barbosa and Terry Borcheller. I even got to meet Patrick Dempsey, who plays Dr. "McDreamy" on the television show *Gray's Anatomy*. It was an all-male field, with some of the best-looking athletes around.

Throughout the next few days and nights, Karen, John and the team got very little sleep. She was a veteran pit crew member and driver changer. The pit boss and John explained as much to me as they could. On racing day when it was his turn to drive, John had a major issue with the car and had to come into the pit to avoid breaking down. It was nerve-wracking for him. Karen and Mom were afraid. I wasn't. John wasn't taking any unnecessary risks. The danger, of course, is enticing; at those high speeds, it's a risk just to get behind the wheel.

But it wasn't like the early days of Formula One racing, when drivers risked their lives every time they were on the track. Those early cars resembled moving coffins, and fiery crashes were the norm. In general, Grand Am had strict rules of conduct and fewer hotheads. A real trooper, my mother sat in the hotel bar with me for hours while I watched part of the race on Speed TV. I loved being at the track and soaking up the ambience, and I found that I was sad when it was over.

From Daytona Beach, we flew to Nassau and to our home in Lyford Cay. I always felt closer to God when I was near the sea. It was odd to be there without Bob, especially since Valentine's Day was approaching. I also visited with Karen Rahming. She shared with me how she was coping with the loss of Kameron; her job helped distract her from the ever-present pain.

I began to do research on Iceland and to acquaint myself with the country I would be representing. I was going to Iceland for the first time in March to attend a briefing at the offices of the Foreign Ministry. My mother and I discussed life after Bob. She urged me to make travel plans and to look ahead; I had to keep marching forward. Over the next few weeks, I came up with a bucket list. Life would pass me by if I let the grass grow under my feet. Stewing and wallowing weren't in my DNA. Travel was definitely on the list, as was getting a walk-on part in a Broadway production.

In fact, while attending a fundraising auction for Dancers in Transition, I discovered I had won a role in *Mamma Mia,* which was playing at the Winter Garden Theatre in New York. I contacted the stage manager and set a date to appear in a July performance. The prospect of a role on stage with a packed audience would galvanize my workout program.

Also on my bucket list were performance driving; attending a Formula One race when the new Circuit of the Americas track opened in Austin; finding another apartment to lease in New York; attending dance classes at the Steps School in New York; taking an acting class at the Julliard School; learning to play the guitar; and taking voice lessons again.

During those first few weeks after Bob's death, I was emotionally drained. I met with an attorney and a CPA to fill out endless forms. There were many times when I just went back to bed. Little things like going to gas up my car overwhelmed me. I made myself leave the house at least once a day. I probably would have been happy watching Lifetime TV all day, but I would have wilted on the vine.

I tried to be gentle with myself, as anything remotely stressful set me off. I had to be careful not to yell at the AT&T representative who put me on hold or the Comcast technician who hadn't fixed my cable channels.

The changes were coming fast and hard. My household employees were also employees of Mosbacher Energy; after Bob died, they were no longer on my payroll. One of his assistants had always helped me with my work. I had hoped that she could help me sort through the pile of condolence letters and phone messages. Bob and I had discussed a three to six month transition before making any major staff changes. However, his request was not put in writing, so his wishes were not honored. It was a new day and one of unanticipated shocks.

A college friend, Martha Blecher, volunteered to help out. She needed a job, and I knew I could trust her. I was juggling insurance, taxes, life insurance forms and more. My calendar was full of obligations, including the release of Bob's biography by Texas A&M University Press.

At times, I felt like I was drowning. There were days when I was flat paralyzed with fear. My dear friends were a phone call away, and my mother was an ever-present rock. There was no perfect way to handle grief. It was sloppy; at times, I was a mess. Irritable and cranky, I wasn't always positive or diplomatic.

I tried anti-depressants, only to have an adverse reaction. Of course, I continued counseling, but I wasn't ready for any kind of group therapy. I was too private. Sharing my innermost thoughts with a group of strangers did not appeal to me.

Several widowed friends reached out to me. I found their thoughtful emails especially helpful. Each person is different and handles grief in a very personal way. What was right for me wasn't right for others. I didn't want to sit around and revisit Memory Lane. I knew I couldn't run from the grief, but I also knew that I would get stuck if I didn't take it on in small steps. I had to keep moving—and grieve while going forward.

The fact that my movement was more of a run than a walk was typical of me, and it served me well then. I discovered that finding a renewed lease on life through a purpose or a hobby is essential in the aftermath of grief and loss.

During those first months after Bob's death, I found that I enjoyed solitude. It was tiring to continually field questions about whether or not I would sell my home (it later became a running family joke) or date again. It was too soon for any major decision. And Bob was a tough act to follow. Someone said to me, "You aren't going to find another Bob." Too true. He was one of a kind.

Besides, I was still deeply in love with him. I didn't define "happily ever after" as finding another man. There were other steps to take to define a happy life. I wanted my independence, and I needed to navigate the world of property deeds, property taxes, the IRS and money management. Bob had done it all for me, even though I'd resisted that brand of being taken care of. I wanted to be an equal partner and know about the business aspects of our lives. I wanted fewer surprises, but that didn't happen. I was in the dark.

Fortunately for me, friends were there to recommend competent, trustworthy professionals. A widow has to be very cautious not to be taken advantage of during those vulnerable early days. There were opportunists waiting in the wings, barracuda types who smell blood and try to press you into uncomfortable business deals. It was a minefield out there, and I learned to exercise extreme caution. I did not want to be the victim of foolish widow-related mistakes. That would prove to be challenging.

Our historic mid-century modern home in
Houston was the scene of many happy events.

CHAPTER EIGHTEEN

SO, ARE YOU GOING TO SELL YOUR HOUSE?

IT WAS THE QUESTION THAT WOULDN'T go away, a real thorn in my side. I heard it every single day. Clearly, those in sales read the obituaries, and Bob's death had been front-page news in several cities. Without the courtesy of a grace period to mourn, realtors began swooping in like vultures targeting a carcass. I kept hearing things like "Do you want to sell your home?", "The market is hot.", and "Yours is a prime property." Of course it was.

To compound matters, this inquiry wasn't limited to realtors. Friends and mere acquaintances asked me the same question. "I'm sorry for your loss" was frequently followed up with, "So, Mica, are you going to sell your home?" Granted, some people were merely curious. Others wondered about my future plans. In many cases, the question was innocent enough—human nature.

While most of the time my response was polite, the question felt like a spike driven through my heart. My home was where my heart was. I might be a bit of a gypsy; however, my home was a retreat. I had poured all of myself into restoring it, so it was like a second child to me. I was terrified to leave it because I would mourn the loss of it, too. There were too many family memories roaming its halls. And I also had Cameron's feelings to consider.

In my opinion, another reason lurked at the center of these inquiries. People were trying to ascertain my financial situation. They were sizing me up to see if I was cash-strapped and seeking a bargain. Like sharks that smell blood in the water, they could then come in for the kill. If there was going to be a fire sale, then they would get a real bargain.

My mother was so fear-ridden after her divorce from my father that she sold our family home for a song. Her attorney bought it, which just didn't feel right to me. She could easily have met the mortgage payments for the next few years. Had she not acted out of fear, she would have had more stability at that difficult time and more security later. I learned from her mistake.

After Bob died, my foundation was badly shaken. He had been my North Star. When I lost him, I lost a lover and friend as well as a savvy businessman and protector. As the lone survivor, I was sagging under the load. There were too many people coming at me from all directions with requests and sales pitches. As I watched monthly expenses add up, my concern grew, too. Wobbly with grief, I had not found my footing yet.

Some people I dealt with, especially some in sales, really were mercenary. I began to recognize that even workers who came out to do simple repairs were charging me outrageous prices. I always got several bids and was shocked at what they thought they could charge. A locksmith who installed Home Depot-style locks, instead of Medco locks charged me four times the normal price. So during this time of grieving, I had to be aware of my finances and watch out for rip-off artists.

As a newly single woman, I was bait. I was walking around in a bubble when I was married to Bob; now my bubble had burst. It seemed to me that any divorcee or widow had certain assets to protect: a car, a property, life insurance payment or stock. Calculating salespeople who made a living by separating women from their assets knew how to cajole or play on their fear. Falling into this category were financial planners, money managers and investment advisers. They all wanted to help me, guide me, profit off me. I remembered from my days at Oppenheimer that brokers were on commission; they all had a quota to make. They made cold calls all day long. Some sales people were really convincing. While many were ethical, there were others who were desperate and simply lacked morals.

I watched several widows walk into the firm and invest all their assets with a broker they had only just met. Instead of hearing their pitch, leaving and giving it some thought, I was surprised at how many of the widows opened a brokerage account and handed over a check. Talk about throwing caution to the wind. These people didn't know and couldn't assess their needs and appetite for risk. It was an eye-opener. Widows are targets for the type of broker who regards them as a meal ticket, a kind of cash cow. Many widows have assets, and the brokers who need the sale are not her friends; they have a motive.

When Bob was ill, I experienced the hard-sale tactic from a man I knew slightly from charity events. President of a financial firm, he had substantial real-estate holdings and was on the board of his son's school. He appeared to be a stand-up guy. I recall our conversation going something like this:

"Mica, if you invest with me, you will double your money. My company, Stanford Financial, has found superior investment vehicles, and I don't want you to miss out."

My motto is, "When in doubt, don't." That small voice I refer to as the Holy Spirit warned me. It came in a whisper. I held off making a decision. A few months later, Robert Allen Stanford, CEO of Stanford Financial Group was indicted for securities fraud. Stanford had been running a $2 billion Ponzi scheme with a shell company in the Cayman Islands. Federal agents found that the computers in the offices weren't even hooked up. As we say in Texas, he was "all hat, no cattle."

Bob would say that I got lucky and cheated the devil. I was shocked, but I wasn't swindled. This close call taught me to be extra wary and cautious of strangers bearing gifts. It didn't matter if I met them at church or in a bible study group. Predator types attend church, too. It's difficult to recognize a wolf in sheep's clothing; some are charming and smooth operators. I felt like I was wearing a sign that said "I am easy. Prey on me."

On the other hand, I wasn't the naïve young woman who had been charmed by a South African creep. I was nobody's fool anymore. At this point, my trust needed to be earned.

My brother's advice was to hold off on any major decisions for at least two years. He said to assume that any decision I made while shell-shocked would be a bad one. There was no *Widowhood for Dummies* book to help me. "Don't dig yourself another grave," my brother said, advising me to avoid making any financial mistakes that could put me in a hole that I couldn't easily get out of.

As the vultures circled, I also tried to navigate the world of consultants. This was the Widow's Walk that was especially hard. As the will was going to probate court, I needed an attorney to represent my part of the inheritance. I would need copies of death certificates; I also needed a new trustee, a banker and a CPA. I had no real business relationships in these fields to turn to. Lawyers and CPAs came in all shapes and sizes. Some had higher fees than others. While they are entitled to earn a living, I did not want to pay exorbitant fees. I soon discovered that some even charged to respond to an email.

John explained that once I hired a lawyer, it would be hard to disentangle myself. I need to choose carefully. He or she would also have intimate knowledge of my net worth. When asking around for names, I also asked about their personality types. I wanted someone who simplified the complexity of my issues. I wasn't afraid to ask what their hourly rate was. In some cases, I might need a partner; in other routine cases, a younger associate who billed at a lower rate would do just fine.

I also got good advice from my son. Lawyers charge by the minute, he told me. "Stick to just the facts, Mom," he said. Women have a tendency to be very talkative. I was reminded of the expression, "Be brief, and you will be invited back." Once I found one I liked, I refused to look for any hand-holding. If the conversation went off-topic and into things that weren't germane to the issue, I asked if we were off the clock. I was paying for a service, so I tried to stay focused and businesslike. It didn't always work, as I was emotional at times. But I had a very satisfactory relationship with this attorney.

I later consulted another attorney regarding a business transaction, and he asked me out. This caught me by surprise. A lawyer should remain somewhat distanced from a legal matter and a client so that there's no conflict of interest in the courtroom. I had trusted this individual with knowledge of my assets; he had come highly recommended and was well-regarded. It seemed unprofessional and like a violation of my trust. I didn't want to be hit on by my doctor, a priest or a lawyer.

Shopping for a CPA was easy. My friend Jay gave me a reference. Again, a CPA would know my total financial picture. I had to trust him or her. It was also important that someone I dealt with understood my financial goals. I didn't want how I invested, saved or spent my money to be dictated to me.

Through my CPA, I was given the names of three bankers at three different institutions. I made the rounds of meetings and settled on one. I could change my mind later, but was looking for a personal service. I didn't want to be just another number. My banker would be a source of financial advice, and I wanted to like him or her. I also hired a trustee but on a temporary basis. I did not want to be bound to any long-term contracts with new business relationships. I was very nervous about my finances. Could I afford to keep my home? I was definitely scared without Bob's income.

All our credit had been in his name—a common mistake. I only had one credit card and was having to fight to establish more. While I liked to feel like his princess, I had turned into a pumpkin. It was an unwelcome wake-up call.

These professionals and my friends helped me navigate the slippery slope of early widowhood. My concentration was not good, but I began to read about finances and investing. I heard internationally acclaimed author and personal finance expert, Suze Orman, speak. She gave sound advice on IRAs, staying out of the credit-card debt trap, mortgage refinancing and the like. I realized that advice from books was free. I spoke to single women friends and asked them what had been the pitfalls in their lives.

An all-too-familiar theme came up: they had been kept in the dark by their spouses. In many cases—like mine—it was not intentional.

Old-fashioned men like to take care of everything, and many women prefer it that way. This is the "head-in-the-sand" approach.

Bob would not share financial information with me. I had implored him to help me establish solid relationships with a bookkeeper, a CPA, a banker and a lawyer. Part of it was that he wanted to be in control. There was a significant age difference between us, and I think that was part of it, too. When I asked him what steps he had taken for my future without him, his response was, "You will be taken care of."

When I asked him how he defined "being taken care of," I wasn't being mercenary. I only wanted to know what future I needed to prepare for. I had married for love, and I'd signed a prenuptial agreement. I was not trying to soften him up to change that agreement, I just wanted to understand what the practicalities of my life would be. My sister-in-law, Karen, calls uncertainty "the iffiness of life." I didn't want any iffiness in my financial future. If I needed to go back to work, I wanted to know sooner rather than later.

These conversations are not very romantic and can be unpleasant. However, they are critical, and women should insist that financial issues be clarified. There should be nothing vague about these details. All wishes for an estate need to be in writing, too. He might have been well-intentioned, but trustees and family could all have different interpretations of exactly what those wishes were. "Dad said I could have his watch." "Mom said I could have her jewelry." Emotions run high after a funeral, and these play out in squabbles at times.

When a subsequent marriage is involved, the situation is more complicated. If the trustee is related to the deceased rather than the survivor, honoring verbal wishes that were not in writing can lead to judgment calls, or rationalizations such as "She has enough," "This is eating into my inheritance," "I never liked her to begin with," or "She got the house, and I didn't." An impartial trustee would work better all around.

In my case, we should have sat down and discussed my financial future, especially once Bob received his prognosis. We had joint bank accounts and property. Was my name on the deed to the house? Or the car? It would have made my first years as a widow much more tolerable if he had helped me form relationships with the right professional consultants. As a prominent businessman, Bob knew the right people and could have ensured that I was not left to deal with complete strangers in my darkest hours.

For wives (or husbands) who are not working or who are not significant breadwinners in their household, the more experienced business person guiding the other in the right direction makes a huge difference. One of my friends was lucky enough to have her husband's best friend and lawyer provide all sorts of help and assistance when she became a widow.

She had an adviser she could rely on, one who had her best interests at heart. Because Bob and I had not clarified these issues, I was thrown to the wolves. I soon discovered I wasn't the only one. The Internet was full of horror stories about this kind of widow blindness. My girlfriends proved invaluable. Incredible women, such as Joanne King Herring, helped inspire and empower me. She shared her past mistakes with me and gave wise counsel. She warned me about dating too soon, and she gave me hope, too.

Robin Craig of the *Houston Chronicle* column, "A Widow's Day," interviewed me. A widow herself, we commiserated. She discussed on her blog some of the tragic widow-related stories. We were all floundering in the dark, it seemed. The "daily-ness" of living was hard enough, but the business-related issues were a nightmare.

During those tender days, I stumbled out of my bed and my cocoon, and went into the new office space I had rented. I was establishing an Icelandic Consulate and was eager to begin a routine. I knew that I would sleep all day if I didn't have a place to go.

I found a breakfast place and felt comfortable eating there alone. Pushing through the heaviness of my grief, I found solace in my new routine. I got to know the waiters, and they stopped to chitchat with me. I read the newspaper and enjoyed the solitude.

Once in the office, I would lose myself in work. I had stacks and stacks of mail—condolence letters and legal paperwork. There were invitations to speak and book-related events coming up that would honor Bob. It was busy, but the work allowed me to bury myself in the distractions and kept me going.

At night, I would take walks. I would do almost anything to avoid coming home. It was lonely, and there were reminders of Bob everywhere. I shed a thousand tears and had trouble sleeping during this adjustment phase. I truly was "Sleepless in Houston." Bereft, I would call widowed friends after midnight. I knew they were up, too. We spoke in shorthand, as we knew exactly what the other was feeling. It was not the best of times. But, as my mother said, it could always be worse.

Sharing a moment at a Scandinavian Ball in NYC
with President of Iceland, Olafur Ragnar Grimsson,
and wife Dorrit who is a longtime friend.
(They were introduced by Gerald and Barbara

CHAPTER NINETEEN

YOU CAN'T CONTROL MOTHER NATURE

WHILE PLANNING BOB'S MEMORIAL SER-*vices, Dianne and I noted wryly that we were like actors in the romantic comedy Four Weddings and a Funeral, which follows the adventures of four friends through the eyes of Hugh Grant's character—who is smitten with a woman and keeps running into her at four weddings and a funeral. While there were no romantic aspects to our situation, in the same day we would often find ourselves selecting an item for her daughter Gretchen's wedding as well as an item for the funeral. Our stationery was ordered at the same time. We represented two important cycles in life: beginnings and endings.*

In mid-April 2010, I flew to London for the wedding of Dianne's daughter, Gretchen. Dianne had been so busy planning "A Wedding and a Funeral" that she had almost forgotten to buy an outfit. On one of our funeral-related excursions, we ran by a store and grabbed a suitable, lovely two-piece ensemble.

Now, Gretchen's beautiful wedding had arrived. I shed happy tears. After the wedding, Dianne accompanied me to Iceland. Neither of us had been before, and we needed a break from the draining months just behind us. With such significant events so recently behind us, we both felt similarly adrift.

I was scheduled to attend a consular training session at the Foreign Ministry in Reykjavik, and Dianne and I planned to tour the countryside. I had made reservations at a famous four-star resort on the Ranga River. It had a celebrated gourmet restaurant overlooking the river that was known for premier salmon fishing. It was a bit late in the season to see the Aurora Borealis, the beautiful northern lights, but we would able to see the glacier-capped mountains and the pristine countryside.

I knew that King Harald V of Norway, George H.W. Bush and Eric Clapton had all been fishing there, and I wanted to experience the best that Iceland had to offer. As a child, I loved to fish, and I was looking forward to trying it again. Darkness came and stayed for only about five hours, so the days were long. We could actually fish at nine o'clock at night.

The Eygafjallajokull volcano was nearby. It had been erupting all month, and I was a bit nervous. For Icelanders, who live with volcanoes all the time, the danger was downplayed. I asked Ambassador Hannanson if there was any reason to be concerned. "It's a so-called tourist eruption," he answered. "Don't worry."

I had attended the training sessions at the Ministry before I came over, and the instructor touched on evacuation procedures. His focus was mainly on hurricanes and tornadoes, as that was what we typically faced in Texas. I left equipped with passports, passport stamps, an Icelandic flag and a consular manual, but not much information on volcanic eruptions. I had met many interesting people and was eager to embrace my duties. Until then, I had a lot of reading to do.

Now, we stopped at the North Face factory to buy suitable clothing for hiking on glaciers and then headed south. We were in a hired "monster truck," an all-terrain vehicle equipped with huge tires so it can navigate well on glaciers. There were large crevasses—large enough for a small car to fall through, as we later learned. The countryside was drop-dead gorgeous; we were enchanted.

On arriving at the hotel, we saw a group of photographers and news reporters packing up to leave. Many had been camped out for several days. There were photos of the eruption with its bright red lava. The hotel was even offering an excursion to the volcano. From the hilarious expressions on many faces in the photos, it looked like a great way to make money.

We considered going on one of the volcano excursions the next day, but a photographer told me not to waste my time. "It was over," he said. "Kaput." That night at dinner and in the little bar, we met several Icelanders and news reporters from all over, including a charming cameraman from NBC who was planning to leave the next day.

During our dinner of salmon and puffin (a local delicacy), we met the hotel manager. In the early hours of the morning, I got a text from Dianne. "The volcano is erupting," her text said.

I called her immediately. "Is this a joke?" I asked.

"No, the manager called me," she said. "Look outside."

I opened the curtains. The sky was pitch black with ash and smoke. Bob had teased me that if I became a Consul General, a volcano would erupt. There was a sign from my weather-watching husband, I thought. I threw on my clothes and went downstairs. Iceland Coast Guard, and Air and Rescue had been brought in. Uniformed personnel were on the ground floor in the pool room. Helicopters were on the lawn. We were surrounded by a small army.

Suddenly, my crash course in evacuation procedures was put to the test. I introduced myself to the captain in charge, and was told that a "ground stop" was in effect. All helicopters were grounded. They had just managed to disable the bridge on the main highway and shove it to one side—effectively saving it. The hot lava pouring off the side of the mighty volcano would hopefully follow the path of least resistance and sweep into the sea. They had successfully rescued the inhabitants, and there would be no loss of life.

At around five o'clock in the afternoon, one helicopter was allowed up in the air, and I was on it. We were going to survey the countryside and observe the volcano. Dianne, my adventurous friend, was allowed to come with me, and she signed a "hold harmless" waiver. Our friend, Mike, the NBC cameraman, came, too. From the air, we could see the lava pouring off the side of the volcano like a giant waterfall. It had created a large river into the land and was running out to sea. That was a relief.

About thirty minutes into our flight, the volcano blew. This time it wasn't small. The ash plume in this phase rose to about 30,000 feet and resulted in the biggest disruption to air travel since World War II. We were the only three people in the world who witnessed it as it happened. Mike was nervously snapping photos as I signaled to the pilot to "bug out." In other words, let's go.

He misinterpreted my hand signals and circled the volcano again. Once back on the ground, Dianne's phone started to ring. It was her husband, Bob, and he was clearly not amused. I doubted that he would ever let the two of us loose again. Meanwhile, Mike loaded his photos onto his laptop and began feeding them to the media. Coast Guard officers, other reporters and I gathered around to view his photos. Until that moment, no one had really understood what had just happened.

Thousands of passengers were stranded everywhere. The trains in Europe were overbooked; ticket machines broke. People were desperate to get home, and car rental companies had no inventory. It was bedlam. I had no idea how the various airlines were handling the coordination of grounded flights.

As we watched the news in shock, Dianne and I realized that we were right in the middle of the action. When we could leave, our driver took us back to the capital. As it happened, Icelandic Air had a few planes left, and we were able to fly to the U.S.—it was, of course, in the other direction.

When I arrived at my hotel in New York, I saw stranded hotel guests in the hallways and in the bar. Most were talking excitedly on the phone. I felt a little guilty that I was even able to get back from Europe. Certainly, nobody else could, except by boat.

I fielded several interviews regarding my adventures in Iceland. The Ambassador emailed me that I'd had a trial by fire. Literally. It was quite a story. For the first time in almost two years, I forgot about my grief and a realization came to me: I needed to make the most of my life and live in such a way that I would have few regrets.

I smiled a real smile for the first time in months. Life would go on, and I would go on with it. I would race forward and live to the fullest.

John takes a break at Circuit of the Americas track with Ally and me—his Godstone MS Heart Car cheerleaders.

CHAPTER TWENTY

LADIES, START YOUR ENGINES

THERE WAS NO GPS SYSTEM to help me navigate my new life. Repairs on my home had been deferred, and I relocated to the Huntington, a nearby high-rise, while insurance-related work on the roof and structure were completed. I felt snug in my new environment and, while sleep still eluded me, I wasn't sleeping with one eye open. After my experiences with break-ins and a stalker, I slept fitfully at night when I was in the house. It had its own particular pops and cracks, and without Bob, it felt lonely. The new apartment felt safe.

It was October 2010. The past year had been an emotional tsunami. Grief had washed me to the shores of the land of unpredictability. I struggled to stay on an even keel. Unfortunately, the emotional highs and lows were part of the process. One minute I was fine, the next minute I was a basket case.

I also faced an endless and unpleasant to-do list created by my attorney. There were other business-related demands, too. Many vendors required proof of death. Every time I was requested to produce the dreaded document, I relived Bob's last days. It was a constant reminder that he was gone, and I was left behind to deal with the aftermath. I was alone. Bob was gone.

There were days when I had to struggle not to give into negative thinking. Unwelcome thoughts and fears popped into my head and brought on waves of despair. They ran the gamut, including thoughts such as, "I will never find another grand passion like Bob" and, "I am too old to date." I knew that I might want to meet a companion or friend in the far distant future, but I simply was not ready yet. It was downright miserable at times. Bob was in heaven, and I was far from it.

My naturally optimistic nature helped me rebound from these destructive thought patterns. I pushed down a sea of unshed tears and forced myself to continue making plans. Having too much time on my hands was unhealthy. After spending one particularly gloomy evening looking at our wedding pictures, I tried on my wedding gown. Sitting on the floor with a glass of champagne, I cried and cried until I had no more tears left to cry. Disgusted with myself and reeling from the pain, I marched out to the trash area with my wedding album and shoved it down the garbage chute. It hurt too much to look at the photos.

The next day, I regretted my emotional decision and called Pete Baatz, the photographer, to ask him to make more prints. If ever there was a turning point that was it. I couldn't turn into a kind of sad spinster. I hadn't been jilted by my suitor and left at the altar. There was no runaway groom. My life had taken its course. It took all my willpower, but I gave myself a "get a grip, Mica" lecture.

With this newfound perspective, I became involved with Pan Can, an organization that raises funds for pancreatic cancer research. In October 2010, while attending their fundraiser in Los Angeles, I met Eileen Littlefield of Nashville, who had also lost her husband, Merlin, to this insidious disease and who would become a great friend. Mutual friend Larry Gatlin later hosted a tribute to honor this ASCAP legend, and Lisa and I attended and cried and laughed together. Merlin, who signed Reba McIntyre, Lyle Lovett and other famous stars, was a Texan like Lisa and me. What's more, Bob, Merlin and Lisa's husband had all known Larry Gatlin. Again this was no coincidence. The three of us—Eileen, Lisa and I—became soul sisters. We could finish each other's sentences.

As we had met on Halloween, I dubbed us the "Widows of Eastwick."

With the holidays looming, I knew I had to be proactive. I resolved then and there to decorate, celebrate and honor Bob by continuing our traditions. He would not want to look down from heaven and see me acting like Scrooge. It was mandatory that I find joy and hope in celebrating Christ's birthday.

Fortunately for me, I had a loving family who was sensitive to my needs. Donnie would enjoy Christmas that year, and all the magic and innocence of Santa Claus. I immersed myself in buying him gifts and choosing a Christmas tree. John and Karen joined me for Christmas Eve and Midnight Mass, and I willed my aching heart to find joy in being with them. I wouldn't let grief win. Life was a gift and, at this time of good tidings, I let my faith carry me forward. "Onward Christian Soldiers" became my mantra.

I had a trip planned after Christmas to Lyford Cay, as was our tradition. While there, I also planned to acknowledge and mark the one-year anniversary of Bob's death. My friend, Lisa, had offered to join me and, as she was grieving too, I knew we would comfort each other on this sad day. It was essential that I prepare to face these painful days with a plan in mind. Without one, emptiness would swallow me whole.

John was going to race again at the Rolex 24 in Daytona Beach. Once again, the race would come on the heels of the anniversary of Bob's death. With plans to look forward to, I would greet the New Year with a lighter spirit. Lisa and Eileen, my "Widows of Eastwick" gang, were planning to come to Florida, too.

The New Year brought new horizons. Lisa and I attended the inauguration of Susana Martinez, the new Governor of New Mexico. I admired her greatly and had hosted a fundraiser for her in Texas. A former Democrat and district attorney, she was part of a new independent breed of Republican. Held in Santa Fe in January 2011, her inauguration took place on one of the coldest days of the year. Lisa and I sat outside during the swearing-in ceremony, bundled in sheepskin and staving off frostbite. I will never forget the scantily clad Native Americans performing without shirts. I was sure they would never thaw out.

In mid-January, Lisa joined me in Nassau. The anniversary of her husband's death had just passed. She was in a reflective mood, as was I. We decided to float two floral wreaths in Clifton Bay. Bob and I had gone swimming there many times, including on our honeymoon. It was as close to a burial at sea as Bob would get. On January 24th, the wind was blowing hard, and it was colder than usual for the time of year. Was this yet another weather-related sign from Bob?

The wind died down the next day, and we went out in a ski boat to pay our respects to the most important men in our lives. Our husbands had never crossed paths, yet we two women from different worlds and the same hometown had somehow been brought together. We tearfully threw our wreaths of roses out to be carried away into the vast ocean. Where they ended up was a mystery.

Secretly, I hoped that Bob and Lisa's late husband, Patrick, were standing together, arm around shoulders, bonding as new friends and watching us memorialize them. I wasn't sure that once in heaven, you could grieve for someone you left behind. That day, I liked to think that he missed me. I wanted to believe that he yearned to come back and comfort me.

Over the next few days, we were introspective and somber—lost in our own thoughts and memories. Soon, it was time to leave. I had walked down Memory Lane and needed to focus again on the future.

Lisa and I planned to reconnect at the end of the month at the Rolex 24 Grand Am race in Florida. It was going to be another grueling race for the drivers. I figured our path of grief was yet another endurance race, so I could relate to what the teams were going through. We had our own twenty-four hours every day to endure.

Lisa, Eileen and I hit Daytona by storm, and became the unexpected center of attention at the track and along pit row. We were two blondes and a redhead, ages forty-nine, fifty-two and fifty-six; we weren't hot, young babes. But racing is a male-dominated sport, and there weren't that many girls of any age at the track prior to race day.

The day after we arrived, we got up early and headed to the track for the start of the race. Having bought pit passes and filled out all the necessary releases, we were thrilled to take our place in Godstone's pit. The German pit boss, however, was none too pleased when he saw us.

"You're not wearing proper gear," he barked at me. "You cannot be in here." I wanted to protest but decided not to make a scene.

"Ladies, follow me," I said. We jumped in the golf cart and drove to Stand 21, which sold official custom-made Nomax suits. I asked the clerk if any ready-made suits were available. He had a few older models, which we tried on. The minute I zipped on the off-white suit with the words Porsche on it in navy blue, I lit up from the inside out. I was electrified. Watching the reactions of my girlfriends, I saw their faces light up as they, in turn, tried on their suits.

"Sold," I said. My friends were tentative, but I insisted they keep them on. Undaunted, we marched back into the pit. I took one look at the by-the-book team manager and suppressed a grin. He was absolutely speechless. I suspected that he really didn't want women in his pit at all and had used our not being dressed properly as an excuse to throw us out. But he seemed to grudgingly admire our resourcefulness.

Throughout that day and the next, we were the flavor of the month. We couldn't walk anywhere without being whistled at, photographed or asked for an autograph. For three widows who felt so beaten down, we were surprised by the attention. It made us feel alive again. I had been so numb for so long, it surprised me that I could feel anything.

Godstone Motorsports team member and inspiration Ally Babineaux also joined us. She had suffered cardiomyopathy as a student at Texas A&M University and had received a heart transplant. She was a shining star and radiated a unique spirit of courage and hope. With her around, I could not feel sorry for myself.

John's team had a good race and finished without an issue. He hadn't been able to finish the year before, so this was a personal best. We celebrated with champagne and toasted our new lease on life. I think we all left there feeling like there was hope again and that life could—and would—get better.

I returned to Houston from Bob's memorial anniversary in Nassau and the race in Daytona Beach, and immediately got busy. Among the events I attended was one near and dear to my heart: a dedication in February for the Tolerance sculptures. This project had come to fruition after four years. Mayor Anise Parker presided over the ceremony; former Mayor Bill White also attended, as work on this iconic public art sculpture had begun during his administration.

With his help, Spanish sculptor Jaume Plensa had installed seven ten-foot kneeling figures made of stainless steel mesh and formed by interlocking letters and symbols from different languages. They were stunning and literally stopped traffic, especially at night. When lighted, they seemed to float up like spirits. These sculptures would eventually serve as the focal point between Rosemont Bridge—spanning Buffalo Bayou—and Harmony Walk.

Dr. Mahmoud Eboo, now Ambassador, was on hand to represent the Aga Khan, who graciously underwrote the project. Sadly, neither my husband nor Peter Marzio, director of the Museum of Fine Arts, Houston who shared my vision and had also died of cancer in 2010, were there to see this project come to fruition. Under Peter's capable leadership, the museum became accessible to people from all walks of life.

A response to a horrible attack in 2006 on David Ritcheson, a Latino teenager, the sculpture was meant to recognize and celebrate Houston's incredible diversity. Tragically, David committed suicide the following year, but his legacy would live on, memorialized in this work of art. I was determined to make sure it did.

This project had fallen apart many times, largely due to the number of stakeholders involved, including City Council. Peter had once remarked to me that, "Public art is a nightmare." But he believed in me, so I had carried on. His widow, Frances, was there that day. Still a curator at the Museum, she would have made Peter proud that day.

None of the Ritcheson family was on hand that day, but David's lawyer, Richard Lion, was. "Something good came out of this tragedy," he remarked. David was just sixteen when the horrendous crime occurred. At the dedication, I spoke about David and my outrage that he had suffered such a horrific attack in a city that I called home. I explained how I had read the headlines after the attack on David and dissolved into tears. It is such a sad story.

"This intolerance is not what Houston represents," I said now. "We are an open city. Diversity is part of our culture." I recalled that in some small way, I wanted to help right a wrong.

This was the most significant project I had ever been involved with. The Plensa figures received significant and worldwide media attention, most of it positive. However, some purists lost sight of the purpose. It was not about establishing a Picasso-worthy art grouping on the banks of Buffalo Bayou. The point was to focus attention on what humanity has in common and to emphasize that in Houston, we have more in common than not. Harmony Walk also became a symbol for gay rights, religious and ethnic differences and human rights. This public artwork was dedicated to all those who had suffered persecution because of their individuality.

I wore my heart on my sleeve that day. For once, I was not trying to be socially or politically correct. I was reminded of my childhood in Morgantown, when my playmate, an African-American child, came to play with me in our segregated playground (she could be there because no one enforced the rules). I was also the girl in Memphis listening to Martin Luther King, whose speeches were so succinct, passionate and logical that I wanted to take on the cause.

I did believe that you could effect change from within the system. Profound change could never be forced. It had taken generations for society to accept African-Americans as equals, yet our country had an African-American president.

Houston had an openly gay mayor, Annise Parker, and her wife, Kathy Hubbard, was widely accepted as Houston's First Lady. Times were changing and one day, a person's color or sexual orientation would no longer matter. Intolerance, I hoped, would be an archaic word in the not-too-distant future.

Dedicating the Tolerance statues took me out of my grief once again. The Ritcheson family had lost a son in the prime of his life. My husband, on the other hand, was in his later years. Bob's death had come at a more natural time in the life cycle. David had chosen to end his life, but only because his pain was too much to bear. His family had provided emotional support; it wasn't their fault. For those who have lost a loved one to suicide, it's easy to have survivor's guilt. But the truth is that there is no fault here. God sees all. He is in charge and we are not. Maybe some of us need to be with the Lord. And maybe it's okay if someone we love chooses to make that journey to be with Him—and therefore find peace.

My mother, now eighty, was as energetic as ever. Except for a mild, but common, heart condition—atrial fibrillation—she was in excellent health. A teetotaler and disciplined eater, her skin was wrinkle-free. I hoped that I would inherit her genes.

My son, his family and I were going to join her in Hawaii in August 2011. With a brother who was a World War II veteran, the war had left an indelible imprint on her life. She had always wanted to visit Pearl Harbor, so I planned a trip. I spent the last week in June in Lyford Cay. Feeling more relaxed with nerves less taut and exposed, I took long bike rides and walks. I could finally concentrate enough to read again and had a duffel bag full of Sandra Brown suspense novels.

Tired of hearing myself voice my emotional pain to my mom, I stopped calling her every day. I was finding some inner peace and trying to concentrate on living in the moment. Friends included me in a couple of dinner parties, and I was reasonably content. I had put my Nassau home on the market, and I was spending much of my time trying to organize my things. For me, selling the home would be very sad but it was too large for a single woman.

On July 1st, I touched base with my mom, and she sounded odd. I had to repeat myself several times and found that she had difficulty following the conversation. She wasn't as crisp as usual, but I chalked it up to age and dismissed it. The next day I called again, and she sounded like her usual self. I promised to come back in time for July 4th, so we made dinner plans for Sunday, July 3rd. While dating my son, Bo had almost been killed in a car accident one July 4th weekend so I was wary about this July 4th too. It was almost a premonition. I was waiting for the other shoe to drop.

Things were so peaceful in Nassau, and I was enjoying being near the sea so much that I nearly extended my stay. But my nagging sixth sense surfaced again. "Best not to disappoint Mom," I told myself. I arrived at our favorite restaurant in Houston and was waiting at the table when my phone rang. "Where are we meeting?" she asked.

Alarmed, I reminded her of where to go. I resolved to take her to the doctor on Wednesday, even if I had to drag her. At dinner, she seemed fine. We laughed and joked and I felt much better; she agreed to join me the next day, July 4th, by mid-afternoon. July 4th arrived and about lunchtime I called her. There was no answer. Probably grocery shopping, I thought. I called again an hour later. No answer. This was not like her.

I hopped into my car and drove toward her condo.

Just as I was making a U-turn, an ambulance went by. It's a sign, I thought. It's hard to explain rationally; I just knew it. Something was wrong with my mom. I hit the gas pedal hard and sped over to her home. I sprinted up the stairs and saw the newspaper on the door-mat—and panicked. I didn't have a key. In a flash, I called 911 and a locksmith. The locksmith came promptly, but an hour later, he still could not pick the high-end Medico lock on the door. I didn't dare speculate too much, like whether or not she was alive.

Meanwhile, I called my brother and 911 again. There were a number of car accidents and fires in the area. Emergency response would be slow. Two agonizing hours later, the police, the fire department and an ambulance came. Using a battering ram, they got in quickly.

"Let us go in first," the police officer commanded. "She's alive, " he called back to me. I ran in behind him. There on the bathroom floor was my beautiful mother. It appeared that she had been there since the wee hours of the morning. She couldn't talk, but she did recognize me. They brought up a stretcher while I called our doctors. «Take her to St Luke's," I said. The officer told me to follow the ambulance.

I arrived at the St. Luke's emergency room. My mother was not there. I was told they had taken her to Memorial Hermann, so I drove there. On arriving, I learned once again that no patient with her name was there.

I was flustered and in a panic. John had flown in by then and called me. Mom was at a different hospital; he was already en route. I floored it and somehow made it to the emergency room in one piece. Right then, I resolved to always insist on riding in the ambulance with my loved one.

The staff was relieved to see me. A very kind physician explained that she had suffered a major stroke and that recovery was unlikely. Sick at heart, I went in to see her. She was miserable but aware.

"Mom," I said to her. "I cannot bear to lose you, too."

We moved her to the hospice floor on Friday, and a good-hearted priest helped me with the paperwork. She did not have all her Powers of Attorney in order, so an attorney was enlisted to help me. She had made it clear that she didn't want life support or any heroic efforts.

Bo's mom Lynn was with me, a comforting presence, when my mother died peacefully on Saturday, July 9th. We had a memorial service in Houston and buried her in a family plot in Florida at a church founded by an ancestor. Afterwards, I returned to Nassau as I had an offer on my home. I felt shattered. This was a knockout punch. I had made one giant step forward in the grieving process, only to take three steps back. For the first time since deciding to live life to the fullest, I felt lost and totally adrift again. First Bob—my North Star—then my mom, my guiding light and confidante.

I was bereft. The undertow of grief was dragging me under. So was guilt. I just had not recognized the classic signs of an impending stroke. Confusion, dizziness and the like. John told me that Mom would never have agreed to let me take her to the hospital that Sunday night we had our farewell dinner. He was right. She would probably have made a scene. I was still her child, and she still ruled the roost.

I spent a miserable few weeks in what usually felt like paradise, dealing with the twists and turns of Bahamian law, but I eventually got our home sold. It was yet one more loss. I flew home feeling like a mere shell of my former self.

John and Karen were a godsend. We all hung together and tidied up Mom's affairs. I had no family left in Houston, and the holidays were approaching.

Driving in a parade of showy steeds in Los Angeles commemorating the 60th anniversary of Ferrari in the USA. The car got lots of attention—it's hard to compete with a beautiful racing machine.

Credit: Joshua Monesson

CHAPTER TWENTY-ONE

FINDING MY BEARINGS

I BEGAN TO SERIOUSLY THINK about moving to a new city and dividing my time between two. I needed a fresh start. Memories of Bob were on every street corner in Houston. Strangers and acquaintances came up to me wherever I went to share a memory about him. At restaurants, private clubs, the grocery store, even the jogging trail at Memorial Park, I would run into someone who had a story about him. It was a real tribute to Bob that he had touched so many lives.

Most of the time, I was pleased to hear my husband receiving accolades. But on bad days, it was hard for me. I was fighting not to fixate on my loss and the constant reminders underscored my pain. Someone once said to me, "Mica, I know you miss him, but I deserve to miss him, too." I was somewhat taken aback. Bob's absence in my life was much greater than it was in that of someone who saw him occasionally at the elevator in his office building.

When it comes to the death of a celebrity or a public figure, people can have an odd sense of connection. There was a condolence book for Bob online, and when I perused it, I was touched by the sentiments expressed about him. His magnetic personality was larger than life, and that made people feel instantly comfortable with him. For some who barely knew him or only knew of him, he had somehow become a friend. People identified with him and admired him. And in our hometown, he was Mr. Houston. I was his surviving spouse, virtually a footnote in the obituary that ran in newspapers across the country.

This distinction was a double-edged sword. I was treated with the utmost deference and respect and included in many social occasions. I also felt that there were too many demands on my time, including countless requests for favors. Without allowing time for the ink to dry on his book, people began to pepper me with emails and phone calls asking for donations, access to the Bushes and the like. While much is asked of someone to whom much has been given, I felt the requests were an intrusion on my private life.

I welcomed anonymity when I could find it. I wanted a place of serenity, a safe spot to feel this new grief and revisit the earlier one that had come back with such force. I discovered that refuge in Santa Fe and in Austin whenever I visited my son and his family. On the lakes and in the lovely scenery of the Texas Hill Country, I could lose myself in nature. Few people recognized me in the grocery store; most of them stumbled over the name "Mosbacher." Over and over, I had to teach people how to pronounce it. "Sounds like Linebacker," I would say.

In restaurants and clubs where patrons were used to spotting Sandra Bullock, Matthew McConaughey and Willie Nelson, political spouses were a dime a dozen. For those who knew me from various press interviews, I mostly got a nod or a hello. Laid back, low-key and casual, Austin was the oasis I needed. Temporary or not, I needed a fresh perspective and a place to heal. I also hoped and prayed that whoever was harassing me and disrupting my peace would not follow me.

I had already run into several old friends and neighbors visiting the state capital during the eighty-second legislative session. As in the past, I would be advocating for TAASA, and I would be representing the University of Houston as Vice Chair of the Board of Regents. State Representative Garnet Coleman (D) of Houston had also asked for my help with some legislation for schools.

Additionally, I had been asked to serve on the Formula One Host Committee for the inaugural Grand Prix in North America on Austin's Circuit of the Americas track. I had a long list of projects that looked interesting and would be a good use of my time. It made sense to me to lease a condo. I didn't want to permanently pull up my Houston roots, and I wasn't ready to sell my home. It was good timing to stick a toe in the Austin water and see how it felt to live there.

On one of my trips there in February 2011, I walked into the sales office at the new Four Seasons high-rise. The broker had one unit available for lease. I looked at it and leased it on the spot. If I was being impulsive, I reasoned, I could walk away in a year. It was neither permanent nor irrevocable. I knew there would be a certain finality to selling my home, as there were very few comparable places in my neighborhood.

Girlfriends warned me that there were few, if any, eligible men in Austin. One friend cautioned me that "everyone is married or in college." Well, I thought to myself, the majority in Houston are married, too. Single women—widowed or divorced—were already fish out of water. There was nothing I could do about that. I had to fly solo now, no matter what.

Austin was a breath of fresh air. It had a small-town vibe, but was on fire economically. There was very little housing inventory, and the music and restaurant scene was booming. I discovered that it was a place where fashion labels weren't as important as the creative way you put yourself together. There were accomplished businesswomen who seemed to carve out niches for themselves that defied the typical glass-ceiling culture.

There were plenty of people with deep pockets in Austin, but conspicuous consumption was less prevalent. At night, jeans, boots and button-down shirts were the norm among businessmen. It was tough to tell who was one of the state's many millionaires and who was a mid-level manager. People were on a first-name basis with restaurant employees, and there was no sense of class-consciousness. I loved the genuine friendliness that pervaded the capital city's culture.

Austin was—and is—also a sports-oriented city with a focus on healthy living. At night, the jogging path around Lady Bird Lake was its own kind of Grand Central Station. I jogged or fast-walked as many evenings as I could. Exercise released those feel-good endorphins, and being lost in a crowd of joggers allowed me space to exhale. While exercising, I often talked on the phone to my Eastwick widow friends. We were experiencing all the same emotions, just not usually at the same time.

We took turns bucking one another up. I got some sage advice from the other two and treasured our deep friendship and the lifeline each one offered me. Truly, I might have been tempted to plunge into the lake and drown my grief if I hadn't had such dear friends. It was important not to isolate myself.

At night, I joined new friends for drinks or dinner. Music always provided solace for me, and with Austin's rich music scene, I found it hard to feel morose when a good country-western band was playing. I loved to dance and would "group dance" with friends. In Houston, I might have been more circumspect; in Austin, no one cared.

The 2012 presidential election was over a year away and Governor Romney was a frontrunner. We were introduced by Houstonian L. E. Simmons, a prominent investor and Finance Chair for Governor Romney.

I had felt an instant connection with Mitt. His wife, Ann, flew in and arrived about an hour later wearing jeans and tennis shoes. The earlier part of her day had been spent with her grandchildren. I related to her immediately. Bob shared some candid advice with them: "Loosen up and don't lose yourself in the campaign bubble."

Mitt was personable and sincere; from what I could tell, he also had a keen intellect and a strong character. I felt that he had been undervalued and dismissed in 2007. It was clear to me after our meeting that he had what it took, but an incumbent would be hard to beat. It would take a scandal and even then, it would be an uphill battle.

In the early months of 2011, I had flown to La Jolla to meet with Governor Romney and a small group for dinner. He was running and needed support. I agreed to help, as Governor Rick Perry was not officially in the race. Privately, I had some misgivings; my loyalty would be tested if Governor Perry did enter the race.

In May, I hosted a fundraiser for Mitt Romney at my home. I gave a brief introduction and presented him with one of Bob's favorite ties, one I had given to him. It was for good luck.

That evening, Romney's campaign raised more than $600,000. I felt strongly that he had hit his stride; he was seasoned and primed after losing the nomination in 2007 to John McCain.

Rick Perry officially threw his hat into the ring in August. I was torn. My friendship with the Perrys went back several years and wasn't based on *quid pro quo*. I did not do business with the state. As Governor, he had been good for business. The state was prospering economically. I supported him because he was the right person for the job.

One night my son and daughter-in-law were visiting me, and Cameron asked what I was going to do.

"I know how you feel about Romney, but you cannot turn your back on the Governor of our state," he said.

"Your friendship supersedes the one you have with Romney, and I know you are a loyal friend," Bo added. There it was. They had articulated my feelings. So I called L.E. to explain and then flew to California to talk it over. After that, I called Anita Perry. I was late to join the Perry for President train, but I went on the road anyway, crisscrossing the country. Florida and California were focal points. I went to the debate at the Reagan Presidential Library and attended numerous fundraisers in California.

In Florida, I introduced the governor to some of my well-connected friends. His message resonated with many. A fantastic "retail politician," he could sell to anyone, "one on one." I could tell at times that he was in pain due to recent back surgery, but he never complained. His schedule was impossible, and I felt that even a racehorse needed rest. I was worried that he had entered the race late and was burning the candle at both ends. It caught up to him in the disastrous debate with the famous "oops moment." He choked. With an overcrowded, crunched campaign schedule like his, anyone might have.

Unfortunately the moment was replayed on CNN and on the web. He couldn't distance himself from it, and New Hampshire was his to lose. I returned home sad, but convinced it was quite simply not his time. Again, it was fate, and armchair quarterbacking was not going to change a thing. I was looking forward to spending more time in Austin and to experiencing my first Formula One race.

Back in Austin, I joined a girlfriend for lunch at the Four Seasons one day. On the way in, I spotted something so sleek, sexy and irresistible that I felt a surge of exhilaration. It was a red Ferrari— the California model—and I was inexplicably in love. I snapped a photo and texted it to my brother with the caption, "It was love at first sight."

My phone rang instantly. It was John. "Buy it," he said.

"What?" I laughed.

"I've never ever heard you express any interest in any car."

It was true. I had driven a series of old clunkers during high school and college. After college, I had an old model, acid-green Fiat that had died on Highway 71 en route to Austin. Another one of my cars had torn cloth seats that looked like they'd been slashed during a police search.

In my twenties and thirties, I had driven practical cars: a Honda Civic, a Toyota Camry and a Ford Taurus station wagon. For a time, I had even driven a "Rent-a-Wreck" after one of my old clunkers died. Indeed, Bob had bought me my first new car—a Jaguar that I drove for almost ten years. I was not a car nut nor enthusiast. To his credit, John saw the beginnings of a fire in my belly, and he helped me ignite it.

Naively, I thought I could simply walk into a Ferrari dealership and purchase a Ferrari of my choosing. Little did I know there was a waiting list. John, however, had racing connections. His friend, Giuseppe Risi, founder of Risi Racing and a Ferrari dealer in Houston, was driving a similar car and John arranged for him to sell it to me. When I took delivery of my steed in Austin, I was too nervous to drive it. So Erik Clover of Ferrari Austin took me for my first spin.

While I wasn't wearing a superhero cape, I was grinning like a fool. In a flash, I was lifted out of the doldrums I had been in for so long. I was obsessed with the car. Certainly, I wasn't risking my life racing on a racetrack, trying to cheat death, but I felt so alive. Inside, I was on fire.

Maybe it was a midlife crisis, but heck, I was in crisis already, midlife or not. I had a new grand passion, one that consumed me. Racing fever was in the Austin air, and I began to read about Enzo Ferrari and racing legends like Ayrton Senna da Silva and Niki Lauda. My brother had named his son for Ayrton; they had once met at a track in France. Ayrton was a three-time Formula One World Champion who was killed at the Autodromo Enzo e Dino Ferrari in 1994.

Niki Lauda was a living legend and the subject of a new Ron Howard movie titled *Rush*. A three-time Formula One champion, he had been seriously injured in a horrific crash during the 1976 German Grand Prix. His Ferrari had burst into flames, and he was disfigured from the fire. His recovery was a miracle, and he raced again just six weeks later at the Italian Grand Prix.

Perhaps it's the closeness to death that gives Formula One drivers the exhilarating thrill. I would never be in that class, of course, but the characteristics of a champion were embodied in drivers like Niki. He had been through a kind of hell and back, and had overcome it to continue his life. Disfigured, he could have retreated after the crash and permanently abandoned racing. But he was a champion. With the heart of a lion, he went on to win two more world championships.

If he and others could overcome such terrible losses, then I could and would go forward. Bob had shown me I needed to live each day as if it were my last. I wasn't going to just survive or exist; I needed to fight for my life. I had to strive to race forward.

I kept my car at the Four Seasons, and the valets and guests got a kick out of her. While it wasn't my everyday ride, I brought out the show pony whenever there was a Ferrari Club activity or a race-related event. There was a large group of Austinites who liked their special cars. There were excursions planned with police escorts and other fun, car-related parties at the dealership.

One night I was thinking about Godstone Motorsports and the potential for it to be much more than a non-profit that raced for a Houston hospital. I dreamed big and contacted the American Heart Association, Central Texas Chapter, about bringing a Ferrari racecar to their ball. The idea was well received; with the help of the Austin dealership, a car was brought into the ballroom at the Hyatt Regency. It was the belle of the ball. No female could compete. Watching man after man pose for a photo with the car, I realized how many men saw themselves as racecar drivers—at least in their dreams.

At the Heart Association ball, Ally Babineaux, as Godstone's Ambassador and heart advocate, spoke about her experiences as a heart transplant recipient and a young bride. Eloquent and passionate, Ally was the highlight of the evening. Francisco Cigarroa, former chancellor of the University of Texas System and a heart transplant surgeon, was a guest and couldn't wait to congratulate her. Many of the doctors familiar with this walking miracle surrounded her after her speech. She was another reminder to me of how precious life was. I wasn't going to waste mine.

Godstone's car was such a success that I agreed to participate in an upcoming Formula One Expo to be held at the Austin Convention Center. Godstone would be the lead sponsor, and we planned to have the car there. Formula One excitement was in the Central Texas air. The Expo would give fans a chance to learn about racing up close. A play area was planned for children. The powerful cars would bring pleasure and entertainment to a large group of fans, young and old.

The racetrack itself was the first to be built in the U.S. for Formula One. Promoter Tavo Hellmund had conceived it. The project stalled out, but Dallas billionaire Red McCombs became the lead investor; together with Bobby Epstein, they came up with a strategy to rescue it. Crews were working around the clock to get it race-ready for the inaugural race in November. It was a nail-biter.

Meanwhile the Formula One Expo came together. Our team was looking forward to participating. I began giving media interviews wearing a Godstone race suit with my Ferrari in the background. One morning, I was booked for an early on-camera interview. I had been up all night with a deep, dull, throbbing pain in my right side. I had my hair and makeup done at 6am and drove my car to the race track. I gave the interview, drove back to the residence and called a cab, which I took to St. David's Hospital.

The doctor there took one look at me, holding my hand like a kind of splint on the right side, and had a staff member drive me to the emergency room. They ran several tests and admitted me. The surgeon said I needed gall bladder surgery.

"Can't it wait?" I pleaded. "I have a group coming to my Houston home for a Circuit of the Americas party, and then there is the kick-off for the Expo on Tuesday."

"You can go home," the surgeon said. "But I predict you'll be back within twenty-four hours." Not again!

My health had a habit of intruding on my plans at the most inopportune times. My brother and his wife ended up hosting the party at my home, and I watched the highlights of the Formula One Expo from my hospital room. John did a wonderful job lighting the book with LED lights and gave a great speech during the fan zone. Erik Clover also did the interviews that I normally would have done. For a girl who didn't want to miss another minute of her life, I was once again sidelined.

Sometimes, racing forward meant idling my engines in bed. Maybe it was God's way of telling me to slow down a bit and take time to smell the roses.

Godstones at an autograph session in Atlanta.
From left, John McCutchen, Jason Hart, me, Karen
Garrett and Ally Babineaux. We are the only mostly
female pit crew team in the United division.

CHAPTER TWENTY-TWO

THE ROAD TO ATLANTA

IT WAS NOVEMBER, and the return of Formula One to the U.S. had arrived. The city and state and law enforcement had choreographed an ideal partnership of cooperation. Austin was now in a new category of international cities like Monaco and Sydney.

The weather gods were smiling that weekend. Friday and Saturday were gorgeous, and race day on Sunday was clear and devoid of Texas humidity. There would be no wet track to complicate things and no need to run on "wets," tires made for rain.

There were many pre-race events, including a fashion show, a party at the Governor's Mansion and many late-night, after-hours parties, including My Yacht nightclub at Austin Ballet. Among the most expensive sports in the world, Formula One offered many venues to please all tastes.

Those of us involved with the Circuit of the Americas (COTA) were praying for smooth sailing and no accidents, both to the track and on the track. It was important for Austin's track debut to go off without a hitch. We did not need public relations to start off with a disastrous catastrophe and a "crash and it bleeds" headline.

The race and the pre-race show were exciting. The University of Texas Longhorn band played; Austin showcased some major talent and was in fine form. An exciting Formula One race ensued, and Sebastian Vettel of Red Bull Racing won. He was now a three-time world champion. Fernando Alonso finished second. It was my first Formula One race, and I was elated. What a weekend—it had all gone so well. Fans lost their hearts to Texas and its hospitality.

My enthusiasm became even more zealous. I read all I could about Formula One drivers. In the spring, Godstone was scheduled to race at the COTA track. We had come to an agreement with the American Heart Association and would be racing officially under their banner to raise awareness for their Hands Only CPR campaign. John had teamed up with Parkplace Motorsports of Dallas. His co-driver would be Jason Hart, a veteran driver and instructor; the other car featured the Porsche factory driver Patrick Lindsey. It was a stellar, top-notch group.

Ally Babineaux had joined our team as an Ambassador. We welcomed racing on our home track and on race day finished in the top ten. Again there were no mishaps and the track received top accolades from *Forbes*. It was technically challenging, but well-engineered.

John and I did several media events on racing, and I signed up for the famous Skip Barber Racing School at Laguna Seca track in California. In the spring, Ferrari owners were offered the opportunity to participate in a COTA track day. I signed up and was eager to learn to race. That day, there were lots of men and two women. We were all required to wear helmets.

Instructors were on hand, but we did the first lap on our own. I crawled around the track. The tight S-turns were intimidating. I didn't know when to accelerate and how to lean into the curves. I was like a toddler riding a bike on training wheels.

I came off the track feeling sheepish. That's when I enlisted one of the instructors. He hopped into the car and began talking me through it. I was tentative at first. But after accelerating, I got my confidence up and then my speed. Before I could exhale, I was flying. I learned to slow down and brake slightly going into a tight turn, then hit the accelerator on the straights. It was a precision dance, and I was hooked.

I couldn't wait to hit the straights. I floored it; I was in control. Perhaps loss was now leading to recovery. I needed to prove that I had courage and had stared down one of my fears. My brother's high-five after I exited the track said it all. "You go, girl!"

On April 19th and 20th, the Grand Am series headed to Atlanta. It was the fifth race of the series. The course, which was located outside the city, was a challenging one. Narrow in parts, there were no "run off" ramps. At the top of turn five were "the esses," uphill turns that resembled the letter S. It had been raining, so wet roads also upped the ante.

John had been working on filming a public service announcement about the American Heart Association at the track. He had brought in a veteran sportscaster from Speed TV. I arrived just in time for the first take.

There was lots of excitement in our part of the paddock. The cars were the usual stars, but the two top drivers in the class were also generating buzz. On our team, two Patricks—Lindsey and Vonn in a co car—were favored to win.

The weather was touch and go on race day. During the autograph session, we all participated and fielded questions from fans. I gave several interviews about the American Heart Association. Our goal was to help prevent deaths due to heart attacks and to raise the profile of CPR. Winning came second.

John stayed conservative on the track during the race and took no unnecessary risks. He held his position all the way, avoiding pointless tactics to overtake another car and erring on the side of conservatism.

After a tough fight, Patrick Vonn, the factory driver, pulled off a victory in our co-car. We all celebrated; we all shared the high. Racing is filled with so many unglamorous moments. Behind the scenes it involves tuning and setting up the car. But when you do win, the triumph is something to be savored.

Sailing after losing Bob was not quite the same although I will always feel his love. It's like the wind, I can feel it even if I cannot see it.

CHAPTER TWENTY-THREE

THIN TREAD ON MY TIRES

WHEN I LEFT THE TRACK OUTSIDE Atlanta, my rental car was buried in the mud. I had parked it on a hill in the grassy parking lot near the paddocks on Friday. It had rained, and there was no way to pull it out without a tow. I was reminded of a favorite mantra, "Move ahead, don't spin your wheels or you will be stuck in the mud."

Yet despite my recent momentum, I was stuck. At the time, I saw it as a kind of a test or biblical trial. Bob and my mother were gone. I kept hitting one roadblock after another.

I called the local tow-truck driver. He knew the spot well and agreed to bring the car back to the hotel. He laughed about my description of the area; apparently, this kind of thing had happened before in the same spot. At least I wouldn't be stuck there all evening waiting for help.

We had planned a celebratory dinner at the Chateau Elan winery, whose chef was renowned in the region. Halfway through dinner, we found out there had been an electrical short and the ovens weren't working. Dinner had to be ferried over from another kitchen.

As the incidents and accidents piled up, I became increasingly convinced that my ride through life was destined to be bumpy. So I braced myself for a kind of metaphorical, high-speed chase—dodging or enduring nicks and bruises along the way. I reminded myself that I was no different from anyone else. We all end up at times in a kind of free-fall through life, and we have to brace ourselves to withstand the impact of crashes along the way.

In my younger years, I had been cautious and measured in my risk-taking. I was less impulsive, the sensible "designated driver." I had played it safe. Now, in my fifties, I decided to throw caution to the wind. I wasn't reckless, but I had come to realize that I could no more control my fate than I could the weather. Waking up every day was almost like jumping out of a plane without a parachute. Life was unpredictable; bad things happened in no particular order, for no particular reason.

About this time there were a series of devastating storms in Alabama. Hundreds of homes were destroyed, and the Red Cross was called in. I felt compelled to go and help. They asked if I could bring in an automatic external defibrillator. I could and did. On arriving at the temporary headquarters, I surveyed the set-up and was amazed by the precision of their organization.

The following day, we handed out hot meals from a trailer in the field and in temporary shelters. While touring a residential block of homes that had been flattened, I saw a young man and his wife picking through the rubble of their home. It was a mess. The rain was still falling, and it was cold. The young man was shivering in his t-shirt.

I offered him food. He took it gratefully, but his attention was focused on recovering some important possessions in his home.

"I need a coat," he said to his wife. I was wearing a Barbour jacket my son had given me for Christmas. Without hesitating, I took it off and put it around his shoulders. He teared up. I hugged him and turned away in tears myself.

I didn't want to embarrass him. He had his pride, and the world had changed me. I was no longer trying to be homecoming queen or the prettiest or smartest girl in the room. Survival wasn't about winning a popularity contest or Prince Charming's hand in marriage. The stakes were much higher.

Life was about forming attachments, emotional intimacy and caring. It was also about helping others. We were meant to do what we could do, to reach out and extend a helping hand to people in desperate circumstances. We might not be able to save the world, but we could help a neighbor. Do one good deed and pass it on.

I was reminded over and over after Bob died that others were also in pain. But as in Clay Walker's song, "The Chain of Love," perhaps that pain could be eased if, instead of always looking inward and thinking about ourselves, we all took the time to help each other change the flat tires.

In October 2012, the folk song "Five Hundred Miles" was on my mind, especially the second verse, which went "Lord, I'm One. Lord I'm two, Lord I'm three, Lord I'm four, Lord I'm five hundred miles away from you." At the time, I felt like the Lord was, indeed, 500 or 1,000 miles away from me.

Things were not going smoothly. I had moved back to Lazy Lane and once again found it impossible to sleep. I knew every creak, groan and squeak of the house. The bar icemaker had a unique, high-pitched whirr; the air-conditioning came on with a kind of engine roar.

Due to the security breaches and stalkers we had experienced, I had police watching the house at night. Still I was uneasy. One night, I fell asleep in the guest room watching TV. I kept dozing off and finally woke up around midnight feeling woozy. I called my son and several close friends and left crazy sounding messages.

The next day, I slept until almost three o'clock in the afternoon. At one point, my housekeeper tried to wake me. I was irritable and groggy. When I finally got up later, I felt drugged. I walked into the kitchen to get coffee, and the stove spontaneously ignited. Yelling to my housekeeper, I ran out of the house and called 911. When the fire department arrived, they called Centerpoint, who came and detected high levels of gas in the kitchen. Needless to say, the gas was turned off.

I went to the emergency room. The attending physician said I had symptoms of toxic inhalation and suggested I go to a hotel. The next day, I called a plumber. He came, ran some tests and called his supervisor. It turned out that my new stovetop had a leaky gas-supply valve. The plumber said it had been improperly installed. As a result, carbon monoxide had been highly concentrated under the hood and was wafting through the air conditioning ductwork. I had carbon monoxide poisoning. I wasn't on drugs or going crazy. No, I was lucky to be alive.

That was the tipping point for me. I took this last incident as a sign that I should sell the house. Without giving it too much thought, I put it on the market. Several friends thought my decision was rash and called me to talk me out of the decision. Truth is, it was rash. My nerves had snapped, and that was it for me.

I resolved to forge ahead and never look back. My plan was to move to Austin and split my time between Austin and New York. I stayed in my Austin condo and in New York and tried to divorce myself from my Houston home. I knew I was deeply attached; it was a place of many wonderful memories. Day after day, I waffled. I wanted to take it off the market; I wanted to sell it. No, it was still too soon to sell.

Then in October, there was a buyer and an offer. It went under contract. The buyer appreciated the architecture and would preserve part of it. This, at least, was some small measure of consolation. The minute the deal closed, I went into mourning. Selling our home was like losing Bob twice.

Had I been too hasty? Yes, it was the top of the market and a sound business decision. But I could afford to keep her. It was one of the most painful decisions I have ever made and one I will always regret. I had sold my Tara, my haven. I caution all widows: Wait and let the smoke clear before you make any irrevocable decisions.

I might have eventually chosen to sell *Reflections,* but at the time I wasn't ready emotionally. I still wasn't clear-headed.

Cameron, Bo, Donnie and I caught the racing bug. F1 Austin had become a family tradition. Donnie loves shiny cars. Life goes on and my grandson has given me a new lease on life.

CHAPTER TWENTY-FOUR

FRESH TRACKS, FRESH STARTS

THE MINUTE I CLOSED ON MY HOME, I was seized by seller's remorse. I had been rash and was acting out of fear. It was a sound investment and would only appreciate over time. I could afford to keep it. I didn't have a sound money management adviser and I had panicked.

As I packed up photos and other memories of the life Bob and I built together, sadness washed over me. Our home was where we had laughed, cried and celebrated married life. We had raised a son there. I could feel Bob's presence in every room. The loss of him, coupled with the loss of the house, hit me full-force.

The movers came and started packing up my things—a stuffed mouse Bob had given me and other precious gifts from family and friends. I walked into a closet, shut the door, and had a good, long wail. It was too much. Clearly, I wasn't ready. I had been warned not to make typical widow mistakes, I thought I was finally healing, but I had just made a colossal blunder.

I also didn't have a place to land in Houston. Buying a new home seemed like a daunting prospect. All of my things were going into storage until I decided where I wanted to live. The future suddenly scary and uncertain again. Like a Formula One driver who hesitates to get behind the wheel after a crash, I had lost my nerve.

By signing on the dotted line of the contract, I had embarked on an unmarked road. Now, the thought of traveling down it was terrifying. My daily mantra during those trying days became, "Get hold of yourself." Making this major change had been premature; it was obvious now that I wasn't emotionally ready. While I'd been living part-time in Austin, I wasn't sure I wanted to make it a permanent move. Houston was still my home.

So I returned to my condo in Austin and beat myself up over my decision. "What was I doing?" I asked myself on my daily walks around the lake. My condo felt uncomfortable, like a shoe that was too tight. I was miserable.

Then one day it dawned on me that I might enjoy spending more time in New York City. Bob and I had spent many happy times there. Even though I was Texas to the core, a different environment might be just the thing to snap me out the doldrums. I reasoned that it was hard to feel lonely in Manhattan; the pace and the action appealed to me. What's more, I was on a couple of boards at performing arts and theatre organizations, so I knew that my time would be well occupied. I had forced more change on myself, so I might as well make it an enjoyable experience. It wouldn't be an irreversible decision.

A few days later, I booked a flight and called Pat, a realtor I knew, about looking for an apartment. It was snowing and a terrible day to be out hunting for a place to live, but we persevered. And it paid off. I found a furnished, two-bedroom place with knockout views of the city and the Hudson River. It seemed perfect, but I hesitated. I had lost confidence in my ability to make smart decisions.

Fortunately, Pat had known Bob and me for a while and gave me some good advice. The apartment was a rare gem in a great building. I balked a little when I found out about all the hoops I would have to jump through to submit references to the Board. It was overwhelming, but not unusual for New York. Pat was my cheerleader and encouraged me through the process. I called on some old friends in Houston and asked if they would provide the Board with what they needed.

Once ensconced in the apartment, I felt a cloud lift. My spirit felt lighter. I was ready to embark on a new adventure. I enrolled in professional dance classes at Steps in the Theatre District; another opportunity for a walk-on role had come up, giving me the incentive to get back into shape.

The class schedule gave me some structure. I also re-engaged with the American Hospital of Paris Foundation and the Iceland-American Chamber of Commerce. On days when I felt sad, I went to mass at St. Patrick's Cathedral. When word got out that I had a spare bedroom, I had a steady stream of visitors. Without hesitating, I also went to the theatre and to concerts by myself.

Mornings were the hardest part of the day. I didn't want to start them off without the love of my life. I missed the sound of his voice and the touch of his hand. Getting dressed and out the door every day wasn't easy, but I forced myself. Lucky for me, the neighborhood had great restaurants. A hot breakfast and the *New York Times* would get me going

I went for long walks, taking in all the sights of the city and getting to know it better. Walking past certain places brought back memories of wonderful evenings with Bob. Far from the fishbowl at home, we had been like honeymooners in our little New York *pied à terre*. I had good days and awful ones. At time, it was hard to run a simple errand. I still wasn't sleeping well, but I tried to stick to a schedule. Finding it difficult to concentrate and stay grounded, I knew the solution for me was to have something to look forward to every week.

My widow friends came to visit often. They were grieving, too, and a change of scenery offered a positive boost. Knowing that we had to get back in the driver's seat at some point, we would force ourselves to go out, usually to Bemelman's Bar in the Carlyle Hotel.

We'd put on makeup, do our hair and try to look our best. It wasn't about attracting the opposite sex—we discouraged any overtures from strange men—it was a kind of therapy. We had to eventually rejoin the human race, so we started with small steps, together. In my mind, I was married. It was crystal-clear that I wouldn't be ready to open my heart for quite some time.

Slowly, over the months, I began to feel a little more optimistic about the future. I wasn't sure what it looked like, but I was approaching everyday life with a more positive attitude. Friends like Eileen Littlefield, who had been widowed longer, told me they were experiencing the same emotions. She had walked the path and blazed a trail for me and others. She validated my feelings and reassured me that I wasn't going crazy.

I returned to Austin and continued my involvement with the American Heart Association. Our racecar was now liveried to reflect the AHA Hands Only CPR campaign; I was in charge of off-track events. CPR has saved many lives, including that of a member of my family. It was important to me to raise awareness of CPR as well as teach it to the public.

As I felt more and more a part of the Austin community, I decided to buy a house. I told myself that it didn't have to be a permanent move. The housing market was on fire, and there wasn't a lot of inventory. It was a seller's market, with many homes boasting multiple offers. While it wasn't the best time to buy, I figured I could sell it in a year if I changed my mind.

Once I faced the fact that nothing was permanent except death, I was more willing to take risks. I called a realtor and found a lovely Georgian-style home that needed no work, no updating, no decorative touches. It suited my taste, and my furniture would fit right in. Best of all, it was new. The last thing I wanted was to be saddled with a money pit; I didn't have the appetite for endless repairs.

I slept on it and made an offer, which the sellers accepted. Was I being rash? It was liberating to buy my first home. I felt seven feet tall when I walked through the front door. This was progress, another step toward building a new life for myself. Bob would have been proud.

Godstone Heart Ambassador Ally Babineaux and I in the pit at COTA track Austin. Far left, drivers John Mccutchen and Jason Hart.

CHAPTER TWENTY-FIVE

EXPECT THE UNEXPECTED

SO THERE I WAS IN UNCHARTED TERRI-tory with my brand-new life, and I was excited. My housekeeper and her husband were planning to move to Austin and live on the property in a few months. In the meantime, I was enjoying my freedom. I didn't need nighttime security guards; I felt safe and snug in my new home. It was exhilarating to walk through the door. My Georgian-style home was all mine.

Even so, I installed an alarm system. Despite having 24/7 security personnel for years, I told myself that if I was careful and set the alarm every night, I would be safe. The stalker and other security problems that occurred on Lazy Lane were part of my past. Bob was the famous one; surely he had been the target, not me. I would be fine. Feeling brave, I tossed off any concerns. While I was still afraid of the dark, I had lived alone before and could do so again.

The first night I spent in the house, the alarm went off at around ten o'clock. I was startled but not concerned. I was not sure at the time if this was a random intruder or a stalker. I had no security team at that point and no reason to assume that anyone was fixated on me. The monitoring company called and said they would send the police to check on me, just to be safe. With the master bedroom doors locked, I stepped out onto the upstairs terrace to wait for the Austin police to arrive. In the process, I locked myself out on the terrace. Shivering in my flimsy nightgown and robe, I told the officers downstairs what had happened. After they checked the premises, they called the fire department. Two cheery firemen showed up and helped down with an extremely long ladder.

I was mortified. The neighbors will think I'm nuts, I told myself. I had no key to the front door, and they had to break in. I was also locked out of my bedroom, so a handsome young officer named Drew Vera picked the lock with a coat hanger. He became my new hero.

The next day, I called the alarm company, and a technician detected a malfunction in the system. It was a motion detector with a bad cell, which was easily replaced. He then checked and rechecked the system and assured me it was working just fine. I didn't need to worry. Just in case, I also had a locksmith disable the automatic lock on the upstairs patio door. I went to bed that night feeling tranquil and content.

Two nights later, my alarm went off again. It was three o'clock in the morning, and this time I had a bad feeling. The police were dispatched, and the caller from the alarm monitoring service kept me on the line. I was panicky. He suggested I go to the upstairs terrace, where the police could see me when they arrived.

Minutes later, an Austin Police car pulled up. The officers got out and found that a kitchen window had been opened. The thought that someone had been on the property unnerved me. I later learned that a ring of professional car thieves was working the area, coming into homes while people were sleeping to find car keys. Most likely, my Ferrari was the target.

After that night, I left the Ferrari keys in the kitchen, out in the open where they could easily be seen. They are welcome to take it and anything else, I thought. I cared about my physical well-being, not my possessions. Fortunately, Celia, my housekeeper, was able to move in sooner than planned, and I would no longer be alone in the house.

I consulted with a private security company I had used in the past. They came out to the house, conducted a thorough assessment, and suggested that I upgrade the alarm system and rekey the locks, among other things. Doing research to determine which locks to use, I was surprised to find numerous videos online showing how to pick certain brands of locks. I also found other how-to videos on hacking alarm systems. It was kind of a wake-up call. Alarm companies were selling alarms, not personal security or peace of mind. Alarms, good locks and lighting could make a home less vulnerable but not totally safe.

After investing in some state-of-the-art equipment, I relaxed. Soon Celia and her husband were in the house, and I wasn't alone. But I was a little angry. I was not going to let bad people rob me of my peace of mind.

A few weeks later, the alarm went off yet again at three o'clock in the morning. I figured that Celia had accidentally tripped it. When I called her she sounded drowsy and confused, so I called 911. The officers came right out and found the front gate swinging open. It had been securely locked when I went to bed.

They also found a back door unlocked, and there was evidence that someone had been in the house. This time, I couldn't get back to sleep. I was resigned myself to hiring nighttime guards. I called Andrew Vera, the young officer who had picked the lock on the master bedroom door, and asked him about the possibility of hiring Austin police officers, whether or not they could moonlight as security guards and if that kind of job would violate any of their contractual obligations. It turned out they could hire out as private security.

I wound up with three officers rotating during the evenings. I hated this infringement on my privacy. It was expensive and took away my newfound sense of personal freedom. But I did hope we'd catch the intruder. That alone would give me a great deal of satisfaction.

Things were fine for a week or two. Then one night the alarm discharged, meaning that it changed status from "armed" to "disarmed." I heard the beep and called the officer on duty. He had left twenty minutes earlier and did not wait for the replacement officer. "Call 911," he said. So I did, shaking.

The police found a door wide open. The thought was chilling. Not only had there been an intruder, but he had also been watching the house. Clearly, he was determined to get in and was undeterred by a police presence. If I hadn't heard the alarm "disarm" itself, he could have been in my bedroom within minutes. This was no ordinary intruder.

The next day, I called the now-retired Houston police sergeant who had investigated the disturbing incidents on Lazy Lane. He told me that I was being too dismissive of the very real danger the intruder posed. He wondered if it was the same predator. The pattern was definitely similar; this was covert, not overt. Bob's stalker, for example, had made herself known through phone calls and letters, and by showing up in person numerous times. This person's profile was of someone who was sophisticated, cunning and brazen.

I told him that I had no sense of being watched or followed. He urged me to continue with guards and to be very aware of my surroundings. It was an unsettling conversation and not a pleasant one. I didn't think I could process one more traumatic occurrence.

The next few weeks I was traveling, so I didn't have much time to worry about the situation at home. When I did return to Austin, I was so jumpy and nervous at night that I was truly scared of my shadow. It took me forever to go sleep. My doctor prescribed a sleep aid, but I found that it made me behave erratically. I had mood swings and became paranoid and aggressive. Obviously, that drug wasn't for me.

A few days later, Officer Vera called to tell me that one of the officers working the night before had seen an intruder on the property. He'd gotten a clear look at him, but the man took off before the officer could catch him. He called for back-up, not wanting to leave me without protection. I had slept through the whole thing. I told them to wake me up from then on.

It was all too familiar. I was reliving a nightmare. Apparently, changing hometowns made no difference to someone who was obsessed. Deranged individuals will cross state lines to get to the object of their obsession.

Being stalked is a harrowing experience. While I had lived with the situation for a while, I never dreamed that someone would fixate on me. It certainly wasn't anyone I thought I knew. I did learn of several anti-stalking organizations and availed myself of their resources and knowledge. I had escaped an abusive relationship, but Willem didn't fit the description. It wasn't his *modus operandi*, either. I had been in touch with some of his victims, and none had heard from him again once he was exposed.

It took tremendous willpower to get on with my life. I resented having to deal with the situation, but peace of mind was critical to my emotional well-being. I knew I would be forced to change my living situation. I would need to rely on my instincts and my faith to carry on. Of course, I would avoid potentially risky situations, like driving alone late at night, but I refused to live my life looking over my shoulder.

Feeling somewhat defeated, I put my beautiful Austin home on the market. I had not renewed the lease on my New York apartment, so I was feeling homeless again. Maybe it's time to go home, I told myself. So I headed east to Houston, and rented a condo in a high-rise. I had come full circle.

With my Austin home on the market, I felt oddly displaced. I had so hoped to find solace in my new hometown. As my mother was fond of saying, "I guess it wasn't meant to be." Now I felt the loss of my Lazy Lane home even more keenly.

In visiting with other widows, I hear that their housing situation is frequently a source of agitation and worry. Most, like me, don't feel confident they can make it on their own resources. Cashing out seems like the right thing to do, but where can you invest the money and do as well? I sold my home and my memories within those walls.

I began to lose confidence in my decisions and second-guess myself. I questioned over and over why the sequence of events had unfolded the way they did in Austin. I had wanted to blaze a new trail and carve out a place to grieve. I wanted off the merry-go-round of life. This part was healthy. Expecting that the stalker would not follow me across county lines was unrealistic. A stalker is obsessive, and my circumstances had gone on for years.

When I was struggling over the decision to sell my Austin home, I called my brother. He said if I wanted to get out of the hole of grief, I needed to stop digging. He said to face my grief—face the music. I needed to accept the unpleasant results of my actions and the reality of the situation.

Moving across county lines was not an antidote. It was all wishful thinking. I resolved to be proactive and prudent, but not to run on fear. Hysteria and paranoia were not helpful emotions. As much as I wanted to hoard memories, it was the end of an era and time to write a new chapter.

DEVELOPING
2016 CAMPAIGN CASH IN FOCUS AS FUNDRAISING EFFORTS HEAT UP

D FOLLOWING ORDER BY IRANIAN COURT AND WIL | DOW IND | 17,924.06

On Neil Cavuto live at 4 in NYC. My life came
full circle as I was now back on the air.

VICTORY LAP

After moving back to Houston, I bought another large house. I took advice from a financial advisor who really did not understand my lifestyle. "Money is cheap." "Interest rates are low." "You will easily qualify for a mortgage." I did not bounce this idea off of anyone. I still did not trust my gut. Einstein said the definition of crazy is doing the same thing over and over and expecting a different result. Bob was not going to come back and walk through the door.

I was living in a kind of haze. My friend Lisa calls it the "widow's fog." I was not thinking rationally. Buying a large home was a mistake. It underscored my loneliness and provided no personal security. Soon I ended up in the same situation—feeling like I was living in a kind of prison. Maintenance and repairs were time consuming. I had dug another hole. There was no time to be creative. A few months into the project, I decided to flip it. Enough was enough.

I wanted to share my experiences and mistakes with other widows, so I began drafting notes for a book. While I was writing, I began to gain clarity. I discerned patterns and realized that my priorities had changed. I did not want to maintain a large home. It was not how I wanted to spend my time. I was never there. My family pointed out that I am a gypsy. Cameron said all I needed was a place to hang my coat.

Many of my friends were downsizing. What I really needed was a lock-and-leave condo in a secure high rise. It was time to realize that I did not need to entertain on a grand scale. It was a time to simplify. I told my family to give me no gift that would not fit in my purse. I was a material girl no more. I had been there done that. I called Laura and put the home on the market. It sold fast, and I wanted to throw a parade in her honor.

Finally, after almost two years, my Austin home sold. I had bought at the top of the market, and it was not the style of home that appealed to everyone. I was so happy to be free of the maintenance, responsibility and carrying costs. These days if anyone asks me if I miss either house, I say *no* without hesitation. I miss Bob and our togetherness, but I do not miss our house. Time has a way of bringing a different lens in which to view the past.

Living up to a middle-age stereotype, I bought a vacation condo in Florida. After all, it is my birthplace, and I love the ocean. This time I bought it at the right price. I also sought advice from some of my wiser friends who know me well. The condo is low maintenance and relatively hassle-free. And it is my retirement place. After all, I do need some place to call home.

Meanwhile my consular duties continued to expand. I have enjoyed being back in Houston and reconnecting with old friends. My brother and his wife recently moved back from Dallas, and I now have family around. I rejoined several boards and was appointed by Governor Perry to steering committee formed with the state of Texas and the Aga Khan Foundation.

Ever the political junkie, I have signed on with another Presidential Campaign for Senator Ted Cruz. Like most Republicans, I was torn among several loyalties. However, I feel that we need a fresh face, and I think he can win. The outcome will be one for the history books, but this race should prove exciting. There are so many qualified candidates, and I think the competition is healthy.

I am concerned that young people are growing up without a sense of what being a patriot means. With the absence of the Pledge of Allegiance and reverence in schools, I fear our nation's core values are in danger of being lost. We all have a right to faith, liberty and the pursuit of happiness. Our families are falling apart and society needs strong family units. As for social issues, I think that those are very personal choices. I am for smaller government and think that we live in a dangerous time with our current terrorist threats. We need a strong leader and I will support whoever our next President is.

Of course I visit Austin frequently and am ready, able and willing to borrow my grandson anytime his parents want to loan him to me. He is one of the many blessings in my life, and I am thankful that I have him. The bittersweet blessing that tragedy brings is newfound appreciation for all the good things that come your way. I find it helpful to begin the day practicing gratitude, and, as I mentioned, I keep a running list of all that I am grateful for, beginning with the basics like my eyesight, my limbs and my health.

I also stopped taking the people in my life for granted. I was frozen for so long on the inside after Bob died. Gradually, I have begun to thaw and open my heart again. I have stopped holding back and try to remember to say "I love you," and "I appreciate you," as often as I can. My friends sustained me during the darkest days, and I am truly grateful for them.

I was so fortunate to share my life with such a wonderful and caring man who truly taught me how to love. Loving him changed me forever. The values of integrity, honor and service permeated every aspect of his life. Before we met, I felt broken and, at times, I was a tortured soul. Life had scarred me. Bad choices had made my life a nightmare. I didn't trust easily.

Bob accepted all the parts of me—especially my edges and sensitive artistic spirit. We had a grand passion and were a match made in heaven. I know he was my destiny. Of course no marriage is easy, but as A-types who couldn't sit still for more than a minute, we were very similar.

It's hard to imagine lightning striking twice. I enjoy the company of a man, but I don't need one to feel complete. Should romance come along, I am sure I will open up my heart. However, I am fortunate to have so many projects to keep me occupied. I don't think I am the hermit type, either.

On our journeys in life, we all struggle with difficulties that can bring unimaginable pain. No one escapes unscathed. When I look around and see how life can grind down the most resilient souls, I realize that there is always someone worse-off than me. During the dedication of the Piensa Tolerance installation, I reflected on young David who was my inspiration for this project. His pain was internalized, and despite his family support, he committed suicide on a cruise. His family suffered a terrible blow.

One of the reasons I wanted to share my story and the often crippling pain that I have felt is that I want others to realize that it is possible to survive pain and move on. Whenever I feel sad, I remind myself of the examples of courage.

There are so many inspirational people who can inspire us. I met former Navy SEAL Marcus Luttrell during my work with T.A.A.S.A. He lost his entire unit and wrote *Lone Survivor* about his incredible experience. But not all these examples are so well known. Within my immediate circle, I am in awe and inspired by friends in Austin who are raising an autistic teenager. While he is non-verbal, he is a straight A student and can compose music by pointing at notes on a letter board. I know that some days his mother must get discouraged, but she keeps a cheerful attitude. She spends her days reaching out to other parents who are in similar circumstances.

After waiting in the hospital room for several months, Goldstone Motorsports team member Ally Babineaux finally received a second heart transplant. She is recovering well and is a walking miracle. Her faith and positive warrior-like attitude sustained her. Her mother, so selfless, observed that she was grateful for Ally's heart but also sad for someone else's tragic loss that provided it.

I also admire my daughter-in-law's mother, Lynn Hoster, who fought breast cancer and beat it. No one escapes life's challenges. The key is how we choose to respond. The Bible says we will be tested and forged by adversity. We are also reassured by scripture that we are never alone. I believe that God protected me from my intruder.

I like to light candles in church for my family and friends. My strength comes from prayer. Like most parents, I worry about my offspring and am constantly asking God to put a wall of protection around them. The ritual of lighting candles is my way of reminding myself that I am not in control of my life. I have been called a control freak. I am a terrible backseat driver. I like to be in control of the ride. Death served to remind me that I am not in control of any of my circumstances. God is in charge, and as scripture reminds me, He will fight the world of spiritual warfare. He is the real superhero in my life. I believe that I am here for a purpose and that God will lead me where I need to go.

Call me a cock-eyed optimist, but I always knew that things would get better. Bob's spirit was so joyful and playful. He knew how to be childlike and fun. With him, I found myself learning to lighten up and be appreciative of all that God had given me. Now, my unwavering faith sustains me and gives me hope.

I can't predict how long I will travel on the road of life or where it will lead me but I know more exciting adventures are in store. I plan to keep moving, even if I stumble and stub my toe. With my eyes focused on the road, the only reason I will glance back is to see how far I have come. As the Serenity Prayer instructs, instead of dwelling on the things I cannot change, I will move forward to a new day and embrace all the unexpected gifts that come my way.

POSTSCRIPT

After losing Bob and my life as I had known it, it was time for rebirth. Anytime I experienced self-doubt or fear or anxiety in the past, I had Bob to lean on. He often said to me, "Tonto, you are not the Lone Ranger"—meaning I was not alone. Now I was the sole survivor. I had been stripped of my soul mate, trusted confidante and lover. Fortunately I am not someone who has to depend on a man to survive.

My fairy tale had come true. I had met my prince. However, my parents also encouraged me to believe in other happy endings too and that included being successful in a meaningful vocation. I had put my writing career on hiatus during my marriage. Now it was time to dig deep and see if I could still put words on paper.

I confess that I experienced a tidal wave of emotions while writing this book. However, I wanted to share the lessons that I had learned from love and loss. I also wanted to share that grief is a process and that while no journey is identical, it is normal to feel disoriented and shattered. After my mom died on the heels of Bob's death, I spent a lot of time asking why. I truly felt alone and abandoned.

During my grieving process, the trauma of a childhood kidnapping coupled with the assault in London intensified. My symptoms of PTSD became more pronounced and I found that in my vulnerable state, I was easily triggered into a dissociative state. I became emotionally flooded on a number of occasions. Emotional flooding refers to an excessive overload of stress hormones that cause the "flight or fight" syndrome. In that state, a trauma victim is reliving the original trauma and is no longer rational. He/she reacts rather than responded and can leave behind a lot of wreckage via words. For those unfamiliar with trauma and its lasting impact, its painful memories buried in the subconscious mind that are blocked—a defense mechanism. My childhood event was too painful to remember and to face.

As my symptoms were impacting those I love the most, I sought help at the Post Traumatic Stress Center in New Haven, Connecticut. Dr. linda Berger is an expert in the treatment of trauma and she helped me immensely. I had survived but a little boy also held captive by my kidnappers did not.

There were many days that I felt strong emotions that overtook me by surprise. I spent time mending fences and trying to explain what I could not explain. Grief just isn't pretty. I am deeply appreciative of all of my patient, loving and understanding friends and family members who thought that I had gone over the deep end. I often say that it's a short trip to crazy.

The power of prayer forged my resolve and over time, I became more centered and felt less fractured. I still have good and bad days, but the bad days are fewer and far between. I never thought laughter would come easily again but one night I could not unzip my dress (my shoulder was injured while playing tennis) and with no one to help me get out of it, I took a pair of scissors and cut off my dress. I stood there in my bedroom and started laughing uncontrollably. It was at that moment that I had an epiphany.

I did not need to take myself so seriously. I have always been so hard on myself. A perfectionist by nature, I am always impatient with my shortcomings. After slogging away through grief and heartache, I realized that the little annoyances in life were unimportant. I stopped getting so impatient with clerks who put me on hold at the phone or cable company and refrained from yelling back at rude drivers. As Taylor Swift sings, I "shake it off." Grief gave me a hard-won new perspective.

I now aspire to be a force for good and to stop being so reactive. I feel that I am more readily able to discern pain that others are feeling. Maybe the rude driver had a rough day at the office. The last thing I need is to succumb to a kind of road rage with life.

These mid-life tires still have some tread on them, and I intend to travel wherever the road leaves me. I still have a lot of love in every corner of my heart, and I will carry Bob with me to the next adventure. If I pass you along the way, it's only because I am racing forward. I still have a lot of living to do. There's still more to do on my bucketlist.

ACKNOWLEDGMENTS

I would like to thank Lucy Chambers and Lauren Adams of Bright Sky Press for believing in me, and my publicist, Lisa Newton O'Neill, for encouraging me when I first thought of writing this book. Indirectly, my gratitude goes to Father Daniel Lahart for helping me during one of the most difficult times of my life—burying my loving husband, Bob.

Thank you to Karen Rahming of Nassau for inspiring me to keep the faith and to Dr. Daniel Von Hoff, Dr. Robert Wolff and all the caring nurses of UltraStaff. I appreciate all of you. Thank you to Kristen and John Perry for bucking me up and to James A. Baker, III, for keeping us laughing during Bob's final days. My eternal gratitude to President George H.W. Bush for his cheery hospital visits. You kept Bob going longer; if it weren't for you, I would never have learned to play golf.

A great big thank-you to the staff at the Four Seasons Hotel and Residences in Austin, including John, George and Tommy Dean. To the folks at Circuit of the Americas, thank you for giving me new purpose. A shout-out to Richard Brooks of Carey Limos for all your assistance. A special hug to Lisa Niemi Swayze and Eileen Littlefield, who provided shoulders to cry on. You were gifts from above. A thank you to my special team, Dr. Chuck Gray, Dr. Alice Gates and Patty Mccullar, LC. I am so appreciative to Margaret Alkek Williams, Jeanie Kilroy Wilson, Heidi and Ted Cruz, Astrid Van Dyke, Diane Lokey Farb, Martha Upchurch Blecher, Alice Gates, PHD, PTSD Center, New Haven and new friend Cammy Jones for reaching out to me.

Last but not least, my eternal gratitude to my wonderful editor, Cristina Adams, who was patient with me when I wrote at times in long hand and suffered through my numerous computer glitches, including lost text. She made my writing look good.

May all of you run forward and live your lives to the fullest with faith and courage. And may you weather every storm with hope in your heart, as even loss has a season—as my grandmother always said, "This too will pass." Life takes some true grit.

Warm wishes to all of you.
Carpe Diem.

ABOUT THE AUTHOR

Mica McCutchen Mosbacher is a fifth-generation Floridian and Texan, with Scottish-Scandinavian roots. An award-winning journalist and public speaker, she currently serves as Honorary Consul General of the Republic of Iceland for Houston and Central Texas. Together with her family, Mica is a sponsor and team member of Godstone Ranch Motorsports, a non-profit car-racing organization, United Division, that uses motorsports to raise awareness for the American Heart Association CPR Campaign and other causes. She also works as an advocate for victims of assault and human trafficking.

Mica lost her husband, Bob, 28th U.S. Secretary of Commerce and chairman of Mosbacher Energy, to pancreatic cancer in 2010. She was accorded an honorary damehood, Knight Commander, by the Royal Order of Francis I in 2011 and was admitted to the Order of St. John by Her Majesty, Queen Elizabeth II in 2012 for her philanthropy in tolerance and humanitarian causes. She divides her time between Houston and W. Palm Beach.